On What Slender Threads

A.A.'s Twelve Traditions from a Historical Perspective

By

Lyn S.

Copyright © 2023 Lyn S.

All rights reserved. This book or any portion thereof may not be reproduced or used in any manner whatsoever without the express written permission of the publisher except for the use of brief quotations in a book review.

ISBN: 9798375108353 (paperback)

Table of Contents

Preface xi
Introduction xiii

Tradition 1 – Unity? What unity? 1
    Lessons from prior movements seeking to help alcoholics 1
    The early days of the Fellowship 2
    The first attempts for unity: group consciences 4
    A glaring lack of unity in the recovery program 5
    Amidst chaos and disappointment and without unity,
        Bill writes "How It Works" 6
    Still no unity once the program is in writing 8
    A slow and discouraging start to selling the Big Book 8
    When the tide changed, it was a tsunami. 9
    From counting members to counting groups 10
    "Leaders" were a barrier to unity in the Fellowship 12
    The idea of unity would not come quickly to the Fellowship .. 13
    Coming up: the Second Tradition 15

Tradition 2 – Who's in charge around here? 17
    For our group purpose 18
    A loving God? Why not a loving Higher Power? 18
    When we speak of God we mean your own conception of
        God 21
    For the A.A. group purpose, the *group's* ultimate authority 22
    Alcoholics' problems with authorities and rules 23
    The problems of power and prestige 23
    Shedding the leadership mantle 26

For our group purpose, our leaders are but trusted servants;
    they do not govern 26
Decision-makers: the earliest group consciences 27
Bill's dream was for *all A.A. groups* to have an A.A. group
    conscience 28
The first Conference that almost wasn't 29
For our group purpose, the General Service Conference is
    A.A.'s group conscience 31
The Conference recommends solutions to the "frozen" texts ... 31
What is an informed A.A. Group Conscience? 31
For our group purpose, we have the Second Tradition 32
Coming up: The Third Tradition 32

Tradition 3 – We don't want you here! 35
    The Fellowship quickly outgrew meetings in homes 36
    A training program for newcomers 37
    A universal and welcoming Fellowship? 38
    The "flying blind" period's first test case – the atheist 39
    The "flying blind" period's second test case – alcoholic
        women 41
    Did the Fellowship forget "A Vision for You?" 43
    Bill's frustration with race and the Third Tradition 43
    The "double stigma" – gay and alcoholic 45
    How are A.A. groups doing today? 47
    A worthy alcoholic? 48
    How do you become an A.A. group member? 49
    Let it begin with me: acceptance, love, and tolerance for all
        who enter 49
    Coming up: the Fourth Tradition 49

Tradition 4 – You can't tell us what to do! 51
    What the Fourth Tradition is and what it isn't 52
    Having a written program of recovery was not enough to
        ensure unity 52

Group autonomy for alcoholics was a fait accompli 53
Autonomy grew from successes and failures 55
Examining motives for special groups in A.A. 57
Akron A.A. and Cleveland A.A.: autonomy and religion in A.A. 59
The motivation not to abuse the principle of autonomy 61
Can "children of chaos" grow up? 62
The Fourth Tradition's emphasis on "affecting other groups or A.A. as a whole" 63
Coming up: the Fifth Tradition 64

Tradition 5 – Don't just sit there! Carry the message! 65
The primary purpose is to carry the message 65
Early dreams for helping struggling alcoholics during the "flying blind" period 67
Another distraction: A program that is a cure for all ills? 68
Statement of unconditional surrender to one primary purpose 70
Going back to our "carry the message" roots: One alcoholic talking to another 71
How can groups reach and help newcomers? 73
Does the group's conduct help or repel struggling alcoholics? 75
Exactly who are alcoholics who still suffer? 76
Singleness of purpose and the A.A. group as a spiritual entity . 79
In summary: A.A.'s *single purpose* and unity 79
Coming up: the Sixth Tradition 80

Tradition 6 – This near-beer is A.A. approved! Really? Nope! 81
What diverts groups from their primary purpose? 82
The toughest nut to crack for A.A. – religious affiliation 82
Alcohol education seemed like a good idea at the time.... 85
Acknowledging early contributions and avoiding affiliation ... 88
Tradition Six's overlap with Tradition Eight 89

Clubs in A.A. evolve to become "related facilities" without
   A.A. affiliation 90
A.A. learns to mind its own business 93
Coming up: the Seventh Tradition 93

Tradition 7 – Thanks for the meeting. Who's picking up the tab? 95
   Problems with money and an unsung A.A. hero, Hank P. 96
   The Fund becomes the Alcoholic Foundation 98
   Desperate times called for desperate measures 99
   Hank's next idea: The One Hundred Men Corporation 100
   The fall-out from the stock scheme begins 102
   Ending the stock scheme does not end A.A.'s troubles 103
   It only got worse 105
   Lessons and principles come from tremendous pain 106
   Tradition Seven and property – the original Big Book
      manuscript 107
   A.A. treasurers, good group practices, and transparency 108
   A.A. members' contributions and our primary purpose 109
   Coming up: the Eighth Tradition 110

Tradition 8 – You get what you pay for! 111
   Introduction 112
   Part I of the Long Form: 113
   Part II of the Long Form: 115
   Part III of the Long Form: 116
   Part IV of the Long Form: 121
   Good old Tom, the fireman 121
   Which brings us to today's paid service workers in A.A. 122
   Alcoholics Anonymous World Services, Inc. 125
   Conference planning and reporting 127
   A.A. World Services Meeting 127
   Those who labor in service for us are worthy of their hire 128
   Business portions of A.A. are "special workers" on a
      large scale and are necessarily incorporated 128

Separating the spiritual from the material 130
Coming up: the Ninth Tradition 131
Tradition 9 – Children of chaos choose orderly chaos............................ 133
How is service defined?... 134
Long Form Part 1: The essentials for individual groups......... 135
Long Form Part 2: The essentials for groups' combined
    efforts: service in Central or Intergroup Committee 138
The G.S.R. connects the A.A. group to the General
    Service Conference.. 140
Long Form Part 3: The essentials for our General
    Service Board 144
In it's early beginnings, A.A. was organized.......................... 145
The Conference laid the groundwork for earning
    Trustees' trust.. 146
Long Form Part 4: We are not organized 152
Caution against confusing service with leadership/
    ownership.. 152
Coming up: the Tenth Tradition.. 153

Tradition 10 – Outside opinions contaminate the solution..................... 155
The Long Form's explicit charge to A.A. members 156
A.A. members had an opinion on World War II 157
Levels of practicing Tradition Ten.. 158
At the personal level: opinions are a dubious luxury 158
Bill tried to avoid outside issues when writing the book........ 160
At the public level: medical opinions about alcoholism......... 160
Medical opinions at the personal level: don't practice
    medicine 161
At the public level: opinions about A.A. and religion............ 162
At the personal level: opinions about religion within A.A. 164
Alcoholics Anonymous grapples with personal opinions
    about drugs 164
Public and personal opinions were the undoing of the
    Washingtonians.. 165

Publicly protecting A.A.'s reputation became an outside issue 166
The Delegate's group conscience protects A.A. from public incorporation 166
At the personal level, Bill's opinions on outside issues 168
Bill's personal opinions on spiritualism 168
Bill's personal opinion on LSD 169
Bill shared his personal opinions on B-3 and niacin 169
At a very public level: Congressional testimony by A.A.s 170
What A.A. does not do 171
In summary 172
Coming up: the Eleventh Tradition 172

Tradition 11 – Alcoholics Anonymous grapples with personal opinions about drugs 173
Anonymity and the Fellowship's early inconsistencies 174
The first publicity stumble 175
The first high-profile anonymity break 176
Bill's struggle with Marty M.'s anonymity break 177
Early A.A.'s heavy hand on anonymity breaks 179
Bill's 1948 anonymity apology 180
Anonymity breaks continued 180
Bill's quandary: save lives or compromise the principles of A.A. 182
How can the A.A. group help? One way is to study this tradition regularly. 183
Understanding Anonymity pamphlet 184
Personal anonymity online 184
Bill's caution 185
Coming up: the Twelfth Tradition 185

Tradition 12 – Equality, vulnerability, and freedom in the spiritual principle of anonymity 187
Appropriate and inappropriate anonymity breaks 188

The origin of the name Alcoholics Anonymous..................... 188
Jack Alexander sets out to expose A.A. 190
Undoing damage already done... 191
A.A. is no one's song and dance routine 191
Bill and Dr. Bob's plea as members of A.A.: Can't we be
    like everybody else? 192
After we're gone, can't we be like everybody else? 192
The Long Form of Tradition Twelve: In Seven Parts............. 193
    Part 1: *We of Alcoholics Anonymous believe …* 193
    Part 2: *The principle of anonymity has an immense*
        spiritual significance – 194
    Part 3: *We are to place principles before personalities –*....... 195
    Part 4: *We are actually to practice a genuine humility –* 197
    Part 5: *That our great blessings may never spoil us –* 199
    Part 6: *That we shall forever live in thankful*
        contemplation 199
    Part 7: *… of Him who presides over us all.*...................... 200
General Service Office pamphlets and statements on
    anonymity... 200
Anonymity – equality, vulnerability, and freedom................. 201
Has A.A. achieved unity? 203
    Why Do We Need a Conference?..................................... 203

Epilogue: Keep coming back! 205
Sources.. 207

Preface

The idea for this book started with a network of women who collectively sought the comfort of an A.A. literature meeting during the pandemic. We studied the Big Book and then moved on to the *Twelve Steps and Twelve Traditions*. I shared some historical background from various sources. Subsequently, one person moved to California and suggested that I have a similar online 'workshop' with her new friends out west. Suddenly, my world of A.A. friends grew very large and incredibly rich with enthusiasm for the Traditions!

In succeeding workshops, I was delighted to be sharing what I had learned from A.A.s who had a much deeper knowledge of its history and the Traditions. As it goes with such explorations, we had more questions than answers. My friends lovingly pushed me to broaden my scope of resources and to seek answers to the questions that arose from our discussions. Together, we found many of our answers in A.A.'s General Service Office's (G.S.O.) wonderful pamphlets and guidelines. A special thanks goes to Steven D'avria in the G.S.O. Archives who so patiently answered my scores of questions.

My workshop family stretches across the United States into England, Scotland, and Spain. In particular, many thanks go to Athena C. for getting the first online workshop started. From this workshop, I met the wonderful Edward, aka "Eduardo," who brought me to the Radford Group in California (even though he was in Ireland) and who said, "You need to write a book!" Eduardo's efforts forged my fortunate friendships with Brea M., Stacy W., Craig T., Beverly J., and Collin; all who hosted workshops, posted my references, and provided a polished and refined platform. Many thanks go to all of the participants like Niecie, Earl, Julie, Jeri, Catherine, Erika, Ian, Thea and so many others who inspired me.

I was fortunate to have a cadre of friends with high expectations who

Lyn S.

helped me to organize the study. Any semblance of polish and quality in this effort is directly attributable to Pete M., Nancy O., David D., Sandy C. Patsy Y., Sarah L., Bob Z., and Julie A. To my "working with others" sister, Sandi: I couldn't have done this without you! Finally, this study would not have been possible without the steadfast faith and encouragement of my husband, Don. Each week, he had me read every chapter to his network of men – probably the most profound expression of his confidence in the study. Much appreciation goes to his crew for hanging in there.

This study is dedicated to all A.A.s and their friends and families. May we trudge the road to Happy Destiny together!

Introduction

WELCOME TO MY HOME! WE'RE going to start a pot of coffee and sit at the dining room table. What are all of those books on the table? Well, you asked me to tell you what I have been learning about A.A. history and how I think it relates to each of the Twelve Traditions. I don't want to just tell you what I have learned; I want to show you my resources. That way, you can look up whatever you want and I truly hope you do that. There is so much more to the story of A.A. as told by these books and pamphlets than I will ever be able to convey in this brief study!

You don't have to tell me whether or not you are an alcoholic. This is a journey for all who are interested in learning about how a raucous group of drunks trying to stay sober succeeded where all other earlier treatments had failed. Because of the Traditions, Alcoholics Anonymous seems to be surviving the test of time – so far.

Why did I do all of this? It began out of my own desire to understand how A.A.'s Twelve Traditions became instrumental to its success and survival. When I started, I only had a superficial appreciation of how the Traditions helped to keep A.A. groups from running amok. Bill's essays were intriguing, but I sensed that he was only scratching the surface of their evolution. Besides, over seventy years have passed since Bill wrote the Traditions. I wondered how they could be relevant after all this time. Through this study, I discovered that, besides being quite relevant, they are critical to Alcoholics Anonymous' *worldwide* ability to carry a message of hope to any suffering alcoholic.

I began my study with reading *Language of the Heart*[1], *Alcoholics Anonymous Comes of Age*[2] and *Pass It On*[3]. All three were tremendously helpful, but historians like Kurtz[4], Schaberg[5], Brown & Brown[6], Borden[7], and so many others revealed to me a story that was not the tale of mistakes and sins that Bill had portrayed in his essays. Through their work, I saw A.A.'s pain-filled missteps become strides toward shaping its future financial and organizational structure. I saw what Bill referred to as A.A.'s sins become miracles that saved it from destruction as it developed and grew. I learned about significant alcoholic and nonalcoholic contributors to the Fellowship's survival. Some were lost to alcoholism while others were overshadowed by the "more glittering achievements[8]" of Bill W. and Dr. Bob. All of the sources that I used led me to cataloguing the experiences of the Fellowship from December 1934 to April 1965 in tandem with the development of each Tradition. Those experiences allowed me to track Bill W.'s chaotic journey to fulfilling his dream of alcoholics in recovery taking full responsibility for Alcoholics Anonymous.

In each Tradition, I will supplement Bill's essay with historical summaries that helped me to fill in the "blank spots" needed to understand better that Tradition's role in the survival of Alcoholics Anonymous. As I progress from one Tradition to the next, I will be developing a continuing story line that will culminate in Bill's last battle for alcoholics; a battle he finally won less than six years before he died.

I find it is more effective to read each of Bill's Traditions essays in the *Twelve Steps and Twelve Traditions* as an accompaniment to this study. Also, I will reference many of the other resources offered by G.S.O. For the chronology of events, I relied substantially on G.S.O.'s literature, Kurtz's *Not-God: A History of Alcoholics Anonymous*[9], and Schaberg's *Writing the Big Book: The Creation of A.A*[10]. I hope I have represented their work, and all other resources, well. Any errors or incongruences are solely my own.

Now I know that the Traditions are more than A.A. groups' "guide to better ways of working and living, and … an antidote for our various maladies[11]." More significantly, I discovered the Traditions were Bill's path to A.A.'s general service structure. I will blushingly admit that, before this study, I had never made that connection. When sharing this work with others, I found that I was not alone in my misapprehension.

If it is not already obvious, now is the perfect time to say the inferences in this historical perspective of A.A.'s Twelve Traditions are strictly my own and in no way reflect the opinions of Alcoholics Anonymous.

My largest thanks goes to you for being willing to 'listen' and let me share what I have learned about the Traditions. I can assure you, I learn so much more with your help.

And so, the coffee is ready. Let's get a cup and begin this frequently funny, and sometimes heart-breaking journey of A.A.'s Twelve Traditions: What it was like, what happened, and what it is like now.

A Few Notes

In keeping with the Eleventh and Twelfth Traditions, I do not use the last names of any alcoholics. "Bill" is used only for Bill W. "Dr. Bob" is used only for Dr. Bob S. I use the first name and last initial for all other alcoholics. More information is available in the references to this study.

I capitalize the word "Fellowship" when referring to A.A. members.

I use the standard name, Big Book, for the texts, *Alcoholics Anonymous: The Story of How Many Thousands of Men and Women Have Recovered from Alcoholism*. Fourth Edition and *Alcoholics Anonymous: The Story of How More than One Hundred Men Have Recovered from Alcoholism*. First Edition. I provide the exact edition and page when citing from the Big Book.

Unity? What unity?

Tradition 1

Our common welfare should come first; personal recovery depends upon A.A. unity[1].

The Long Form: *Our A.A. experience has taught us that:*

Each member of Alcoholics Anonymous is but a small part of a great whole. A.A. must continue to live or most of us will surely die. Hence our common welfare comes first. But individual welfare follows close afterward[2].

Synopsis of Bill's essay in the 12 & 12

Bill emphasized the independent nature of alcoholics as people who cannot be *told* what to do. However, alcoholics cannot stay sober without the group so their *common welfare* must come first. Acknowledging that alcoholics must conform to spiritual principles or perish, they must sacrifice individual wants for the good of the group. Bill stressed the importance of individual sacrifice to A.A. as a whole. The Twelve Traditions ensure *unity* of the groups and *unity* of Alcoholics Anonymous as a whole society[3].

Lessons from prior movements seeking to help alcoholics

Past crusades to solve America's alcohol problem included the Washingtonians of 1840 to late 1880s, the Emmanuel Movement of the 1910s, and the Peabody Method of the 1920s. Each endeavor initially had substantial success but none could endure the difficult test of time[4]. Like past movements, the early Fellowship of Alcoholics Anonymous was initially experiencing success. However, how would it survive the test of time when all of its predecessors had failed?

For the Fellowship to endure there had to be a code of conduct for the movement that would outlive its founders. Furthermore, there had to be complete agreement by all alcoholics in the Fellowship to abide by that code. Given these two seemingly impossible constraints, Bill's solution was the Twelve Traditions.

Ironically, the miracle of A.A. today is that the Traditions, so far, have been instrumental to the Fellowship's survival even without *all* A.A. members' compliance and without *complete* agreement to its principles.

So far.

The First Tradition is the foundation of that code of conduct. A.A.'s ability to survive the test of time depends on unity and the common welfare of its members.

In his October 1949 article, "We Approach Maturity," Bill referred to 80,000 A.A. members when he said, "In each life, unity has risen far above former chaos[5]." In a similar way, Bill hoped that A.A.'s Traditions would help A.A. rise far above the chaos of its early and adolescent Fellowship when he went on to say, "… we may if we are worthy, surely expect an equal unity for A.A. as a whole[6]."

Bill's expectation for unity was at best aspirational given the chaos of A.A.'s early and adolescent years.

The early days of the Fellowship

Since there was not an articulated program of recovery, it is no small wonder that Bill referred to the time from when he stopped drinking in December 1934 to the First Printing of *Alcoholics Anonymous* in April 1939 as A.A.'s "flying blind" period[7].

Bill attributed his sober beginnings to a visit by his friend, Ebby T. Ebby, Bill's fun and then fun-with-trouble drinking companion for many years, shocked Bill with the news that he was no longer drinking due to an intervention by members of the Oxford Group[i]. Ebby's visit, one alcoholic talking to another, was not new having been a part of the earlier Washingtonian, Emmanuel, and Peabody treatments. Nonetheless, this visit led to Bill finally getting sober and in a subsequent visit, Ebby shared with Bill a rough plan for staying sober[8].

Bill doggedly worked with other alcoholics during his early months of recovery. Dr. Silkworth[ii], who attended to Bill during his recent hospitalizations, may have inspired him; but the real impetus was the relief that working with drunks gave Bill from his depression and from the desire to drink[9].

Finally, Bill found success with Dr. Bob and the two men promptly started working with whomever they could find. When Dr. Bob's Oxford Group friend, T. Henry Williams, commented on how hard Bill and Dr. Bob worked in the early days to sober up drunks, Bill's reply was simple, "We had to.... We were under awful compulsion, and we found that we had to do something for somebody or actually perish ourselves[10]."

For early A.A.s, carrying the message was a matter of personal survival.

By October 1937, in just over two years, the fledgling Fellowship had approximately thirty-one sober members in Akron and around ten members in New York City[11]. This was an astonishing rate of recovery in the context of treatment for hopeless alcoholics during those years. Most hospitals avoided taking difficult alcoholic cases. Furthermore, hospitals that took such patients could not boast the number of successes that Bill and Dr. Bob were experiencing.

Bill and Dr. Bob were keenly aware that they had discovered an effective solution for struggling alcoholics. They certainly had multiple failures. It was

---

[i] American Lutheran minister Frank Buchman founded the Oxford Group, a Christian fellowship, in 1921. It was particularly successful in the 1930s. Buchman renamed the group in 1938 Moral Re-Armament and led the group until he retired in 1961. See the section, "A glaring lack of unity in the program" in Tradition One of this study.

[ii] Dr. William D. Silkworth specialized in the treatment of alcoholism at Charles B. Towns Hospital for Drug and Alcohol Addictions where he treated Bill W. Dr. Silkworth wrote "The Doctor's Opinion" in the Big Book. See Tradition Ten in this study under "At the public level: medical opinions about alcoholism."

not unusual for prospects to relapse, sometimes repeatedly. Bill and Dr. Bob's immediate concern was to determine whether such prospects were serious about getting sober again. Since everyone had less time than Bill, the idea of continuous sobriety would not be nearly as important as helping an alcoholic to get sober, whether a first-timer or one who was prone to relapse.

In those first two-years, forty-one alcoholics recovered by a word-of-mouth program fueled Bill's dream of carrying the message to as many alcoholics as possible.

The first attempts for unity: group consciences

Out of a desire for unity, although not named as such, one of the earliest group consciences occurred when Bill met with the Akron squad promptly after his and Dr. Bob's tally of sober alcoholics. Bill sought the Akron squad's support to find better ways to spread the message of recovery. After a heated discussion and a contentious vote, Bill received a very grudging approval to find money to build hospitals, train missionaries, and write a book[12].

Bill secured the Akron group's approval by agreeing not to approach the Akron alcoholics for financial support. He would have to seek support where the money was – New York City.

If there was unity, at best it was only half-hearted!

Six months later, Bill and his sober friend, Hank P., secured some funding albeit far short of their expectations. John D. Rockefeller, Jr.'s $5,000 donation[iii] awarded on March 17, 1938 was barely enough to help Dr. Bob continue his work in Akron. Thus, their dream of hospitals, sanitariums, or paid missionaries was unattainable[13]. A book would be Bill's only hope for getting the word out

---

[iii] Fund raising hopes hinged on John D. Rockefeller, Jr. who continued his wealthy family's practice to donate money to jumpstart a wide range of initiatives such as temperance movements and education for minorities. For more information, read Ron Chernow's *Titan: The Life of John D. Rockefeller, Sr.*

to alcoholics who could not make the journey to Akron or New York. He went back to Akron in April of 1938 to present his case for writing a book.

Oh no! Another group conscience!

The Akron squad was even more resistant, arguing that they would be flooded with requests for help and that the program was working perfectly well by word-of-mouth testimony. With such vociferous objections, wisely, Bill did not call for a vote knowing he would lose and would not get 'permission' by the squad to write the book[14]. Undeterred, Bill went back to New York and found the support he needed to begin writing. Without achieving the unity he truly desired, Bill wrote his story in May 1938 while Hank P. focused on finding more funds[15].

The Akron group assumed that writing the book was off the table. It should come as no surprise to alcoholics that, Akron protestations notwithstanding, Bill started the book without their approval. Dr. Bob would not know what Bill was up to until five weeks after the "no-vote-called" Akron visit. It was then that Bill sent Dr. Bob a very polished version of his story and the chapter, "There is a Solution[16]." Anticipating confrontation, Dr. Bob decided to withhold this information from most of the Akron squad, at least for the time being.

A glaring lack of unity in the recovery program

By November 1938, the Fellowship was growing in Ohio and New York, and spreading out to other states. Bill was approaching his third year of sobriety and already the unwritten program of recovery was morphing in substantively different ways. The approach was dependent on where and with whom one got sober.

- The program in Akron was the Oxford Group's Christian-based Four Absolutes (honesty, unselfishness, love, and purity) and five Cs: confidence, confession, conviction, conversion, and continuance[17];
- In New York, the program was a more secular six-step style that Bill described in his story[18];

- Hank P. had his own method using four steps derived from the Oxford Group's Four Absolutes and[19];
- Depending on who was carrying the message, more simple variations were surfacing that could be summarized with three steps:

1. Admit you're licked.
2. Surrender your life to God
3. Act accordingly (i.e. pray, meditate, help others)[20].

If Bill did not get a program down in writing and published quickly, A.A. would become a hodge-podge of approaches to recovery. Unity would not be possible, and there would never be a cohesive Fellowship.

Amidst chaos and disappointment and without unity, Bill writes "How It Works"

While variations of the program were having some success, clearly there was little unity on how it worked. Through the summer into the fall of 1938, Bill appeared to avoid writing the portion of the book that would lay out the recovery program. Instead, he slowly produced other chapters, and started seeking input from the Fellowship so that there would be buy-in. Though Bill urged Dr. Bob to seek feedback from the Akron squad, Dr. Bob was selective in who saw the drafts. As a result, very few comments came from Akron. In the meantime, Bill shared what he had written up to that point at the weekly meetings in New York where members hotly debated Bill's Christian-oriented references[21]. Bill later recalled, "So, we fought, bled, and died our way through one chapter after another[22]."

In short, one part of the Fellowship, Akron, was non-committal while the New York alcoholics were arguing over every word!

To make matters worse, Bill was facing one financial letdown after another. Besides struggling with his own monetary woes, he and Hank P. repeatedly hit brick walls in terms of getting support for the book. The Trustees of the Alcoholic Foundation, who managed the Rockefeller donation, refused their pleas to seek any further sources of funding. Finally, in a desperate move to raise money to print the book, Hank and Bill devised an ill-conceived scheme to sell stocks. But, nobody was buying the stocks!

In November 1938, Bill suffered what was perhaps his greatest heartbreak, yet another relapse by Ebby. Specifically, after returning from drying out all summer on Fitz M.'s farm, Ebby went on a roaring bender taking with him two sober members who were living with Bill and Lois. Bill was furious and promptly threw the two residents out[23].

Shortly thereafter, as poignantly portrayed by Ernest Kurtz, "it was a not-very-serene [Bill] who, after much hesitation and even stalling, finally set out to put down in words the heart of the program[24]." In "How It Works," it is not surprising that, with the pain of Ebby's disastrous relapse, Bill first focused on people who do not get this simple program[25]. Bill seemed to etch his dismay and bewilderment in his introductory paragraph.

> Rarely have we seen a person fail who has thoroughly followed our directions. Those who do not recover are people who cannot or will not completely give themselves to this simple program, usually men and women who are constitutionally incapable of being honest with themselves. There are such unfortunates. They are not at fault[26].

Then, setting aside his despair, Bill laid out his version of how the first one-hundred men and women got sober with a Twelve Step program.

Wait a minute! Twelve Steps? Yes! Twelve Steps!

If there were heated debates about the earlier chapters, the first draft of "How It Works" provoked outrage. As Bill shared some years later, "… and boy, pandemonium broke loose[27]." A sizable amount of compromise and bargaining resulted in the final draft, but disagreement and strife over Bill's heavy use of Christian references and directives persisted up until days before the First Printing of the book.

The idea of unity was tenuous as reflected in these early confrontational "group consciences." It would only get worse.

Still no unity once the program is in writing

If there was very little unity before, the completion of the book left a wake of dissension and disagreement. Bill had great difficulty getting the earlier members in Akron to submit their stories to include in the book. Some claimed the book was a commercial enterprise, a taboo for a program in which service is freely given. Bill D. (alcoholic number 3) and Earl T. (the cofounder of the Chicago groups) exhibited their disdain by withholding their stories; stories that Bill desperately wanted, but ultimately did without. After the book's unquestionable merit was established, both men submitted their stories for the Second Edition printed fifteen years later[28].

By the end of the "flying blind" period, Bill's attempts to foster unity in the Fellowship fell far short of the ideal. Ironically, none of the recovered alcoholics of that day had worked the *Twelve* Steps of Alcoholics Anonymous.

Perhaps that was why Bill wrote in "There is a Solution," that the Fellowship had found a recovery program "upon which we *can join* (emphasis added) in brotherly and harmonious action[29]."

Without the unity he desired, he was clearly unable to write 'upon which we *have joined* in brotherly and harmonious action.'

Bill's wish for unity was not a reality. It was a dream.

A slow and discouraging start to selling the Big Book

On April 10, 1939, Cornwall Press printed 4,650 books[30]. Inquiries about the newly published book barely trickled into Hank P.'s New Jersey office where Bill worked with Ruth Hock. In May 1939, Lois and Bill's worsening financial difficulties resulted in the loss of her childhood home. They shuffled from family to family in the Fellowship and ultimately moved into the first AA clubhouse in New York City.

Four months after the book's publication, Hank relapsed. The bitterness between the two former friends resulted in a firestorm that very much informed A.A.'s current Sixth and Seventh Traditions[31]. As Bill struggled to hold the Fellowship together, requests stemming from the publication of the book continued to be few and far between.

Bill had less than five years sobriety. And the first few months after he published the Big Book were miserable.

When the tide changed, it was a tsunami.

After multiple failed efforts to get publicity, *Liberty* magazine published a piece called "Alcoholics and God" in September 1939. Then the program began to attract attention. Rockefeller, impressed with the early Fellowship's tenacity and perseverance, began to host dinners, which helped to attract more attention and funding. Finally, The *Cleveland Plain Dealer* published a series of articles starting late 1939 and continuing into 1940 causing escalated growth in membership particularly in Ohio[32].

If Dr. Bob and Bill were delighted when in 1937 when they had 40 or so members in two years, they must have been reeling in shock at acquiring 2,000 members in the two years after publication of the Big Book. These promotional boosts were A.A.'s first forays into their evolving public relations policies.

The 2,000 newly declared alcoholics, in essence, were the first products of the Twelve Step program outlined in the book. Many of them were not the "real alcoholics" that Bill thought would benefit most from the program. They were "hard drinkers" who were enjoying the fruits of successful sobriety except for one common concern: they did not have the spiritual upheaval described by "real alcoholics" in the First Edition.

Were they doing something wrong? Bill responded to their concerns in the Second Printing of the First Edition, which was the last substantive adjustment he would make in the Big Book. Bill changed the wording of the Twelfth Step from "spiritual experience" to "spiritual awakening" and, in "There is a Solution" and "More about Alcoholism," directed the reader to an essay in "Appendix II" which would later be called "Spiritual Experience[33]."

The tide had been rising, but the tsunami began in March 1941, when Jack Alexander's *Saturday Evening Post* article[iv] made Alcoholics Anonymous a

---

iv See in this study Tradition Twelve under the section "Jack Alexander sets out to expose A.A."

household name. In just over eight months, the 2,000 members increased to 8,000. As Bill described it:

> A real Niagara [Falls] then broke loose, and we were deluged with letters and with alcoholics by the thousands.
> This sudden growth ushered in a period of awful uncertainty. The big test of A.A.'s unity began in earnest[34].

Was there A.A. unity? Not really. Not yet.

From counting members to counting groups

Surely, Bill was happy that there was a single program of recovery after he published the Big Book. Furthermore, he must have taken a great deal of pleasure in the knowledge that groups were springing up across the United States, Canada, and overseas with the help of business travelers and newly sober World War II soldiers. However, that pleasure was short-lived as Bill quickly discovered that groups were self-destructing almost as fast as they were forming.

In *Alcoholics Anonymous Comes of Age*, one early member's story captured Bill's dream of what would happen when the Big Book landed in the hands of a struggling alcoholic.

In September 1939, Mort J. was very drunk in Denver, Colorado where someone gave him a copy of the Big Book. Mort tossed it into his suitcase and continued to drink his way across several states arriving in Palm Springs, California in November. One can easily imagine a hung-over and trembling Mort starting to read the book. However, that was not all that happened. Mort actually got sober as a result of reading the Big Book. He then followed Bill's suggestions in "Working with Others" and started the first Los Angeles group in the Cecil Hotel.

As new groups frequently did, the newly formed Los Angeles group sought guidance from A.A.'s New York Headquarters. As was its practice, Headquarters sent help in the form of recovering salespeople who were traveling on business to the areas of need. Apparently, the trip from New York to Los Angeles was too long for these helpers to make without relapsing. The Los Angeles group reported:

Well, we've got a lot of people sober out here. But we do sometimes wonder if anybody is sober east of the Rocky Mountains. We haven't seen a single Easterner who is really dry. They've all been drunk, every one of them[35].

Again, relapse was not unusual among the early members. Sadly, Boston alcoholic, Paddy, was a case in point. Paddy's first two successes were Bert C. and Jennie B., but Paddy could never stay sober. Though he continued to work with others, his heartbreaking relapses culminated in his alcoholic death. Bill pointed out that, "This very sick man left behind him a great group and a triple-A rating for valor[36]." Bert and Jennie continued to stay sober as trusted servants of the Boston group.

The Los Angeles group and the Boston group are snapshots of what was starting to unfold rapidly in the early 40's. In *Alcoholics Anonymous Comes of Age*, Bill wrote:

> The pins on our office wall map showed scores of new groups springing up every week. Sometimes experienced A.A.'s moved away from established centers to make their homes in other cities. Such localities were the lucky ones. But in most cases the newly formed groups had no experienced guidance whatever, except for the A.A. book, an occasional traveler, and correspondence with Headquarters[37].

Bill continued to describe the turmoil and confusion that resulted in a steady stream of correspondence between these struggling groups and Headquarters that would contribute to *The Twelve Points to Assure Our Future*, a prequel to A.A.'s Twelve Traditions. He said:

> Their worries and problems seemed endless. Committees quarreled, new clubs had unheard of headaches, orators held forth, groups split wide open. Some members turned professional, selling A.A. therapy for money to new prospects. Sometimes whole groups got drunk, and local public relations went haywire. Such was the beginning of a truly frightening experience that lasted a long time[38].

It lasted for a long time because the idea of unity was not particularly appealing to those who started their own groups.

"Leaders" were a barrier to unity in the Fellowship

The "flying blind" period was challenging because Bill was struggling with individual recovered alcoholics who had their own ideas of what the program of recovery should be. Unfortunately, having a written program of recovery was helpful, but it was not a solution. Like all books, the Big Book was subject to interpretation. More frequently than not, the interpretation that prevailed was usually delivered and reinforced by the person who started the group.

For example, in Cleveland, Clarence S. held forth that the A.A. program was derived from "two sources in the Bible: The Sermon on the Mount and Saint James on faith without works being dead and the healing ministry[39]." Akron and Cleveland literature sales offerings today include publications that support Clarence's and the Oxford Group members' beliefs.

In 1940, Bill sent a New York member, Ray W. to start a group in San Francisco while there on business. Ray was an affirmed atheist, but he seemed broad-minded enough to use the Big Book in this endeavor. Ray contacted the list of San Francisco alcoholics provided by Headquarters and asked them to meet him at his hotel. Bill did not anticipate what Ray would say to these new prospects.

> Now, boys, this A.A. is great stuff. It really saved my life. But there's one feature of it I don't like. I mean this God business. So when you read this book, you can skip that part of it[40].

Less than two weeks later, Ray departed leaving behind a divided and frightened group. Fortunately, a local psychiatrist, Dr. Poliak, and a non-alcoholic woman, Mrs. Oram, continued to support the faltering group. While slipping and backsliding were common amongst the members, the group somehow held together[41].

In *Alcoholics Anonymous Comes of Age*, Bill wrote that early A.A.'s first big fear was that of slips or relapses. Fortunately, the disposition of the early members was to help all who wished to stay sober. The next big fear was out-of-bounds romance, but they soon learned that these perils would not "do us in after all, and our fears in this area subsided[42]."

The worst perils were "the desires for power, for domination, for glory, and for money." Bill was gentle in his Traditions essays when he described bleeding deacons. However, in *Alcoholics Anonymous Comes of Age*, Bill spoke more plainly about difficult "leaders" of groups:

> They were all the more dangerous because they were invariably powered by self-righteousness, self-justification, and the destructive power of anger, usually masquerading as righteous indignation.
>
> Pride and fear and anger – these are the prime enemies of our common welfare[43].

Such power-driven members, no matter what their motives, threaten the common welfare of the group. Bill then emphasized the backbone of unity in A.A.: the Twelve Steps:

> True brotherhood, harmony, and love, fortified by clear insights and right practices, are the only answers. And the purpose of A.A.'s traditional principles is to bring these forces to the top and keep them there. *Only then can our common welfare be served; only then can A.A.'s unity become permanent* (emphasis added)[44].

The "flying blind" period was followed by what Bill called "the big test of A.A.'s unity," which lasted into the late forties. By 1944, Bill had contended with 10,000 alcoholics many of whom were in 360 groups, most of whom knew far better than he how A.A. groups should operate[45].

It must have been out of some sense of desperation that, in 1945, Bill started to formulate the *Points* to assure A.A.'s future.

The idea of unity would not come quickly to the Fellowship

Under these conditions, how could A.A. ever hope to pass the big test of unity, which was critical to surviving the test of time? That is, how would he ever get the groups to identify as a single Fellowship of Alcoholics Anonymous?

Lyn S.

Just as there was a desperate need for the Fellowship to have a single program of recovery, its survival depended on a single code of conduct to which all A.A.s would agree. Thankfully, Bill did not hesitate to take on the impossible dream of A.A.'s unity and common welfare.

In the April 1946 issue of Grapevine Magazine, Bill wrote *The Twelve Points to Assure Our Future*, which he said were "codified into a set of principles [that] could offer tested solutions to all our problems of living and working together and of relating our society to the world outside[46]."

With hundreds of groups already functioning, Bill anticipated the need for selling the *Twelve Points*. While battling depression and resistance from old-timers and the Trustees on the Alcoholic Foundation's board, Bill traveled the country for over three years peddling the *Points*. The reception by the existing groups was at best disinterest, if not outright rejection[47]. Ironically, adoption of the *Points* was made possible by the desperate need of new groups, not out of the need for change by established groups. Established groups would take a while longer to recognize the value of the *Points* for solving their problems.

Bill had hoped the *Points* would serve as a study guide to help groups pass the "big test of A.A.'s unity." Like woefully underprepared students, the Fellowship would need another five years to demonstrate at the very least, a promising potential to achieve unity by accepting Bill's idea for a Conference. After that, the Fellowship would need almost fifteen years to be willing to take full responsibility for Alcoholics Anonymous. We will explore this rocky journey as we discuss the rest of the Traditions.

Members should heed Bill's reminder in the First Tradition essay, "So at the outset, how best to live and work together as *groups* became the prime question[48]." Bill did not say "as a group" but "as *groups*." *Working* the First Tradition includes a commitment to be part of general service for groups in the United States and Canada. Groups do this by having an active General Service Representative. We will learn in the Second and Ninth Traditions why a General Service Representative is important to A.A. unity[49].

Is today's Fellowship passing A.A.'s big test of unity?

Coming up: the Second Tradition

In the Big Book, *There is a Solution,* reminds alcoholics of the two fundamentals of recovery:

> "But the ex-problem drinker who has found this solution, who is properly armed with facts about himself, can generally win the entire confidence of another alcoholic in a few hours. Until such an understanding is reached, little or nothing can be accomplished[50]."

and

> "When, therefore, we were approached by those in whom the problem had been solved, there was nothing left for us but to pick up the simple kit of spiritual tools laid at our feet.[51]"

The Second Tradition makes these two fundamentals possible when alcoholics come together as a group and when the groups come together as a Fellowship.

Who's in charge around here?

Tradition 2

> *For our group purpose there is but one ultimate authority – a loving God as He may express Himself in our group conscience. Our leaders are but trusted servants; they do not govern*[1].

The Long Form: *Our A.A. experience has taught us that:*

> For our group purpose there is but one ultimate authority – a loving God as He may express Himself in our group conscience[2].

Synopsis of Bill's essay in the 12 & 12

In this Tradition's essay, Bill tracked the natural path followed by many alcoholics after successfully starting groups and becoming 'leaders.' As the membership grew in these new groups, resentments increased against the 'leaders' until members pushed for rotation of leadership. After nursing bruised egos, some founding 'leaders' became elder statesmen; others relapsed or continued to be bleeding deacons. Bill provided clear guidance for how A.A. members can be trusted servants. Using this essay as an opportunity to help newly forming groups, Bill provided an overview of possible group service positions. Finally, to illustrate the wisdom of a group conscience, Bill tells the story of how, with the guidance of his group, he turned down a job as an A.A. lay therapist[3].

For our group purpose

The first phrase, "For our group purpose." is indispensable in that it binds the Second Tradition to the First Tradition.

To illustrate its importance, a restatement of the Second Tradition could be:

> *A.A. ensures its unity and protects the common welfare of its members* by having but one ultimate authority *for the group* – a loving God as He may express Himself in our group conscience. *A.A. groups' leaders* are but trusted servants; they do not govern.

Upon closer examination, "For our group purpose" might evoke questions about Bill's wording of the Second Tradition. Given that A.A.'s membership included the non-religious from its earliest beginnings, why did Bill continue to use his deist "loving God" and "Himself" instead of the more inclusive spiritual Higher Power when he wrote the Traditions? Why did Bill add, "Our leaders are but trusted servants; they do not govern" when he revised the original *Twelve Points*? Finally, how did the group conscience become A.A.'s process for shaping policy and making decisions?

For each of these questions, we will see how the spirit of the phrase, "For our group purpose," evolved to become a standard for *inclusivity* when practicing the spiritual principle of the Second Tradition.

A loving God? Why not a loving Higher Power?

While Bill wryly referred to his own awakening as a "hot flash" or 'white light" spiritual experience, it was a very personal and profound event that irrevocably confirmed his belief in a Higher Power he called God. When Bill started working with Dr. Bob, they predictably turned to religious literature, meditations, and prayers with which they were familiar. Naturally, Bill would draw on those resources most comforting to him when he drafted the book.

A.A. owes a great debt to two of Bill's New York Fellowship members, Hank P. and Jim B., who fought constantly to temper Bill's heavy-handed use of Christian references in the draft copies of the Big Book. Bill answered with stubborn resistance against changing *his* text.

On What Slender Threads

In desperation, Hank shared the religiously weighted prepublication manuscript with a New Jersey psychiatrist, Dr. Howard[i]. The doctor was intrigued by the draft but recommended that all coercive words, like 'must' and 'should,' be removed to make the program more appealing to alcoholics. In the psychiatrist's view, the text was far too directive and dogmatic particularly through its pervasive use of Biblical phraseology[4].

According to Jim B., "…disaster nearly overtook us, for it threw Bill into a terrific mental uproar to have his baby pulled apart by an outside screwball psychiatrist, who in his opinion knew nothing about alcoholism[5]."

Still, Bill was determined not to make any changes until Hank threatened to convene a *committee* of alcoholics to weigh in on the text. After all, Bill was claiming that one hundred men and women wrote the book. The undesirable prospect of a group conscience forced Bill to relent 17 days before the prepublication manuscript went to press. He frantically started replacing the mandate-oriented text with prose that was more suggestive and he counterbalanced some of his Christian-based language with allowances for other spiritual pathways[6].

Some, but not all.

Many of Bill's Biblical expressions remained without qualifiers. This was also true in the *Twelve Steps and Twelve Traditions*. As an A.A. member expressed in the pamphlet, *The "God" Word: Agnostic and Atheist Members in A.A.*, "The God in the Big Book is the God of Bill W.'s understanding[7]." One can say the same of the *Twelve Steps and Twelve Traditions*.

To be fair, Kurtz wrote that for the first forty years of A.A.'s history, most alcoholics, including atheists and agnostics, ultimately adopted an understanding of God very similar to Bill's perspective[8].

But "most" does not mean all.

---

i Historians have been unable to identify conclusively who Dr. Howard was. See Schaberg's *Writing the Big Book*, 566 – 567.

Lyn S.

When Bill presented the Traditions at the 1950 International Conference, he had been sober 15 ½ years. He continued to believe that atheists, agnostics, and other multi-deist or non-deist alcoholics who came into A.A. eventually would believe in a God similar to his own. Hence, his Christian references continued in the 1953 publication of the *Twelve Steps and Twelve Traditions*. Specific to this discussion, the Second Tradition invoked the ultimate authority as a loving *God* rather the more generic loving *Higher Power*.

Bill less-than-half-heartedly tried to be more inclusive in his essay on the Second Step when he said: "Relieved of the alcohol obsession, their lives unaccountably transformed, they came to believe in a Higher Power, and *most of them began to talk of God* (emphasis added)[9]." Later on, in his essay on the Twelfth Step, Bill reverted to his old ways. He wrote that the member who was the "doubter … who still considered his well-loved A.A. group the higher power, *would presently love God and call Him by name* (emphasis added)[10]."

Indeed! Jim B. might have disagreed. His story in the Big Book, "The Vicious Cycle," concluded with Jim having a spiritual experience of the educational variety[11]. There is no indication Jim called God by name.

It would take many more years for Bill to acknowledge that the spiritual path was wider than he imagined. Bill and his friend, psychiatrist, and Trustee, Dr. Harry Tiebout[ii], were surprised with the success of Buddhists in Southeast Asia getting sober using the Big Book while maintaining their non-deist beliefs. Furthermore, like the recovering Buddhists, many A.A. alcoholics who remained atheists or agnostics were getting and staying sober[12].

Was it enough for Bill to consider making changes to the literature?

Ironically, Bill was frustrated by the Fellowship's enshrinement of the Big Book, which was the primary reason he wrote the 1953 *Twelve Steps and Twelve Traditions*. He desperately wanted to write more about the Steps, but he could not overcome the members' objections to making even the smallest edits to the Big Book. Eight years after the publication of the *Twelve and*

---

ii Dr. Harry Tiebout was a psychiatrist who promoted Alcoholics Anonymous. He treated Marty M. and Bill W. He served as Trustee from 1957 to 1966.

Twelve, he revisited his frustration by saying, "As time passes, our book literature has a tendency to get more and more frozen – a tendency for conversion into something like dogma[13]."

Did this mean he might have been open to tempering his earlier religious references, had he been able to do so? Probably not, because through his own spiritual pursuits over the years, Bill believed he had evidence that God existed[14].

Was he being at all self-reflective when he said, "We may as well face the fact that A.A. will always have its fundamentalists, its absolutists, and its relativists[15]"? Maybe, especially since he did not openly share with the Fellowship that he believed he had proof of the existence of God. He practiced restraint when, in later years, he acknowledged that faith *must* be an individual experience[16].

Bill had clearly come to terms with differences in the fundamental idea of a Higher Power by 1965 when he wrote:

> We have atheists and agnostics. We have people of nearly every race, culture and religion. In A.A. we are supposed to be bound together in the kinship of a common suffering[17].

Bill continued with an admonishment for the Fellowship and perhaps for himself:

> Let us not, therefore, pressure anyone with our individual or even our collective views[18].

Nonetheless, Bill's change in perspective came long after the Fellowship had effectively halted any substantive editorial changes to the Big Book.

When we speak of God we mean your own conception of God

Which again, is why A.A. owes so much to the tenacity of Hank P. and the stubbornness of Jim B. Because of their persistence, there are multiple 'religious disclaimers' in the Big Book. One of the more important concessions is in the chapter "We Agnostics":

When, therefore, we speak to you of God, we mean your own conception of God. This applies, too, to other spiritual expressions which you find in this book. Do not let any prejudice you may have against spiritual terms deter you from honestly asking yourself what they mean to you[19].

However, a few disclaimers counter-balanced with a plethora of Biblical terminology were not enough. Two years after the First Printing of the Big Book, an expanded 'spiritual experience' qualifier was added to alleviate the anxiety of some of its 2,000 readers who became A.A. members. They were worried about not having a 'white light' spiritual experience. In response to their concerns, Bill apologetically added to the Second Printing of the First Edition an alternative to the 'white light' spiritual experience:

He finally realizes that he has undergone a profound alteration in his reaction to life; that such a change could hardly have been brought about by himself alone… . With few exceptions our members find that they have tapped an unsuspected inner resource which they presently identify with their own conception of a Power greater than themselves[20].

There is no question that, without any substantive changes since 1941, the Big Book is unparalleled in effectively giving religious and non-religious alcoholics a path to continuous sobriety through a spiritual transformation – an experience that is based on each individual's understanding of the path to spirituality.

They need only ask what the prose means to them.

For the A.A. group purpose, the *group's* ultimate authority

Thus, members of a group can apply the same advice in "We Agnostics" to the wording of the Second Tradition. Therefore, when approaching a group conscience, do not let the terms in the Second Tradition "deter you from honestly asking yourself what they mean to you."

Practicing the First Tradition's principles of unity and common welfare, all members of the group should take a moment to acknowledge the authority that is derived from their *combined spiritual understanding as they begin the group conscience.*

This works very well if no one is trying to dominate the discussion. What is a group's best defense from those who would be leaders rather than trusted servants?

Alcoholics' problems with authorities and rules

After Bill set out to "sell" the *Points* to the groups from 1947 through 1950[21], he found that while some groups were struggling, many had been thriving without any guidelines. This made his "sales job" difficult knowing that without the groups' support for the *Points*, Bill's long-range ambition to make alcoholics fully accountable for A.A.'s survival would never come to fruition.

Dealing with disinterested and apathetic groups led Bill to follow Earl T.'s advice to condense and give another name to the *Twelve Points*. Bill wisely avoided calling the *Points* 'laws,' 'rules,' 'by-laws,' or 'regulations,' knowing the Fellowship would reject any code that reflected a heavy authoritarian hand[22]. Thus, he chose the *Twelve Traditions*.

However, as much as alcoholics abhor authoritarians, no one loves being an 'authority' more than alcoholics do. Bill's observations while on the road and responding groups' problems while at Headquarters inspired him to expand the second *Point*, now the Second Tradition, to include, *Our leaders are but trusted servants; they do not govern*[23].

Leaders scrambling for recognition in A.A. was a very familiar problem to Bill.

The problems of power and prestige

A.A.'s early struggles with 'leadership' and 'credit for the founding of Alcoholics Anonymous' persisted for many years. Founder and co-founder status were not just for applause, but also for control of the program. Indisputably, Bill secured his co-founder designation by writing the Big Book and by having the longest continuous sobriety.

Predictably, with the exponential growth of Big Book sales, the competition to share Bill's co-founder status escalated.

Bill opened the floodgate when he tried mightily to give credit to as many people as he could while telling spellbound audiences his 'A.A. beginnings' stories. He did this by first illustrating his own continuous struggle with ego and grandiosity when he shared about his self-serving proposal that "Alcoholics Anonymous be named "The B. W. Movement[24]." Bill said members' rejected this folly through the wisdom of a group conscience, which added a bonus lesson to his tale. Bill then grandly attributed A.A.'s origins to such "diverse people as William James[iii], Dr. William Silkworth, the Reverend Sam Shoemaker[iv], [Dr, Bob's wife, Anne], and Sister Ignatia[v] [25]." Some early supporters not mentioned by Bill were quick to chastise him for deliberately forgetting their contributions and those of other non-alcoholic friends; a charge he found himself repeatedly denying throughout A.A.'s early adolescence.

Struggles for control of the newly developing Fellowship also surfaced in Akron. The Akron A.A.s were linked to the Oxford Group from their earliest beginnings through the stewardship of Henrietta Seiberling[vi]. Clarence S., having separated from the Oxford Group-driven Akron squad, boasted about forming the first group named 'Alcoholics Anonymous' in Cleveland in May 1939. Bill repeatedly acknowledged Henrietta and Clarence for their multiple contributions to A.A., which may have prompted both to proclaim themselves as co-founders of A.A[26].

There were others who might have been co-founders had they stayed sober.

Up until his death, Bill always acknowledged Ebby T. as the man who consistently encouraged him to apply "spiritual principles and rules of practice[27]."

---

iii William James was a renowned American Philosopher who wrote *The Varieties of Religious Experience* (1902), a favorite resource for Bill W.

iv Rev. Sam Shoemaker was a popular Episcopal priest and avid supporter of Alcoholics Anonymous.

v Sister Ignatia worked closely with Dr. Bob as a nurse for alcoholics.

vi Henrietta Seiberling, a member of the Akron Oxford Group, introduced Bill to Dr. Bob at the Gatehouse on the Seiberling estate. She remained a key supporter of Alcoholics Anonymous for many years after.

In later years, when 'sponsor' became part of the A.A. vernacular, Bill faithfully referred to Ebby as his sponsor. While Bill continued his work in A.A., Ebby occasionally dropped in, but never fully engaged with the Fellowship[28]. He eliminated himself as a co-founder with his on-and-off drinking and his disinterest in working with other alcoholics. Ebby was sober when he died of emphysema on March 21, 1966.

According to Schaberg, there was another "Co-founder who Drank":

> Hank [P] is the most forgotten man in A.A. history. Had he stayed sober, he would surely be hailed today as one of the movement's co-founders.... Hank's slip was catastrophic and the price he paid – both personally and emotionally – was severe[29].

Schaberg did not stop there. He emphasized Hank's contributions when he described Hank as:

> ... a man whose direct contribution allowed A.A. to first survive and then emerge from its "flying blind" period with a clearly articulated program of recovery that was accessible, accommodating, and far more effective than the one Bill [W.] would have supplied had he been left on his own[30].

As we continue this study of the Traditions, we will learn more about Hank P.'s significant contributions to the overall structure of A.A., particularly its self-supporting philosophy and financial transparency protections.

Had Hank promptly returned to the Fellowship, members might have overlooked the fact that he drank four months after the publishing of the Big Book. Unfortunately, Hank continued drinking. His animosity toward Bill deepened and his bitterness toward A.A. grew. Hank not only lost any hope of cofounder status, his contributions faded in the background of A.A. history. He died at the age of 57 on January 18, 1954[31].

Finally, Dr. Bob was the most important recipient of Bill's self-effacing attempts to assign credit to others for the founding of A.A. A key player in

Akron during A.A.'s formative years, Dr. Bob stayed continuously sober after his relapse in June 1935. Besides Bill, this made him "the 'last man standing' among the important and effective early members[32]."

Without question, Dr. Bob's contributions more than earned him his co-founder status. He was the boots-on-the-ground 'Twelfth Stepper' who helped so many alcoholics find sobriety while Bill was raising money and writing the book. While others competed for co-founder status, Dr. Bob was quiet about his accomplishments.

With so many alcoholics and non-alcoholics clamoring for cofounder status, it was not until sometime between 1945 and 1947 that Dr. Bob rightfully rose to the top over all other competitors[33].

Shedding the leadership mantle

Establishing a co-founder did not completely minimize Bill W. as a 'leader' of A.A. Bill had multiple battles on that front, exacerbated by A.A. members' adulation that included hanging his picture on the walls in meetings.

In an attempt to lessen his visibility, he modified the story of the creation of A.A. to make it sound like a "hundred men and women" had actually founded the movement and created the book[34]. His on-the-road 'yarns' purposefully amplified early members' role in writing the basic text and diminished his leadership role to one of being a trusted servant.

In an indirect way, one hundred men and women writing the Big Book was a vehicle for encouraging groups to rely on group consciences, rather than individuals, for their decisions.

For our group purpose, our leaders are but trusted servants; they do not govern

Bill reflected that relinquishing his 'leadership' to A.A. members was inevitable but "a little hard on the old ego[35]." He then made a statement that is a core subtext in the Second Tradition.

> Here are people lifted up by their principles rather than by their preachers. How well this all [augurs] for the long future[36]."

Bill knew that alcoholics, especially those with good intentions, might regress by proclaiming their authority particularly over groups. Understanding this pervasive nature of alcoholics, especially himself, led to the heart of the Second Tradition – that of establishing unambiguously *who was the authority* (a loving Higher Power) and *who was not* (individual A.A. members).

This would only be possible through an *informed group* conscience.

Decision-makers: the earliest group consciences

While in Akron in April 1938, Bill had valiantly attempted to use the group conscience to get approval for writing the book. When he could see that he was not going to win a vote of approval from the Akron group, he appeared to resign from the issue by not calling for a vote. Thus, without Akron's support or knowledge, Bill went back to New York to start writing the book. The idea of honoring a group conscience was off to a rough start by A.A.'s earliest member!

Thankfully, in spite of his rebellious move to continue with the book, Bill intuitively understood that seeking counsel from the growing membership was essential to A.A.'s unity and ultimately its survival. His own maneuverings notwithstanding, Bill kept his eye on the prize – A.A.'s common welfare and unity were possible only by reliance on the group rather than reliance on an individual, especially himself.

The decision-making impact of group consciences definitely had a trial-by-fire moment when Bill told the New York Fellowship of his job offer from Charles Towns[vii] of Towns Hospital. While he alluded to the attractiveness of the offer in his Second Tradition essay, Bill does not adequately portray his and Lois's financial pressures. On hearing Bill tell the story in a meeting, Jack N. captured the depth of Bill's concession to the group conscience by saying sadly, "For a man to be supported by his wife in those days – well, for a Vermont Yankee – was a disgrace[37]."

---

vii Charles B. Towns experimented with cures for alcoholism and founded the Charles B. Towns Hospital in 1901.

Had Bill accepted the job at Towns Hospital, A.A.'s philosophy of non-professionalism and non-affiliation with outside enterprises would be non-existent because other A.A. members would shortly thereafter scramble for the same opportunities. As Schaberg indicated, this decision, based on the wisdom of a group conscience, was pivotal to A.A.'s future. It was a future not yet seen by Bill and Lois. Faithful to the wisdom of the group, they lived under impoverished conditions while Bill continued to direct his energies to writing the Big Book[38].

As much as Bill valued the group conscience, he did not always follow the early Fellowship's recommendations. According to *Pass It On*, when it came to group consciences during A.A.'s formative years, Bill was "… selective, using only those experiences that went to the heart of A.A. problems. Since his desire was always the best interest of A.A., his so-called manipulations always worked for the good of the Fellowship[39]."

A case in point is that of the co-founders' royalties from the sale of the Big Book. Had Bill listened to the group conscience at the time the book was published, it would not have been sold at all, but given away. In this case, Bill overrode the group conscience, insisting that the Fellowship sell the book[40]. Certainly, Bill deserved royalties just for writing the Big Book. Furthermore, he was correct when he reasoned years later that, without his receiving royalties, there would be no Headquarters, no Traditions, and ultimately no A.A. Bill would more than earn his keep for many years afterwards.

However, Bill demonstrated an inordinate faith in his own judgement when he said, "My personal life may not be exemplary, but I have never made a mistake about A.A[41]."

In fact, he did occasionally make mistakes. At heart, he must have known this given his desire to take decision-making out his hands or of the hands of a few and into the hands of the groups.

Bill's dream was for *all A.A. groups* to have an A.A. group conscience

When Bill was peddling the *Points*, he had a much larger purpose in mind. Bill promoted his dream for A.A to have a structure of elected trusted servants who would steer A.A.'s course[42]. Members were unimpressed and as years went by, Bill was having little success selling his dream of autonomy[43]. The complexity of trying to achieve a buy-in from members was compounded by the rapid growth of groups and their increasing reliance for guidance from Headquarters (Bill W. and Dr. Bob) and the Trustees of the Alcoholic Foundation.

The conundrum was that these overly reliant groups were, at the same time, resistant to the suggestions given by the Foundation and Headquarters; especially since groups had no say in crafting those suggestions. If this were to continue, Bill feared groups would lose interest and become disenfranchised from the Trustees, Headquarters, and A.A.

The groups were not the only ones to resist this idea. The Trustees were not happy that Bill was pushing a model they had not approved. When he broached the idea of an annual convention of groups' representatives, the Trustees protested vehemently. Such a cumbersome structure would incur undue hardships on the representatives and on the Foundation causing fractured political maneuverings and unnecessary expense.

The first Conference that almost wasn't

As we will learn later, some Trustees did not believe that recovered alcoholics would ever be mature enough to rise to such a task. Bill argued that the Foundation would ultimately lose A.A. groups if they were not included in these important discussions. Why should groups in other states care about decisions made by an unknown and remote group of non-alcoholic Trustees in New York?

Bill admitted to using sledge-hammer tactics on the Trustees as reflected by a scathing letter he wrote that included, "When I was in law school, the largest book I studied was the one on Trusts. I must say, gentlemen, that it was mostly a long and melancholy account of the malfeasances and misfeasances (sic) of boards of trustees[44]." Clearly, this was a solid demonstration of an immature alcoholic not getting his way. Bill was ashamed of his outburst saying, "I had written this to a group of the best friends I had in the world, people who had devoted themselves to A.A. and to me without stint. Obviously, I was on a dry bender of the worst possible sort[45]."

After intense arguments, apologies, and more arguments, non-alcoholic Trustee Leonard Harrison, who opposed the idea, compromised with non-alcoholic Trustee Bernard Smith, who supported Bill. Together, they convinced the Alcoholic Foundation to give the annual Conference a five-year test run[46].

In April 1951, the first General Service Conference met in New York City. Even today, all trusted servants should embrace that year's theme: *Not to Govern, but to Serve*. Bill noted that about a third of the delegates were real old-timers, and the rest were active members sober four to eight years. He said:

> We all sensed that something momentous was happening; that this was a historic moment. "… The delegates inspected A.A.'s finances and listened to reports from the board of trustees and from all of the services. There was warm but cordial debate on many questions of A.A. policy[47].

Thus, began transparency in A.A. affairs. Bill continued:

> The trustees submitted several of their own serious problems for the opinion of the Conference. With real dispatch the delegates handled several tough puzzlers about which we at headquarters were in doubt. Though their advice was sometimes contrary to our own views, we saw they were frequently right[48].

The first Delegates laid the groundwork for an informed group conscience; one that included background research and allowed all views including the minority opinion. Bill concluded:

> They were proving as never before that A.A.'s Tradition Two was correct. Our group conscience could safely act as the sole authority and sure guide for Alcoholics Anonymous. As the delegates returned home, they carried this deep conviction with them[49].

It was at this first trial run that the Delegates proposed changing the name of the Alcoholic Foundation to the General Service Board. This recommendation and the Delegates' General Service Conference structure of Alcoholics Anonymous was formally approved in 1955.

For our group purpose, the General Service Conference is A.A.'s group conscience

So began a seismic shift in how A.A. shaped policy through the five-year test run of its annual General Service Conference attended by Delegates, hereinafter referred to as the 'Conference.' In keeping with the Second Tradition, Delegates are not leaders, but trusted servants of their respective Areas' A.A. groups. Furthermore, the Conference continues to rely on a loving Higher Power as expressed by the Delegates' group conscience.

In short, the Conference is A.A. groups' group conscience for the United States and Canada.

The Conference was only a fractional part of giving responsibility for A.A. to alcoholics. It would take years for Bill to achieve his dream of alcoholics taking full responsibility for A.A.

The Conference recommends solutions to the "frozen" texts.

Even though the Big Book and the *Twelve Steps and Twelve Traditions* became "frozen" as described by Bill, the Conference responded to societal changes with pamphlets and literature that address evolving issues in race, ethnicity, sexual orientation, gender differences, spiritual variances, age (whether younger or older), problems other than alcohol, and many others.

The timeliness and effectiveness of every pamphlet depends upon A.A. members' careful use and study. All pamphlets are subject to revisions and updates as recommended by the Conference. Scan the pamphlets in the General Service Office's literature catalogue[50]. If you identify a need or have recommendations for changes in existing pamphlets, contact your General Service Representative to raise the issue.

What is an informed A.A. Group Conscience?

The AA Group pamphlet, provides guidance on an informed group conscience:

What is an Informed A.A. Group Conscience?

The group conscience is the collective conscience of the group membership and thus represents substantial unanimity on an issue before definitive action is taken. This is achieved by the group members through the sharing of full information, individual points of view, and the practice of A.A. principles. To be fully informed requires a willingness to listen to minority opinions with an open mind.

On sensitive issues, the group works slowly – discouraging formal motions until a clear sense of its collective view emerges. Placing principles before personalities, the membership is wary of dominant opinions. Its voice is heard when a well-informed group arrives at a decision. The result rests on more than a "yes" or "no" count – precisely because it is the spiritual expression of the group conscience. The term "informed group conscience" implies that pertinent information has been studied and all views have been heard before the group votes[51].

The AA Group pamphlet also provides detailed descriptions of the roles that trusted servants may serve with the reminder that rotation is best. We will discuss these in detail when we study the Ninth Tradition.

For our group purpose, we have the Second Tradition

An effective group conscience is the spiritual principle of *A.A. groups* that practice unity and prioritize the *common* welfare of all members. That statement alone should be sufficient to protect groups from heavy-handed leadership. However, knowing the nature of alcoholics, Bill added to the Second Tradition for emphasis, "Our leaders are but trusted servants; they do not govern."

Drawing on some of the promises in the Big Book, the group conscience is the group's opportunity to join in "harmonious action[52]," to allow our "common sense to become uncommon sense[53]," and to "enter the world of the Spirit" as an A.A. group[54].

Coming up: The Third Tradition

The *AA Group* pamphlet provides the information needed to join an A.A. group:

"The only requirement for A.A. membership is a desire to stop drinking" (Tradition Three). Thus, group membership requires no formal application. Just as we are members of A.A. if we say we are, so are we members of a group if we say we are[55].

We will learn in Tradition Three that the road to that very simple requirement was long and rocky.

We don't want you here!

Tradition 3

The only requirement for membership is a desire to stop drinking[1].

The Long Form: *Our A.A. experience has taught us that:*

Our membership ought to include all who suffer from alcoholism. Hence we may refuse none who wish to recover. Nor ought A.A. membership ever depend upon money or conformity. Any two or three alcoholics gathered together for sobriety may call themselves an A.A. group, provided that, as a group, they have no other affiliation[2].

Synopsis of Bill's essay in the 12 & 12

Bill began this Tradition with the reminder that the early Fellowship met in private homes. Their concerns and efforts to control who entered their homes naturally resulted in "rules for admission." Bill provided two examples of people who were not within the norms of the early Fellowship. The first story illustrates how the Fellowship's fears were baseless. The second emphasizes how barring alcoholics from the program could be tantamount to a death sentence. Eventually all rules were eliminated. Thus, the only requirement for membership is a desire to stop drinking. Bill summarized and emphasized his points with his last sentence: "So the hand of Providence early gave us a sign that any alcoholic is a member of our Society when *he* says so[3]."

Lyn S.

The Fellowship quickly outgrew meetings in homes

During the Fellowship's earliest years, alcoholics and supporters of the newly forming program quite naturally gathered in private homes. At that time, no one could have anticipated the rapidly growing demand that would occur in just a few years. That demand became more evident after the publication of the Big Book.

In the First Edition of *Alcoholics Anonymous*, "Bill's Story" described the numbers and settings for gatherings as of early 1939 in Akron and Cleveland:

> In one western city and its environs there are eighty of us and our families. We meet frequently at our different homes, so that newcomers may find the fellowship they seek. At these informal gatherings one may often see from 40 to 80 persons[4].

Two years later, in the Second Printing, Bill replaced the phrase, "eighty of us and our families," with "five hundred of us and our families." In addition, he changed the size of these gatherings from "40 to 80 persons" to "50 to 200 persons." For obvious reasons, there was no more mention of meeting in homes! The scramble for non-residential venues had begun.

Finally, in the June 1942 Third Printing of the First Edition, Bill increased "500 of us and our families" to "one thousand of us and our families[5]." That amendment remained for all future printings and editions.

Bill must have been excited with each revision as he penciled in the growing numbers. However, his own story provided a cautionary tale about opening one's home to alcoholics:

> An alcoholic in his cups is an unlovely creature. Our struggles with them are variously strenuous, comic, and tragic. One poor chap committed suicide in my home. He could not, or would not, see our way of life.[6]

Nonetheless, impressed by the program's success with impossible cases, many alcoholics and non-alcoholics generously opened their homes so that alcoholics could work together. For example, early Akron A.A. owes a tremendous debt to T. Henry and Clarace Williams, non-alcoholic members of the Oxford Group.

On What Slender Threads

The Williams had already opened their home for Oxford Group meetings where Dr. Bob first openly confessed his inability to stop drinking[7]. Members prayed for him, but his confession and their prayers appeared not to work. Dr. Bob's recovery began in earnest when he met Bill, the self-described "rum hound from New York[8]." Out of a genuine desire to help Dr. Bob and Bill, the Williams allowed newly recovering alcoholics to meet every Wednesday night in their home with their Oxford Group friends. The Williams kept their home open up until 1954, even though most of the alcoholics, also known as the Akron squad, had "spun off[9]" to form their own group by late 1939.

The spin-off was very much a function of growing pains for the early Fellowship. There were tensions developing between non-alcoholic Oxford Group members and the alcoholics who had joined them for support. As Bill indicated years later, even though the Akron squad had not been calling themselves the Oxford Group, they would always carry the Oxford Group label as long as the squad attended meetings at the Williams house. By December 1939, simmering tensions and the Oxford Group members' objections to the Big Book compelled Dr. Bob to offer his own home as a meeting place for the Akron squad. Some went with Dr. Bob immediately; others continued meeting at the Williams's house only to eventually join their recovery companions[10].

Coinciding with the squad's departure from the Williams house was the sudden and rapid growth of people seeking help from A.A. Dr. Bob wrote Bill, "Had 74 Wednesday in my little house, but shall get a hall soon[11]." It was only a matter of a few weeks before Dr. Bob moved the growing group to the King School in Akron.

A training program for newcomers

In residential and in non-residential venues, there were a number of problems with prospects who were indeed "unlovely creatures." Some early A.A.s sought to manage the influx of newly recovering alcoholics by requiring that they attend beginners meetings before they were allowed in A.A. meetings. The format for these early beginners meetings offered some assurance that prospects were serious about the program.

In *Back to Basics*, Wally P. wrote that Cleveland's Crawford Group started one of the earliest beginners meetings in 1941[12]. Many other groups quickly followed.

In June 1943, the North-West Group of Detroit required prospects to attend four sessions of beginners meetings with the following themes: "(1) Admission (2) Spiritual (3) Restitution and Inventory (4) Working and Message[13]." The Detroit and Cleveland groups' expectation that newcomers "be familiar with the 'basic principles' before ever attending a 'regular' meeting of Alcoholics Anonymous" helped ease Fellowship members' anxieties by controlling who got in to their meetings[14].

Today, while most meetings are in non-residential venues, some groups continue to sponsor "Back to Basics" workshops, although they are no longer 'tickets' for entry to A.A. meetings. Additionally, many areas offer beginners meetings that vary in format but are oriented toward providing newcomers the jump-start needed to proceed with the program. In offerings that target beginners, experienced A.A.'s are essential to their success. In the spirit of 'working with others,' these are ideal venues to find newcomers to help.

A universal and welcoming Fellowship?

In the Third Tradition essay, Bill wrote about the fears early A.A. members had when a newcomer who was 'different' from the norm arrived. He went on to say that when groups realized their fears were unsubstantiated, the Fellowship replaced its accumulation of restrictive rules with a very simple requirement for membership. To illustrate how far A.A. had progressed, Bill painted a rosy picture of A.A.'s open-door policy in *Alcoholics Anonymous Comes of Age*. He said, "Since that early time literally all kinds of people have found their way into Alcoholics Anonymous. Our inclusiveness is now very broad indeed[15]."

Bill went on to describe the range of members, from a Countess to a, hopefully former, member of Al Capone's mob. He concluded, "That's how universal A.A. is today[16]."

Was A.A. a truly universal and welcoming Fellowship?

We will examine the Fellowship's stumbles with two membership test cases during the "flying blind" period; after which, we will explore later challenges to A.A.'s inclusivity. Then the more important question will remain.

Is A.A. a truly universal and welcoming Fellowship?

The "flying blind" period's first test case – the atheist

The Third Tradition essay included a story about "Ed" a pseudonym for avowed atheist, Jim B. Jim was fortunate to have found his way into the New York Fellowship rather than the Akron Fellowship. Bill had already pulled away from the Oxford Group's tenets realizing that a fundamentally Christian program might deter struggling alcoholics. Schaberg observed, "[Jim] was, in fact, the kind of man who would not have a chance of getting sober in Akron[17]." Schaberg continued:

> There wasn't a glimmer of hope that [Jim] would ever make a personal surrender to God (either in public or private), and in Akron, as already noted, a new member was not admitted into the group until he had fulfilled that basic requirement[18].

As Bill portrayed in his essay, Jim angered the New York Fellowship with his profane declarations about his disbelief and his vocal contempt for those who did believe. At five months, Jim relapsed and disappeared for five days, after which he called his Fellowship friends for help. In an unusual move for the Fellowship in those days, the members ignored his calls. Jim finally reappeared by sneaking into Hank P.'s home late at night. The next morning found Jim contrite and willing to do anything to be allowed to stay in the Fellowship.

Almost anything.

Years later, Jim B. reinforced that part of Bill's essay:

> When the others saw my altered attitude, they took me back in, but for me they *had* to make it tough; if they hadn't, I don't think I ever would have stuck it out. Once again, there was the challenge of a tough job, but this time I was determined to follow through[19].

However, Bill's conclusion in the Third Tradition essay implied that "Ed" had a religious awakening. Bill wrote:

As he tossed on his bed, his hand brushed the bureau near by, touching a book. Opening the book, he read. It was a Gideon Bible. Ed never confided any more of what he saw and felt in that hotel room. It was the year 1938. He hasn't had a drink since[20].

In reality, Jim had a slightly different view:

For a long time the only Higher Power I could concede was the power of the group, but this was far more than I had ever recognized before, and it was at least a beginning. It was also an ending, for never since June 16, 1938, have I had to walk alone[21].

As much as Bill loved embellishing to make a point, he may have gone a bit too far. Clearly, Bill was firmly entrenched in his Christian beliefs and "Ed" was a metaphor for Bill's fixation that all who followed the A.A. program would find the God of Bill's understanding.

It is unfortunate that Bill didn't use Jim's story in the Big Book, "The Vicious Cycle." Jim provided a moving example of how an alcoholic atheist had a spiritual experience of the educational variety. Jim wrote that after getting sober and moving to Philadelphia:

I found myself in the middle of a brand-new group. When I started to tell the boys how we did it in New York and all about the spiritual part of the program, I found they would not believe me unless I was practicing what I preached[22].

What better example is there for the A.A. adage, 'Your actions speak so loud, I can't hear what you're saying!'? In his story, Jim continued to share the benefits of 'acting as if.'

Then I found that as I gave in to this spiritual or personality change, I was getting a little more serenity. In telling newcomers how to change their lives and attitudes, all of a sudden I found I was doing a little changing myself[23].

In the May 1968 *Grapevine*, "Sober for Thirty Years," Jim said that reliance [on the group] evolved to "… a belief that God and Good were synonymous" and, finally to "meditating and trying to tune in on my better self for guidance and answers[24]."

The truth is better than the myth. At the very least, Jim's real story made the spiritual path broad and roomy for agnostics and atheists. At the heart of this Third Tradition, belief in God is *not* a requirement for membership.

The "flying blind" period's second test case – alcoholic women

While society did not particularly appreciate alcoholic males, alcoholic women were considered the lowest of the low. In late 1935, one of the first women to seek help from the early Akron group *just might* have contributed to Dr. Bob's concerns about women in the Fellowship. Lil came to the Akron squad for help and promptly caused a disruption that was a distressing combination of alcohol, sex with another member, and the ensuing destruction of Dr. Bob's office to seek out and gobble down pills[25]. According to an Akron member's wife, Lil eventually got sober without A.A. but her impact on the Fellowship remained[26].

Not a stellar start for women in A.A.!

As indicated earlier, wives and family members also came to recovery gatherings. According to Schaberg, wives were the biggest barriers to the acceptance of women in early A.A as they were afraid of what these women might do to their families. Women from lesser social standings had a particularly difficult time as demonstrated by a Cleveland group barring a woman from going to their homes because she was "so bad[27]." Unfortunately, this event was not the only time that A.A. groups turned women away from the recovery program.

However, trouble did not solely arise from alcoholics' wives. Schaberg wrote, "the men could be just as bad and often acted in ways that did nothing to alleviate their wives' fears[28]." When a young, beautiful, and very rich divorcee, Sylvia [K], travelled from Chicago to Akron desperate for help with her alcohol problem, the husbands were enthusiastically welcoming, much to the chagrin of their wives. Sylvia was so excited about the help she received from the squad, she hinted she might move to Akron permanently. Someone suggested Sylvia could do more good by starting a group in Chicago. Schaberg said, "Sylvia was summarily escorted to the train station by several members and she left for the Windy City, much to the relief of Dr. Bob and all of the A.A. wives in Ohio[29]."

Sadly, Sylvia relapsed on the way back to Chicago. The 'solution' proposed for the 'Sylvia problem' could have resulted in her alcoholic death. Fortunately, she knew Earl T., who had been traveling back and forth to Akron. Together, they became the most active founding members of A.A. in Chicago[30]. Her story, "The Keys to the Kingdom" is in the Fourth Edition of the Big Book.

It is easy to see why Dr. Bob was particularly frustrated with the difficulties of working with women. Frank Amos[i], a nonalcoholic Trustee articulated Dr. Bob's concerns in February 1938 report when he said, "The sex problem makes it difficult. He, as a physician, can and has helped, but his wife and other wives must handle most of these for which there is a growing need[31]."

However, pushing an alcoholic woman into a room of non-alcoholic wives just wasn't ideal! Over time, Dr. Bob's cynical view eventually softened at his own wife's urging. Because of Anne's influence, he came around to the realization that women needed the help of other recovering alcoholics. According to Elgie T, Dr. Bob reflected, "Why not? What difference does it make? They're just as drunk as the men are[32]."

New York A.A., during that period, seemed more receptive to helping alcoholic women as evidenced by Florence R. Florence's ex-husband took her to Lois who in turn, took Florence to Bill. Bill readily worked with her. Florence's story, "A Feminine Victory," was the only alcoholic woman's story included in the First Edition of the Big Book. Wistfully, she wrote, "To my lot falls the rather doubtful distinction of being the only 'lady' alcoholic in our particular section[33]." Florence helped many women in the A.A. program, but sadly, she relapsed and died in 1943[34].

---

i Frank Amos was the Rockefeller associate who first investigated the potential for providing a donation to the early Fellowship. He remained a long-time friend, Trustee, and supporter for many years thereafter.

Did the Fellowship forget "A Vision for You?"

The two "flying blind" test cases underscored the importance of A.A.'s requirement for membership in those early days. As Schaberg noted:

> Both the women and the atheist [Jim B.] were in one way or another seriously out of step with the rest of the group, but they were admitted to their meetings nonetheless[35].

Unfortunately, efforts by members to block people who were "out of step" would continue after the "flying blind" period and, unfortunately, well into the period of A.A.'s great test for unity.

Were the struggles of women and other 'different' alcoholics what Bill had in mind when he wrote the following in "A Vision for You" in the Big Book? Maybe it should hang on the walls of A.A. meetings to remind members of the Third Tradition.

> No one is too discredited or has sunk too low to be welcomed cordially – if he means business. Social distinctions, petty rivalries and jealousies – these are laughed out of countenance. Being wrecked in the same vessel, being restored and united under one God, with hearts and minds attuned to the welfare of others, the things which matter so much to some people no longer signify much to them. How could they[36]?

How could they, indeed! Unfortunately, they could and they did.

Bill's frustration with race and the Third Tradition

A sad chapter in A.A.'s history, described poignantly in *Pass It On*, occurred when Bill had invited two black alcoholics to come to a New York area meeting, which resulted in a firestorm. A member of the group, Bobbie B. said the reaction was divisive and contentious with members' views ranging from welcoming to threatening to storm out.

Most group members agreed Bill had overstepped by not consulting them first. Obviously, it did not occur to Bill that including anyone in the meetings would be a problem. Realizing this mistake, Bill backtracked by asking the group a challenging question. Would those who protested including the two men in the meeting at least agree that they had a right to A.A. just the same as everyone else? Of course, the objectors had to agree in principle. With that wedge, Bill managed to get the group to concede, "that Negroes should be invited to attend open or closed meetings *as visitors* (emphasis added)[37]."

As visitors, blacks could come to meetings as silent observers.

In this and many other similar instances, A.A. fell far short of Bill's "A Vision for You" claim that social distinctions are laughed out of countenance!

According to *Pass It On,* many black alcoholics found sobriety and each other by the mid-1940s. Jim S., whose story, "Jim's Story," is in in the Second, Third, and Fourth Editions of the Big Book is believed to be the originator of A.A.'s first black group[38].

However, Bill was far from satisfied with this passive-exclusion policy as was indicated in his 1943 letter:

> Along with you, I feel very deeply about this race business. Save this one question, I suppose A.A. is the most democratic society in the world. All men should have an equal opportunity to recover from alcoholism – that is the shining ideal.
>
> But, unhappily, my own experience suggests that it may not be achieved in our lifetimes. In all the South and in most of the North, whites refuse to mingle with blacks socially. That is a stark fact which we have to face. Nor can they be coerced or persuaded to do so, even alcoholics[39]!

Referring to the obstructive actions in his own New York group, Bill said he had already been "slapped down" and he realized pressuring the group to do otherwise would only cause harm. Bill continued sadly, "It falls grievously short of our ideal – but practically speaking, what can be done about it? I don't know – I'm still looking hard for the answer[40]."

Three years later, Bill's answer would be in the statement of the Third Tradition. *The only requirement for membership is a desire to stop drinking.* Unfortunately, it would not be the answer for all A.A. groups for many more years.

Bill seized every opportunity he could to avoid the 'silent observer' option. In 1945, Barry L. called Bill when a black man with a multitude of other differences (bleached hair, ex-convict, homeless, wearing make-up, and dope-fiend) showed up at the clubhouse. Barry had spoken to older members and no one knew what to do about the unusual visitor. On behalf of the group, Barry called Bill and rather than Bill relating what his New York group did, he asked Barry to repeat once more what the peculiarities were for this particular visitor. Then, as the story is told in *Pass It On*:

> "Now," said Bill, "did you say he was a drunk?" "Oh yes," Barry replied. "There's no question about that. He's certainly a drunk." "Well, I think that's all we can ask," said Bill[41].

The group welcomed the man. Even though they never saw him again, Barry said this moment in A.A. created a precedent for the Third Tradition.

The "double stigma" – gay and alcoholic

Barry L. recounted Bill expanding on the portion of the Third Tradition essay about the man with the double stigma. When the man asked to join the Akron group, he candidly identified himself to Dr. Bob as a "sex deviate[42]." Unfortunately, the positive outcome as portrayed in Bill's essay on the Third Tradition did not set the standard for the future of gays in A.A.

Barry, who came to A.A. in 1945, recalled in a 1985 talk, the comfort level for gays in early A.A. by wryly saying:

> We did the best we could with what we had, and I was lucky enough to fall into the hands of two homosexual persons in AA, one man and one woman. And in those days, we were not closeted. In 1945, we were sealed in vaults[43]!

It was a telling reflection of A.A.'s failure to practice one of our most important principles, love and tolerance. In the same 1985 talk, "The Gay Origins of the Third Tradition," Barry said unhappily,

> I'm not going to talk much more about the old days because I don't like talking about the good old days. I don't think those were the good old days in AA; I think *these* are the good old days[44].

To underscore his point about the not-so-good-old-days, Barry L. recalled the firey discussions at the 1973 General Service Conference about whether to list gay groups in the *World Directory*. Sad to say, many delegates argued vehemently against this. According to Barry, the least harsh criticism was, "… What about the tradition of inclusiveness? If you set up gay groups, would they exclude other people[45]?"

This question breathes life into the word 'disingenuous' given early A.A. groups forced Negroes into forming their own special groups, and the Conference had already approved other special groups! Barry went on to say,

> … the discussion got going hot and heavy; it was really very distressing. Finally, at the end of the afternoon discussion, which was so hot and heavy, the chairman had a very smart idea – a very smart AA idea: he tabled the matter until next year[46].

That meant that the issue was on the agenda for the 1974 Conference and there would have to be a resolution. Regrettably, a year later, the fiery argument continued. On the heels of another long and heated debate, the chair cleared the agenda for the next day so that it was the only item for that day. It was no better then, until a nonalcoholic Trustee spoke up. In Barry's words,

> [The non-alcoholic trustee doctor] walked to the microphone and said, "I understand that when you listed young people's groups, you did not go through these shenanigans. Is that right?"
>
> And everybody said, "Yes…"

"And that when you listed women's groups you didn't go through all this folderol did you?

And everybody said, "No, we didn't do it then."

Well, what in the world are you picking on *these guys* for?" and he took his seat[47].

Barry went on to say there was a tangible change in the room. Seizing that palpable moment, the chair called the question. The recommendation to list Gay groups in the World Directory passed with 128 out of 131[48].

We will delve into special groups as they relate to group autonomy in the Fourth Tradition.

How are A.A. groups doing today?

In its early days, A.A. fell far short of the spirit of what Dr. Bob said that resolved the conflict about the man with the double stigma: "What would the Master do[49]?" Bill articulated a dream for A.A. unity in his Third Tradition essay when he said:

> Could any then imagine a society which would include every conceivable kind of character, and cut across every barrier of race, creed, politics, and language with ease[50]?

The long form of the Third Tradition was an expansion of Bill's dream.

> Our membership ought to include all who suffer from alcoholism. Hence we may refuse none who wish to recover. Nor ought A.A. membership ever depend upon money or conformity. Any two or three alcoholics gathered together for sobriety may call themselves an A.A. group, provided that, as a group, they have no other affiliation[51].

Has A.A. achieved Bill's dream? Does the common welfare of all newcomers come first? Can all alcoholics depend on A.A. unity?

A worthy alcoholic?

In the GSO pamphlet, *AA Tradition: How It Developed*, "Who is a Member of Alcoholics Anonymous" cautions members to avoid being the worthy alcoholic who judges the less worthy. All people who have a desire to stop drinking are worthy including chronic relapsers, young people, people who drank only a little, homeless, and people with other issues[52].

The A.A. Traditions have no provision for enforcement. They rely on members practicing spiritual principles. This particular Tradition calls on the principle of complete acceptance. It implicitly charges A.A. group members not to judge anyone's desire to stop drinking other than their own. As the pamphlet reminds the group:

> Our A.A. door stands wide open, and if he passes through it and commences to do anything at all about his problem, he is considered a member of *Alcoholics Anonymous.*
>
> He signs nothing, agrees to nothing, promises nothing. We demand nothing. He joins us on his own say-so[53].

Bill noted that some A.A. groups take this Tradition a step farther:

> Nowadays, in most groups, he doesn't even have to admit he is an alcoholic. He can join A.A. on the mere suspicion that he may be one, that he may already show the fatal symptoms of our malady[54].

This does not mean that prospects or members can disrupt the meeting. Bill goes on to say:

> … If a member persists in coming to meetings drunk he may be led outside; we may ask someone to take him away. But in most groups he can come back next day, if sober[55].

However, Bill's most important point of all invokes the "We" part of A.A.'s Traditions: common welfare and A.A. unity:

We do not wish to deny anyone his chance to recover from alcoholism[56].

How do you become an A.A. group member?

The requirement for membership applies not only to the A.A. Fellowship. Per A.A.'s First Tradition, it applies to the A.A. group. In the *A.A. Group* pamphlet, Tradition Three suggests that "group membership requires no formal application. Just as we are members of A.A. if we say we are, so are we members of a group if we say we are[57]."

Let it begin with me: acceptance, love, and tolerance for all who enter

> On a personal note: *Years ago, Fred walked in to my group one evening and scared the daylights out of me. He was filthy, ragged, and clearly disturbed. He straggled in and angrily scoped the room. Almost immediately, two of our old-timers ran up to Fred and greeted him like he was royalty. They talked to him excitedly while they gave him a cup of coffee.*
>
> *Well, because of those two beautiful old-timers, poor Fred didn't have a chance. He got sober even with his mental challenges. Over time, his appearance improved and his demeanor became relaxed.*
>
> *I gave him a ride home after a meeting one night and was struck by how grateful he was for his sobriety. Fred died a year later still sober. His family loved A.A.*
>
> *I am so grateful for the old-timers who showed me the true spirit of this Tradition, unconditional love and acceptance to all who enter.*

Coming up: the Fourth Tradition

When we study the Fourth Tradition, we will learn that Bill was dismayed when he discovered some groups used the autonomy of the group as an excuse to keep struggling alcoholics out.

Quite the opposite, the Fourth Tradition was intended to reach as many alcoholics as possible.

You can't tell us what to do!

Tradition 4

Each group should be autonomous except in matters affecting other groups or A.A. as a whole[1].

The Long Form: *Our A.A. experience has taught us that:*

With respect to its own affairs, each A.A. group should be responsible to no other authority than its own conscience. But when its plans concern the welfare of neighboring groups also, those groups ought to be consulted. And no group, regional committee, or individual should ever take any action that might greatly affect A.A. as a whole without conferring with the trustees of the General Service Board. On such issues our common welfare is paramount[2].

Synopsis of Bill's essay in the 12 & 12

Bill wrote, "every conceivable deviation from our Twelve Steps and Twelve Traditions has been tried." He provided two "storm signals" for groups considering the conduct of their activities: avoiding anything that could affect A.A. as a whole, and avoiding affiliations outside of A.A. Bill provided the Middleton case study to underscore his point that groups frequently went against Headquarters' advice and, while the results were disastrous, not all was lost. The leader turned trusted servant seized the lesson with humor and passed his experience on in the form of Rule #62: "Don't take yourself too damn seriously." Bill wrote the Fourth Tradition essay with a cautionary tone, but expressed his complete confidence that members would ultimately have to conform to principles[3].

Lyn S.

What the Fourth Tradition is and what it isn't

To paraphrase a past A.A. Trustee, invoking the Fourth Tradition usually means someone is getting ready to back a tractor over four to six of the other Traditions! To the contrary, practicing the Fourth Tradition is not a license to overrule any of the other Traditions.

In fact, following the wisdom of *The Twelve Traditions Illustrated*, the Fourth Tradition is like the Fourth Step:

It suggests that the A.A. group should take honest inventory of itself, asking about each of its independently planned actions, "Would this break any Tradition[4]?"

The Fourth Tradition with the other Traditions allows groups to establish their own customs and practices for their meetings and other activities, all with the aim of carrying out A.A.'s primary purpose – to help alcoholics who still struggle.

More to Bill's way of thinking as revealed in his writings, autonomy allowed groups to experiment – to be innovative – in their quest to serve the struggling alcoholic.

Having a written program of recovery was not enough to ensure unity

The publication of the Big Book may have given Bill a brief sense of security that all future A.A.s would "trudge the road to happy destiny" together. However, over the next few years, Bill witnessed new groups falling apart almost as rapidly as they were forming. He said, "As the *Saturday Evening Post* crop of alcoholics tried to form themselves into hundreds of new groups, the specters of disunity and collapse grew to frightening proportions[5]." To make matters worse, there was little or nothing Bill could do about it.

To illustrate early groups' struggles, Bill gave the example of meetings starting in Japan. In Tokyo, meetings had started with the help of American alcoholics and rapidly spread out to include the Japanese. One day a Japanese member visited Headquarters in New York, and declared that "awful things" were happening in Japan and, as a result, there were two kinds of A.A.! To make matters worse, there was one group leader who decided there should be only ten steps and charged alcoholics 100 yen to attend meetings[6].

As frightening as this and many similar willful departures from the program seemed, Bill learned over time that while such deviations ultimately proved ruinous for groups, they had little impact on A.A. as a whole. Like the Rule #62 analogy in his essay, Bill's hope was that when such flare-ups occurred, groups would see the value of returning to the principles of the program. He said,

> Today it is only amusing. We know that they will soon be infiltrated by common sense and experience. They will find that nobody can professionalize A.A.s Twelfth Step and the elder who means well and does badly will mend his ways[7].

Bill then concluded with a statement that is, in fact, an implicit question for all groups to consider when shaping their customs and practices:

> He will finally see that alcoholism is a quest for survival in which the good is sometimes the enemy of the best, and that only the best can bring the true good[8].

Nonetheless, the Japanese member's comment, "They have two kinds of A.A.," underscored how the Big Book alone would not be sufficient to ensure unity in A.A. Without some written guidelines for groups, loose interpretations of the Big Book intertwined with prideful egos spelled doom for A.A's unity. How could Bill craft guidelines for a group of alcoholics who are already prone to anarchy? Ironically, the answer was to encourage autonomy.

To an 'outsider,' this Tradition may seem to be contradictive to A.A. unity. To Bill, the problem was not whether groups should be autonomous; it was whether one could have a philosophy of autonomy and, at the same time, unity in A.A.

Applying Tradition Four in conjunction with the other Traditions was only a partial solution. The real solution was in Bill's dream for alcoholics or "children of chaos[9]" to take responsibility for A.A.

Group autonomy for alcoholics was a fait accompli

Ironically, Bill tried to use his position as a leader at A.A. Headquarters to manage newly forming groups. It did not take long for him to learn that leaders of groups, under the same influence of power and prestige as he, could not be told what to do. He said,

> As one of the people who helped start this movement, I thought for a long time that I ought to be able to manage it from New York. But I soon found that I could do no such thing. Neither could anybody else at A.A.'s Headquarters[10].

Bill summarized his correspondence with headstrong leaders, like himself, when he said:

> The groups said to us, "We like what you are doing. Sometimes your suggestions and advice are good. But whether to take you or leave you alone is going to be our decision. *Out in the groups, we are going to run our own show* (emphasis added). We are not going to have a personal government in New York, or anywhere else. Services, yes. But government, no[11]."

Bill painted a vivid picture of the obstinacy of A.A. members in established groups or in new groups that may have been very true in some instances, but certainly not all. Newly forming groups relied heavily on Headquarters, which was a metaphor for Bill and Dr. Bob. Bill and Ruth Hock faithfully answered their queries. Most of the correspondence required sending literature, connecting groups with sober alcoholics, and providing other general information. On the other hand, some questions were more philosophical in nature. Bill, having already observed the turmoil of the Fellowship during and after the "flying blind" period, prudently used what he learned from groups and encouraged autonomy. Bill wrote:

> If I understand correctly, your problem sounds similar to ... On that occasion, these good people, now years sober, can only relate to you what we seem to have learned from past experience. Perhaps you and your group will choose to follow this, but whether you do or not, please let us know how it comes out[12].

Bill's invitation to experiment provided some evidence of his own humility and open-mindedness. A declaration that there was only one path to a spiritual experience would have turned many away from the program. Similarly, mandating how groups must conduct their activities would have destroyed any chance for unity in A.A.

Autonomy grew from successes and failures

In what *Pass It On* referred to as the "boomerang incident," Bill's grandfather challenged him to make a boomerang, telling Bill that was something only Australians could do. Bill spent six months with multiple failures one of which he cut from his own bed's headboard. Successful at last, Bill threw his boomerang, which indeed circled back, but nearly hit his grandfather on the head[13]!

Like the 'boomerang incident,' informed as much by their failures as their successes, Bill and Dr. Bob experimented with getting newcomers sober and with the conduct of their early meetings. Dr. Bob handpicked members of the Akron squad based on commonalities and personalities to work with newcomers. In meetings, Bill's use of dark but empathetic absurdity managed to elicit raucous laughter setting the tone for humor in A.A. Borrowing from the Oxford Group, Bill introduced himself in New York meetings as "My name is Bill W. I'm an alcoholic," which quickly became and remains a custom in A.A. meetings[14].

Experimentation extended to the newly forming groups as well. The first beginners meetings started in Cleveland as an experiment to filter out the less than sincere prospects. The Cleveland groups introduced the value of personal sponsorship in their beginners' meetings along with using the Big Book as a study guide for newcomers[15].

However, like the "boomerang incident," members' efforts sometimes resulted in the metaphorical experiment circling back and hitting, or almost hitting, someone in the head.

The earliest case was Bill's attempt to allow struggling alcoholics to stay in his home. It didn't take long for Bill and Lois to realize that such generosity, known today as enabling, served more as a deterrent to recovery. Not knowing what to do with women resulted in pushing them into the same room as the alcoholics' wives; a plan that was not very well thought out. Additionally, as mentioned in Bill's Third Tradition essay, creating rules for who could attend and who could not attend A.A. meetings quickly became a quagmire of impossible processes for screening and enforcement.

San Francisco groups had a rough start when a member from New York, sent by Headquarters, urged the newcomers to disregard the "God business" in the Big Book. In the chaotic aftermath, Headquarters tried to help by sending letters of encouragement but replies were sparse and less than positive. A rather inebriated woman from the early San Francisco group visited New York and somewhat exaggeratedly reported, "Bill, we've been going a whole year in San Francisco and do you know that at Christmas time we were all drunk[16]." Shortly afterward, enough alcoholics finally stayed sober and contributed to the rapid growth of those groups.

Sometimes members' methods seemed heavy-handed but garnered unexpectedly good results. Headquarters had severe reservations about Irwin, a Southern member who, with the passion of a missionary, imposed his overbearing desire to help alcoholics by breaking "all the rules of caution and discreet approach to newcomers[17]." The list of calls to Headquarters for help in Irwin's area only got longer, so Bill reluctantly sent it to him. Bill wrote, "Irwin ran them down, every single one, with his home-crashing tornado technique[18]." However, to Bill's surprise, Irwin's tireless efforts produced results as evidenced by Headquarters getting letters of thanks from "stunned but happy Southerners[19]."

In short, allowing groups and individuals to take the lead in how they conducted their A.A. affairs occasionally had all the makings of a three-ring circus. Bill, as the point of contact for early A.A. groups, assimilated the results of failed and successful efforts. Therefore, no one was better qualified than he to make the following statement about autonomy:

> But this ultra-liberty is not so risky as it looks. In the end the innovators would have to adopt A.A. principles – at least some of them – in order to remain sober at all[20].

Bill went on to acknowledge the rewards that come with innovation:

> If, on the other hand, they found something better than A.A., or if they were able to improve on our methods, then in all probability we would adopt what they discovered for general use everywhere[21].

After Bill had already expressed his frustration about being unable to make any changes to the Big Book after its Second Printing, he went on hopefully:

> This sort of liberty also prevents A.A. from becoming a frozen set of dogmatic principles that could not be changed even when obviously wrong. Healthy trial and error always have their day and place in A.A[22].

'Healthy trial and error' and sometimes 'unhealthy trial and error' contributed to *The Twelve Points to Assure Our Future*. Bill said, "This was the welter of exciting and fearsome experience out of which A.A.'s Twelve Traditions were drawn and first put to paper in 1946[23]." He went on to say:

> Implicit throughout A.A.'s Traditions is the confession that our fellowship has its sins. We confess that we have character defects as a society and that these defects threaten us continually. Our Traditions are a guide to better ways of working and living, and they are also an antidote for our various maladies[24].

In terms of autonomy, is innovation dangerous? It is if it affects other groups or A.A. as a whole. This is most likely to happen if groups disregard any one or more of the other Traditions when experimenting with an innovation. It is also very likely to happen if groups act out on their collective character defects, usually born out of fear.

Examining motives for special groups in A.A.

From Bill's perspective, alcoholism was an egalitarian affliction and to turn anyone away from the help the Fellowship had to offer was tantamount to pronouncing a death sentence. Bill dreamed in "A Vision for You," that A.A. groups would warmly welcome anyone. No one would be too discredited and social distinctions would be "laughed out of countenance[25]."

Thus, it might seem that Tradition Three's simple membership rule would preclude the need for special groups in A.A. Unfortunately, according to *Pass It On*, "One of the obstacles was that [the Third Tradition] was sometimes seen to contradict the Fourth Tradition[26]." In other words, groups used autonomy to support discrimination and, as a result, denied help to struggling alcoholics who did not fit their members' particular profile. A.A. groups' early history of offering outcasts the option of creating their own special group was at best a bandage to cover up bias if not outright rejection.

For example, Bill's ideal groups would have set aside problems with sex and race when women and Blacks sought help. In reality, alcoholic women were greeted with anxious discomfort and Blacks were met with passive, if not outright, hostility. It was no wonder the first A.A. groups for women started as early as 1942 and for Blacks in 1945[27]. Whatever the precipitating factors were, at least there was the benefit of women and Blacks having a safe haven to encourage recovery for each other.

Obviously, Bill's ideal did not hold up under the reality of societal constraints within the United States, particularly during the 1940s and, unfortunately, for far too many years after. With two special groups already in place, it was not long before others followed. However, the reasons for starting such groups shifted. It is not a stretch to see why young alcoholics would have difficulty relating to older alcoholics. For all millennia, generations have their own language and their own problems that are peculiar to their age group. Thus, special groups for young people began in 1946[28].

Over time, forming special groups as a discriminatory practice gave way to particular populations seeking the comfort of being with others who shared their common experiences or professions. Consequently, the number of post-Traditions special groups continued to increase. International Doctors in A.A. was created in 1949 and Birds of a Feather (for pilots) formed in 1975[29]. In both cases, these groups provided a secure space for professionals who, understandably, did not feel comfortable sharing their foibles to lay persons outside of their fields.

In post-Traditions A.A., group autonomy provided the opportunity to offer a wide array of special groups for alcoholics including, but not limited to, atheists, dual-diagnosed (depression and alcoholic), lawyers, and gays. All serve the important need of providing a safe haven for prospects whose issues are familiar to the members of their special group.

There is only one caveat.

Recalling the highly charged vote at the 1974 General Service Conference that allowed 'Gay Meetings' to be listed in the *World Directory*, Barry L. said:

> And then to put the icing on the cake, immediately after the vote was announced, somebody said, "I want to propose a resolution. That it is the consensus of the conference that no [A.A.] group, anywhere, of any kind, should ever turn a newcomer away from his or her first meeting." And that was passed unanimously[30].

As it applies to special groups, the spirit of this important resolution was articulated in the *A.A. Group* pamphlet.

> Some A.A.s come together as A.A. groups – for men, women, young people, doctors, gays and others. If the members are all alcoholics, and *if they open the door to all alcoholics who seek help* (emphasis added), regardless of profession, gender or other distinction, and meet all other aspects defining an A.A. group, they may call themselves an A.A. group[31].

Akron A.A. and Cleveland A.A.: autonomy and religion in A.A.

For all of the problems A.A. had as groups were growing in numbers, with many invoking autonomy in troubling ways, Bill articulated his faith in the Traditions with remarkable bravado. He declared:

> Some may think that we have carried the principle of group autonomy to extremes…. [Autonomy] means that these two or three alcoholics could try for sobriety in any way they liked. *They could disagree with any or all of A.A.'s principles and still call themselves and A.A. group* (emphasis added)[32].

Akron A.A. and Cleveland A.A. serve as examples of how group autonomy may allow for a departure from some of the Traditions. Akron A.A.[33] and Cleveland A.A.[34] summon their role in A.A.'s history to sell publications from the pre-Traditions era that one will not find in A.A.'s conference approved literature.

Some of the literature is unambiguously Christian-based. Akron A.A. does provide an explanation and qualification on the binder of a package of these publications.

> This historical literature was written by Evan W. at the request of Dr. Bob. He felt that the newly written Big Book was too difficult for the blue-collar worker to read. Evan was a former writer for the newspaper and wrote *A Manual for Alcoholics Anonymous* in 1941, followed by *A Second Reader for Alcoholics Anonymous*. These pamphlets were completed by 1950 and reflected the early mindset of Akron's earliest members.

The binder then makes a very important disclaimer and interesting justification:

> This literature is pre-conference and is still serving members of AA around the world.
> Published and distributed by the Akron Area Intergroup primarily for its historical value; but also to serve the purpose for which it is originally written – to help us all better understand the program of Alcoholics Anonymous.

Pamphlets posted on the Akron A.A. literature sales site include *The Four Absolutes*, a philosophy that Bill W. believed would make recovery impossible and frustrating for alcoholics[35]. Other pamphelets are:

Second Reader for Alcoholics Anonymous which includes the statement:

> There is NO MYSTERY in the Spiritual side of A.A. As a matter of fact, the good active member is practicing Christianity at all times whether or not he knows it[36].

Spiritual Milestones in Alcoholics Anonymous which says:

> The unselfish helping of others is the practice of love, upon which Christian philosophy is based. Remember at all times Our Lord's two

commandments. "Thou shalt love the Lord thy God with all they heart, and with all they soul and with all thy mind. And thou shalt love thy neighbor as thyself. On these two commandments hang all the Law and the Prophets[37]."

Akron A.A. and Cleveland A.A. also sell General Service Conference-approved literature. Keeping in mind that members are free to purchase whatever they like, one may still argue that these resources do not meet the spirit of what Bill wrote in his essay on the Fourth Tradition. He said:

> A group ought not do anything which would greatly injure A.A. as a whole, nor ought it affiliate itself with anything or anybody else. There would be real danger should we commence to call some groups "wet," others "dry," still others "Republican" or "Communist," *and yet others "Catholic" or "Protestant"* (emphasis added)[38]."

On the other hand, Akron and Cleveland clearly cherish their historical and irrefutable contributions to early A.A. For many members, attending Akron's Founders Day in June is closely equivalent to attending an A.A. International Convention. There certainly is no denying Akron and Cleveland's role in the success and rapid growth of Alcoholics Anonymous.

A.A.'s complex beginnings and the preservation of this history may be a case of how our Traditions achieved Bill's dream – group autonomy and unity of the Fellowship.

The motivation not to abuse the principle of autonomy

For Bill, struggles with race, gender and other societal differences demonstrated the misuse of Tradition Four. Nevertheless, he had faith that as more groups practiced all of the Traditions, A.A. would survive isolated cases of abuse of the Fourth Tradition and of the other Traditions. Wisely, Bill recognized the nature of alcoholics when he said, "A code of traditions could not, of course, ever become rule of law[39]."

Bill's faith depended on the individual member, the group, and A.A. as a whole. In his view, all three have the positive motivation to align their will with a spiritual Higher Power combined with the aversion to the disease of alcoholism. Bill said:

> So there is authority enough, love enough, and punishment enough, all without any human being clutching the handles of power. Such is A.A.'s backstop against dissolution, and its final guarantee of survival under any conditions. For us, it is to do or die[40].

For many years after the Traditions were adopted by the Conference, Bill's faith was not sufficient to convince those who had the "handles of power" in A.A. to turn it over to "children of chaos."

Can "children of chaos" grow up?

By the time the General Service Conference assumed custody of the Traditions in 1955[41], Bill's five-year experiment successfully gave A.A. groups a voice through their Delegates on matters affecting A.A. as a whole. However, groups did not have the final authority over A.A. That belonged to the Trustees, the majority of whom were non-alcoholic.

Unfortunately, there were very influential voices in A.A. mostly in the form of some non-alcoholic and alcoholic Trustees on the Board and some Delegates who were convinced that, even in recovery, alcoholics would never be able to adhere to the Traditions and be fully responsible. At least, not enough to lead A.A.

This obstacle stood in the way of Bill's last hope for unity, which was for A.A. groups to take full responsibility for A.A.'s future.

Bill would struggle for years trying to convince the naysayers that alcoholics could be responsible for A.A. And he firmly believed that would prove true even with Traditions that were unenforceable and appeared to encourage anarchy. His most difficult opponent would be one of his dearest non-alcoholic friends, Dr. Harry Tiebout.

Tiebout had a stellar career in studying alcoholism and had published multiple scholarly papers on the subject. He supported the theory that the "disease" of alcoholism was a dependency and, more specifically, was marked by immaturity as demonstrated by over-dependency. Much of Tiebout's analyses evolved from his therapeutic work with Bill. Kurtz wrote that Teibout used a Freudian expression to point out to Bill, "that both in his active alcoholism and in his current sobriety he had been trying to live out the infantile grandiose demands of "His Majesty the Baby[42]."

Bill did not disagree. In fact, he referred to Tiebout's summation in his Twelfth Step essay when he said "[eminent psychologists and doctors] had the nerve to say that most of the alcoholics under investigation were still childish, emotionally sensitive, and grandiose[43]."

"How we alcoholics did resent that verdict!" was Bill's very next line in that same essay, which spoke more to his own frustration in his inability to provide a substantive rebuttal on behalf of sober alcoholics and especially himself.

Tiebout served as a trustee for the Alcoholic Foundation and eventually the General Service Board from 1957 through 1966. His was a critical vote that prevented alcoholics from becoming the majority on the General Service Board. After the 1955 A.A. themed *Coming of Age* Conference, a 15-year battle of wits continued between the two friends that in many ways served Bill in terms of understanding his own emotional maturity.

When we study Tradition Nine, we will learn how Bill finally convinced unbelievers that "children of chaos" could not only come of age but also could be responsible even with a code that encouraged autonomy.

The Fourth Tradition's emphasis on "affecting other groups or A.A. as a whole"

When making substantive changes, groups should carefully consider the Long Form of this Tradition. The first sentence calls upon the spiritual principle of the Second Tradition.

> With respect to its own affairs, each A.A. group should be responsible to no other authority than its own conscience[44].

The next sentence asks for courtesy and concern for groups that are neighbors. Sensitivity to issues such as conflicts in meeting times, space, and availability of other meetings for different populations might be among the considerations for discussion.

> But when its plans concern the welfare of neighboring groups also, those groups ought to be consulted[45].

Then the group is charged to carefully and objectively examine all of the Traditions and any other relevant literature provided by the General Service Office. If there is doubt, it suggests seeking the Board's guidance.

> And no group, regional committee, or individual should ever take any action that might greatly affect A.A. as a whole without conferring with the trustees of the General Service Board[46].

Keep in mind that the group is not asking the General Service Board for permission! Groups are free to do what they think is best. Consulting the Board is an opportunity to tap into the vast experience, strength, and hope of past A.A. groups. With careful research, the group can conduct an *informed* group conscience.

Finally, in the spirit of the First Tradition, On such issues our common welfare is paramount[47].

Coming up: the Fifth Tradition

Next, we will explore the Fifth Tradition. If the Fourth Tradition needs all of the other Traditions as an anchor to prevent drifting on a sea of anarchy, it is the Fifth Tradition that steers the ship.

Don't just sit there! Carry the message!

Tradition 5

> *Each group has but one primary purpose – to carry its message to the alcoholic who still suffers*[1].

The Long Form: *Our A.A. experience has taught us that:*

> Each Alcoholics Anonymous group ought to be a spiritual entity *having but one primary purpose* – that of carrying its message to the alcoholic who still suffers[2]. (12 & 12, p. 190)

Synopsis of Bill's essay in the 12 & 12

Bill stressed the importance of the *group* in carrying the message. He made a particular point to emphasize that every member in the group can carry the message – no matter how educated or uneducated, no matter how skilled or unskilled – all have the same valuable gift to share. He then illustrated through the story about the 'conceited Irishman' how the principles in A.A. can help all members to work with skeptical prospects[3]. In a humorous way, this story echoed his admonishment in "Working with Others" to approach prospects with candor and humility; to not speak from any spiritual hilltop[4].

The primary purpose is to carry the message

A frequent misquote of the Fifth Tradition is, "Our primary purpose is to help the alcoholic who still struggles." This is understandable given the A.A. Preamble's repeated use of the phrase "help others." More specifically, the Preamble says in the beginning "help others to recover from alcoholism" and in the end "help other alcoholics to achieve sobriety." Alcoholics help by offering their own experience, strength, and hope, which is in keeping with the Twelfth Step's clearly stated principle of *trying* to carry the message. In the wording of the Fifth Tradition, Bill echoed that same spirit of humility for the group: "Each group has but one primary purpose – to *carry its message* (emphasis added) to the alcoholic who still suffers."

The wording of the Twelfth Step and the Fifth Tradition seem to align with a fundamental concept in "How It Works." That is, "That probably no human power could have relieved our alcoholism[5]."

This is not a surprise to friends and family in A.A.'s companion program, Al Anon.

Certainly, Bill was not concerned with semantics during his first six months of sobriety! He was frantically trying not to drink by attempting to 'help' other alcoholics, but with no positive results other than the fact that he stayed sober. Bill finally met Dr. Bob and then there were two alcoholics desperately trying to stay sober by working with others. Hands-on experience quickly taught them that their prospects genuinely had to want to stay sober. All Bill and Dr. Bob could do was carry the message.

In the early days of the Fellowship, carrying the message was a simple process of one alcoholic talking to another. However, who better than alcoholics can take a simple idea and make it complicated! That started when Bill began to dream about hospitals for alcoholics and missionaries to spread the good news. He wasn't alone in conjuring innovations to share the good news. Over the next few years, many excited members believed they could improve the A.A. program with their financial, educational, or other schemes for carrying the message.

As a whole, alcoholics, including Bill and Dr. Bob, were ambitious, inspired, and smart. With such innovative talent behind potentially creative A.A. projects, how and why did the Fellowship circle back to its humble beginnings – when the primary purpose depended on one alcoholic carrying the message to another?

Early dreams for helping struggling alcoholics during the "flying blind" period

When Bill and Dr. Bob did a head count in October 1937, forty-one recovered alcoholics fueled Bill's dream of trying to expand their program so that they could save as many lives as possible[6]. Hospitals and institutions in that day were not nearly as successful, so it was not a stretch for a grandiose alcoholic to believe he could outdo professionals in that field. All he needed was funding (a popular battle cry of seasoned alcoholics)! After coaxing and cajoling reluctant Akron alcoholics to agree to his plan, Bill went back to New York to raise the money for paid missionaries and for writing a book, but his vision was to carry the message through A.A. hospitals and sanitariums.

Bill and Hank P. hoped for a flood of funding when a representative for Rockefeller, Frank Amos, visited Akron to see what their small start-up Fellowship was accomplishing. Amos considered three proposals before writing his final February 1938 report to Rockefeller. The most expensive option was to create a small hospital led by Dr. Bob in Akron at a cost of about $100,000. Concerned that Rockefeller might consider the cost excessive, Amos added a second, less expensive option. Dr. Bob could continue his work in City Hospital and a $30,000 donation would be sufficient to create a rehabilitation home supervised by him and overseen by a couple of recovering alcoholics[7].

Henrietta Seiberling claimed that she told Amos that money would ruin the Fellowship and that she convinced him to eliminate the first proposal, which probably lessened the chance that he would put forward the second proposal. Whether it was Seiberling's influence or another deterrent, Amos struck down both proposals and recommended instead only $5000 spread over two years to provide a car, a secretary, and support for Dr. Bob to continue his work with alcoholics and to offset the toll his work was taking on his struggling practice[8].

Amos's final proposal was a devastating blow to Bill and Dr. Bob's dream of A.A. hospitals. With Rockefeller's approval of the $5000 request in March 1938, Dr. Bob's hospital "that would have served as a first big step in the expansion of their movement – was dead and it would never be seriously considered again[9]."

Not fully giving up on the idea of a hospital but focusing more on writing a book, Bill and Hank continued to seek additional funds using as bait Bill's first two chapters, "There is a Solution" and "Bill's Story." There was mild interest, but without a chapter on the program of recovery, no one would commit to supporting the fledgling Fellowship. Raising more funds was off to a bad start.

In October 1938, Fitz M.'s contact with a Washington, D.C. judge who was intrigued with the Fellowship resurrected Bill's ambitious vision for a chain of A.A. hospitals. However, a series of missed opportunities and the judge's sudden debilitating illness brought the matter to a full stop. Nevertheless, Bill would stubbornly cling to his belief "that a chain of sanitariums, sponsored and staffed by A.A. members, would eventually prove to be their best hope for carrying the message of recovery out into the greater world[10]."

It would be several more years before Bill finally and completely gave it up.

It is understandable why Bill thought A.A. sanitariums would help more alcoholics than the word-of-mouth approach of the early Fellowship. However, naive and inexperienced, he had no way of knowing such complex institutions required a deadly combination for alcoholics – money, property, and power. That realization was at the expense of the newly formed, over-ambitious A.A. group whose Rule #62 story is in the Fourth Tradition essay. Clearly there was too much diverting that group from its primary purpose! Who among bankrupt idealists like A.A.'s have not bemusedly sighed, "It seemed like a good idea at the time…?"

Another distraction: A program that is a cure for all ills?

In less than three years, fortunes changed from bad to good for the struggling program; all without hospitals, sanitariums, and other early schemes for getting the word out. After the publication of the Big Book and as the indisputable value of A.A. started to permeate society, many recovered alcoholics and non-alcoholics gushed over the potential for the program to be a panacea

On What Slender Threads

for *all* of the world's ills. In an April 1948 Grapevine article, Bill wisely, and with very intoxicating prose, responded:

> Fortunately, most of us are convinced that these are perilous speculations, alluring ingredients of that new heady wine we are now being offered, each bottle marked "Success[11]!"

Obviously, Bill was thoroughly enjoying the metaphorical image of an inebriating taste of wine. He continued:

> Of this subtle vintage may we never drink too deeply. May we never forget that we live by the grace of God – on borrowed time; that anonymity is better than acclaim; that for us as a movement poverty is better than wealth[12].

Finally, Bill ended his allegory with the soul of the Fifth Tradition:

> And may we reflect with ever deepening conviction, that we shall never be at our best except when we hew only to the primary spiritual aim of AA. That of carrying its message to the alcoholic who still suffers alcoholism[13].

Apparently, by 1955, Bill had witnessed still more alcoholics giving in to the misapprehension of being able to solve other problems through A.A. In his admonishment to his well-intentioned but overzealous friends in recovery, and partly to himself, he said, "Let us resist the proud assumption that since God has enabled us to do well in one area we are destined to be a channel of saving grace for everybody[14]."

Notice the phrase, "proud assumption." In other words, a little humility, please!

We will learn in upcoming Traditions that Bill continued to have his own struggles with straying from A.A.'s primary purpose.

Statement of unconditional surrender to one primary purpose

In the end, Bill saw the futility and hazards of any endeavor that diverted A.A.s from carrying the message to struggling alcoholics. He waved a white flag not only for himself, but also for the A.A. Fellowship by emphasizing the importance of unity through his repeated use of the word "We." Bill said,

> We think we should do one thing well rather than many things to which we are not called. That is the central idea of this Tradition. *Our society gathers in unity around this concept* (emphasis added)[15].

So that there was no confusion about A.A. members pursuing fields directly or peripherally related to alcoholism, Bill continued,

> Of course we might interest ourselves in fields of education, research, neurosis, and the like[16].

Then, emphatically, Bill draws a clear line for A.A. groups:

> But, as a society ... [o]ur experience says that we definitely should not. We can and we do help, as individuals, in those fields. That is good. But, as a fellowship, we know that we must not be diverted[17].

Bill then laid the groundwork for the Sixth and Tenth Traditions in terms of distractions from carrying the message: affiliating with outside entities and opinions on outside issues:

> Though A.A. is obligated to both medicine and religion, we cannot become experts in either. We know that theology is for clergy men and that the practice of medicine and psychiatry is for doctors. Certain that we can do together what we cannot do separately, we shall always co-operate but never compete[18].

Finally, he reemphasized unity not only for the group, but for A.A. as a whole when he said:

> We shall direct our energies where they count most. Most emphatically, then, A.A. has but one single purpose: *to carry its message to the alcoholic who still suffers.* That is our basic objective, our real reason for existence[19].

Going back to our "carry the message" roots: One alcoholic talking to another

There is probably no better telling of when Bill met Dr. Bob than Ernest Kurtz's version in *Not-God: A History of Alcoholics Anonymous*[20]. Kurtz's recreation of that pivotal moment in A.A. history is a well-researched masterpiece that portrays the meeting particularly from Dr. Bob's perspective.

As Kurtz indicated, even though Dr. Silkworth urged Bill to give prospects "the medical business and give it to them hard," Bill was understandably nervous about giving a medical professional the "medical business." As providence would have it, there was a solution. Kurtz wrote:

> One look at the twitching, trembling surgeon as they were introduced solved Bill's problem about what to say first. "You must be awfully thirsty, Bob. Say, let's talk a little while first – it won't take long." Moving off to a side room, [Bill] began telling [Dr. Bob] the tale of his experiences with alcohol[21].

Kurtz continued the tale of how Bill shared about his drinking, what happened after Ebby's visit, and what he learned from Dr. Silkworth. Kurtz poignantly described Dr. Bob's reflections as he realized he stayed and listened well beyond the fifteen minutes he promised his wife:

> ... here was someone who did understand, or perhaps at least could. This stranger from New York didn't ask questions and didn't preach; he offered no "you must's" or even "let us's." He had simply told the

dreary but fascinating facts about himself, about his own drinking. And now, as [Bill] moved to stand up to end the conversation, he was actually thanking Dr. [Bob] for listening. "I called Henrietta because I needed another alcoholic. I needed you, Bob, probably a lot more than you'll ever need me. So, thanks a lot for hearing me out. I know now that I'm not going to take a drink, and I'm grateful to you[22].

Bill simply carried the message and thanked Dr. Bob for listening. Dr. Bob must have thought, "Wait a minute! He's leaving?" The effect was transformative. Kurtz continued the story from Dr. Bob's viewpoint:

While he had been listening to Bill's story, Bob had occasionally nodded his head, muttering, "yes, that's like me, that's just like me." Now he could bear the strain no longer. He'd listened to Bill's story, and now, by God, this "rum hound from New York" was going to listen to his. For the first time in his life, Dr. Bob [S] began to open his heart[23].

In the context of the Fifth Tradition, the story of when Bill met Dr. Bob is important as it reminds alcoholics that the "ex-problem drinker, who is properly armed with facts about himself, can generally win the entire confidence of another alcoholic in a few hours[24]."

This story is A.A.'s first successful instance of carrying the message.

Bill and Dr. Bob continued to carry the message to others at great personal sacrifice. Compared to A.A. today, the process for carrying the message then was arduous and frequently discouraging. It involved going to other peoples' homes, going to hospitals, or driving to another town sometimes many miles away. There were always multiple failures. Some newcomers would try working with others again and again for years before successfully carrying the message. With this perspective of what it was like, every A.A. member should read "Gratitude in Action[25]" (Dave B., one of the founders of A.A. in Canada in 1944), "The Man Who Mastered Fear[26]" (Archie T. who started A.A. in Detroit), and "He Sold Himself Short[27]" (Earl T. who started A.A. in

Chicago). Because of A.A.'s early pioneers, individuals carrying the message transitioned to groups carrying the message.

Now A.A.s don't have to painstakingly seek out struggling alcoholics. They come to A.A.!

How can groups reach and help newcomers?

Bill gave up his dreams for A.A. hospitals and, in his disappointment, he settled for the hope that if the book were widely distributed, it would serve to carry the message. His vision was that the reader of the book would then carry the message to another alcoholic, and then another, and then another. Reminiscent of his first meeting with Dr. Bob, Bill included a guideline for carrying the message in "Working with Others."

> Outline the program of action, explaining how you made a self-appraisal, how you straightened out your past and why you are now endeavoring to be helpful to him. It is important for him to realize that your attempt to pass this on to him plays a vital part in your own recovery. Actually, he may be helping you more than you are helping him. Make it plain he is under no obligation to you, that you hope only that he will try to help other alcoholics when he escapes his own difficulties[28].

Bill then wrote a passage that could very well serve as a paradigm for the overall climate of an A.A. meeting.

> Never talk down to an alcoholic from any moral or spiritual hilltop; simply lay out the kit of spiritual tools for his inspection. Show him how they worked with you. *Offer him friendship and fellowship* (emphasis added). Tell him that if he wants to get well you will do anything to help….If he is to find God, the desire must come from within[29].

Besides keeping the early Fellowship's experience, strength, and hope in mind, A.A. groups that want to conduct a self-examination vis-a-vis the Fifth

Lyn S.

Tradition should consult the *A.A. Group Pamphlet*. In particular, there is an inventory for groups with the first four questions focusing particularly on the Fifth Tradition.

1. What is the basic purpose of our group?
2. What more can our group do to carry the message?
3. Is our group attracting alcoholics from different backgrounds? Are we seeing a good cross-section of our community, including those with accessibility issues?
4. Do new members stick with us, or does the turn-over seem excessive? If so, why? What can we as a group do to retain members[30]?

Promising newcomers safety and privacy is paramount and assured through A.A.'s principle of anonymity.

> At the personal level, anonymity assures privacy for all members, a safeguard often of special importance to newcomers who may hesitate to seek help in A.A. if they have any reason to believe their alcoholism may be exposed publicly[31].

During a group's self-examination, mindful application of the Second Tradition is essential. That is, such an endeavor requires an ultimate higher authority as expressed in the group conscience.

Of course, the group conscience itself can be the arena where personalities may override principles. Again, invoking the Second Tradition and relying on an ultimate authority, the group can examine the conduct in its group consciences and business meetings. Practicing the principles of recovery in group consciences and business meetings is how members continue to carry the message together *and to each other*.

In a wish for the future of the A.A. Fellowship, Bill wrote in "Working with Others:"

> Life will take on new meaning. To watch people recover, to see them help others, to watch loneliness vanish, to see a fellowship grow up

about you, to have a host of friends – this is an experience you must not miss. We know you will not want to miss it. Frequent contact with newcomers *and with each other* (emphasis added) is the bright spot of our lives[32].

In short, are meetings a bright spot for all?

Does the group's conduct help or repel struggling alcoholics?

Naturally, meetings have disruptions occasionally. Some planning can help to circumvent such events, but over-planning can drive newcomers and regulars away. A group may want to survey its meeting guidelines to be sure they contribute to carrying the message.

For example, a crosstalk policy can be helpful or it can be harmful. Groups might consider its history and then think about what is appropriate for carrying the message. An overview of crosstalk was published in the 1994 Holiday issue of Box 459[33]. The General Service Office (G.S.O.) staff first identified an original definition of crosstalk:

> … it is traceable to a list of guidelines for "World Service" – that appears in 1992 in a central office newsletter and has since been reprinted and circulated more widely.
>
> The guidelines state, in part, that "Any comments negative or positive, about another's share, experience, life, program or remarks are crosstalk – that is interference."…" The only appropriate comment about anyone else's share – a speaker's or another member's – is 'Thank you for your share.'"…Even comments such as 'When you talk about…it reminded me of my own experience…' are possibly inappropriate[34].

Then the G.S.O. staff made a very firm disclaimer:

> The so-called guidelines did *not* emanate from the General Service Office. What random investigation reveals is that they may have

filtered into some A.A. groups through members who also attend other Twelve Step recovery groups[35].

Then added for emphasis at the end of the article:

[Groups are free to have "crosstalk" guidelines]....But please do not say that such guidelines came from the General Service Office[36].

The G.S.O. staff shared their own experience as members of the program:

Comparing notes, many of us realized that nonjudgmental suggestions we had received in meetings, in response to something we had shared, was very beneficial to our recovery. It is how we learn, and that's what 'sharing experience, strength and hope' is all about[37].

Finally, the article provided a reminder that alcoholics tend to rebel against mandates:

Also, there is a thin line between guidelines and rules; and experience suggests that in A.A.'s benign anarchy,' rules, rigidity and attempts to control don't work very well[38].

In short, a policy of crosstalk may help to moderate disruptive comments but could be counterproductive if a group enforces it rigidly or belligerently.

Incidentally, invoking autonomy in the Fourth Tradition, some groups make crosstalk part of their meeting conduct. For example, one group has a weekly Big Book reading and discussion in which questions, comments, e.g. crosstalk, are encouraged. It has its raucous moments, but there is a large following and its members are devoted to the structure claiming it has done much to increase their understanding of the Big Book.

Exactly who are alcoholics who still suffer?

Marty M. may be one of the first alcoholics to work the Twelve Steps of Alcoholics Anonymous. She received a draft copy from Dr. Tiebout, which she promptly tossed out the window upon learning that the solution was spiritual. Marty proceeded to go on a bender, but came back, read the draft copy, and restarted her bumpy journey into sobriety[39]. Marty's story in the Big Book, 'Women Suffer Too,' held nothing back in terms of sharing with others the dominance of alcoholism in her life[40]. At the end of her story, she wrote:

> ... I feel myself a useful member of the human race at last. I have something to contribute to humanity, since I am peculiarly qualified, as a fellow-sufferer ...[41].

Marty understated her positive influence as she spent over forty years working to educate the public about alcoholism. As we will discuss later, her contributions to the Traditions and to A.A. policy were invaluable.

After twenty years of sobriety, Marty relapsed. Little is known about what triggered the relapse because she managed to keep a shroud of secrecy around this episode that was sustained for many years. Her biographers noted:

> This relapse of Marty's has remained a closely held secret among AAs who were aware of it at the time. Some of them didn't even know that others knew[42].

Why such secrecy?

Was it possible that Marty knew, because of her celebrity status, the adage "Who we see here, what we hear here, let it stay here," would not be respected in her particular case? Why was she reluctant to seek the comfort of her group? Worst of all, was she uncertain that she would be able to share her despair safely and anonymously?

Marty's biographers speculated that she kept this secret to avoid negatively affecting the National Council on Alcoholism, her own creation. She also may have felt a heavy responsibility in that her relapse could deter other women from seeking help in A.A.

Whatever her reasons, secrecy prevented her from getting comfort from the very people who were "peculiarly qualified," the Fellowship of A.A.

Marty's biographers provided some insight that all should consider if ever tempted to over-simplify any alcoholic's relapse as a failing on their part.

> Alcoholic relapse is dangerous, of course, because the outcome is unpredictable, and the person risks death or permanent disability to self or others. But relapse need not be a moral issue…[43].

Marty's biographers go on to say that being an A.A. dropout:

> … is too simplistic an explanation today for relapse. Contemporary and continuing research into the phenomenon of relapse shows it to be a multifactored, individualized occurrence[44].

Fortunately, Marty became active in A.A. again, and seemed to reach a peace with her alcoholism as was underscored by her remarks on responsibility at the 1965 International Convention in Toronto. Her biographers wrote:

> Marty said it took her many years to understand she bore a rock-bottom, indivisible, personal responsibility for AA's great gift of life so freely given – to realize that how she conducted herself mattered to the future of AA …[45].

Who has not heard of someone with 9 months, 3 years, 7, 10, 15 or more years relapse? Does A.A.'s primary purpose apply only to newcomers? Are members paying attention when *anyone* stops going to meetings?

Shouldn't members always remember that, sober or not sober, all A.A.'s are alcoholics who still struggle?

Does the group carry the message to the newcomer and to *all* of its own members?

Singleness of purpose and the A.A. group as a spiritual entity

Bill used the word "primary" to describe carrying the message as our most important purpose. He probably did not imagine that alcoholics would construe primary purpose to mean that there are second and third purposes for the Fellowship. However, in the Fifth Tradition essay[46] he used variations of "singleness of purpose" three times and did not use "primary" at all.

> There is another reason for this singleness of purpose [Bill goes on to say we can't keep it unless we give it away.] (page 151)
>
> Highlighting the wisdom of A.A.'s single purpose, a member tells this story: [Bill tells the story of the conceited Irishman] (page 151)
>
> Thank heaven I came up with the right answer for that one. It was based foursquare on the single purpose of A.A. [Bill answers the Irishman's accusation about being a religious sect.] (page 153)

The singleness of purpose is emphatically stated as "one primary purpose" in the Long Form of the Fifth Tradition:

> Each Alcoholics Anonymous group ought to be a **spiritual entity** *having but one primary purpose* – that of carrying its message to the alcoholic who still suffers[47].

The Long Form charges the group, as a *spiritual entity*, to invoke the Second Tradition when it decides how it will carry the message. That is, an ultimate authority as expressed in an informed group conscience will guide the group's conduct in how it carrys the message.

In summary: A.A.'s *single purpose* and unity

In October 1949, Bill joined the First Tradition with the Fifth Tradition in his article, "As We Approach Maturity[48]." He harkened back to his original dream of carrying the message to as many suffering alcoholics as possible.

....we are sure there must be a million alcoholics who would join Alcoholics Anonymous tomorrow if only they knew what we do[49].

Bill underscored the foundation of A.A.'s Traditions, unity, as essential to carrying the message:

We keenly realize that any fundamental disunity among us could instantly disillusion tens of thousands who would again turn their faces to the wall[50].

Bill named the chief threats to A.A.'s unity and our common welfare:

Hence, those disruptions common to great wealth, power, or controversy ought never be for us. Too many of the "million who don't yet know" would surely die[51].

Bill concluded that the Fellowship's unity and common welfare are essential to its one and only purpose:

Therefore, our Fifth Tradition states: "Each AA group ought to be a spiritual entity having *but one primary purpose* – that of carrying its message to the alcoholic who still suffers[52].

Finally, in Bill reminded members that there is no better way to carry the message than with an attitude of gratitude!

So long as *we remain grateful for what has be fallen us* (emphasis added), and for so long as this Tradition of high and single purpose is indelibly emblazoned on our hearts, our destiny will be assured[53].

Coming up: the Sixth Tradition

Through A.A.'s first five Traditions, members and groups learn how to better relate to each other. Now we can explore the Tradition that helps the Fellowship to relate to the world outside of A.A. – the Sixth Tradition.

This near-beer is A.A. approved! Really? Nope!

Tradition 6

> *An A.A. group ought never endorse, finance, or lend the A.A. name to any related facility or outside enterprise, lest problems of money, property, and prestige divert us from our primary purpose*[1].

The Long Form: *Our A.A. experience has taught us that:*

> Problems of money, property, and authority may easily divert us from our primary spiritual aim. We think, therefore, that any considerable property of genuine use to A.A. should be separately incorporated and managed, thus dividing the material from the spiritual. An A.A. group, as such, should never go into business. Secondary aids to A.A., such as clubs or hospitals which require much property or administration, ought to be incorporated and so set apart that, if necessary, they can be freely discarded by the groups. Hence such facilities ought not to use the A.A. name. Their management should be the sole responsibility of those people who financially support them. For clubs, A.A. managers are usually preferred. But hospitals, as well as other places of recuperation, ought to be well outside A.A. – and medically supervised. While an A.A. group may cooperate with anyone, such cooperation ought never to go so far as affiliation or endorsement, actual or implied. An A.A. group can bind itself to no one[2].

Lyn S.

Synopsis of Bill's essay in the 12 & 12

Bill's essay provides a review of early A.A.'s intoxicating ambitions, including hospitals, educational endeavors, and legislative reform. It includes a liquor-trade job offer story that was similar to the Towns Hospital job offer. Bill used the Towns Hospital story to illustrate the power of the group conscience and he used the liquor trade story to focus on affiliating A.A. with outside entities. They both offer a cautionary tale on professionalizing Twelfth Step work[3].

What diverts groups from their primary purpose?

In Tradition Five we learned that, for the sake of A.A.'s unity and survival, the Fellowship must not be diverted from its primary purpose. Tradition Six explicitly describes activities that are distractions: *"An A.A. group ought never endorse, finance, or lend the A.A. name to any related facility or outside enterprise, lest problems of money, property, and prestige divert us from our primary purpose*[4]*."*

Notice Bill made a particular point to apply non-affiliation not only to "outside enterprises," but also to "related facilities." Based on his own experience, enthusiastic A.A.'s with all good intentions wanted to help by creating or promoting other alcohol-recovery related enterprises. Before we explore A.A.'s "related facility" difficulties, we will examine "outside enterprises," the first of which continues to be problematic – religion in A.A.

The toughest nut to crack for A.A. – religious affiliation

A.A.'s earliest beginnings and its own text, the Big Book, linked the Fellowship with religion. Jim B. and Hank P. doggedly tried to get Bill to moderate his references to God, but Bill wrote as if he wanted to have it both ways: non-affiliation with religion and spiritual affiliation with Christianity.

Careful as Bill was to avoid any association with the Oxford Group in the First Edition, disconnecting it from A.A.'s origins proved more difficult given its undeniable role in A.A. history. Bill's disclaimer in the Foreward (sic) to the First Edition did not eliminate the perception of A.A.'s religious association, but it did clearly articulate a disassociation to that perception.

> We are not allied with any particular faith, sect or denomination, nor do we oppose anyone. We simply wish to be helpful to those who are afflicted[5].

For multiple reasons, Bill pulled away from the Oxford Group when he returned to New York after his first extended stay with Dr. Bob. Among his concerns was that a connection with the Oxford Group would deter alcoholics associated with other religions, particularly Catholic alcoholics, from getting involved with the new Fellowship. However, religious neutrality did not come easily. Bill explained:

> In Akron, they [the local A.A. members] were the Oxford Group, or at least many thought they were, until the book came out in 1939. Not only it, but the Fellowship was named 'Alcoholics Anonymous.' We had consciously withdrawn from the Oxford Group, in fact, definitely here in New York at a much earlier time, and although the older people in Cleveland or in Akron realized that it wasn't any longer an Oxford Group, we carried the label as long as the meetings were on at T. Henry William's house[6].

Perception about the Fellowship's association with the Oxford Group also came from the outside. Bill had hoped a positive review by the American Medical Association (AMA) would provide the momentum needed to propel sales of the book. Unfortunately, in October 1939, the AMA published a tepid review that condescendingly described the program's method as one of intriguing the alcoholic "into the acceptance of divine guidance in place of alcohol[7]." While the AMA acknowledged the book's "recognition of the seriousness of the addiction to alcohol," it compared the program to the Dale Carnegie and Oxford movements, thus having "no scientific merit or interest[8]."

The review must have disappointed Bill in the face of months of less than stellar sales of the book. To make matters worse, the Akron Oxford Group and its alcoholics continued to be rankled with Bill albeit for conflicting reasons.

If the alcoholics in Akron had their problems with the Big Book, members of the Oxford Group had even more. There was the impression that it was commercial, for one thing. Another reason they were disappointed was that there was no mention of the Oxford Group in the book. Furthermore, the Twelve Steps had replaced the four absolutes, which were not mentioned either[9].

Wait a minute! It was bad that it was a commercial venture, but they didn't get credit for it? That must have been a head-scratcher for Bill!

Moreover, in Akron, the very people who put Bill and Bob on their "Fellowship" feet were at odds with each other. Dr. Bob was in the middle of a rapidly developing maelstrom. Disenchanted with Oxford Group members, Clarence S. and his hometown alcoholics separated from the Akron group in May 1939 forming in Cleveland the first group named Alcoholics Anonymous. Finally, with mutual hard feelings and sadness, Dr. Bob broke off from the Oxford Group in early January 1940 and started A.A. meetings in his own home. His regrets could not have been too overwhelming as he referred to the event, in a letter to Bill, as finally "… shaking off the shackles of the Oxford Group[10]."

Fifteen years later with the publication of the Second Edition of *Alcoholics Anonymous* in 1955, A.A. was secure enough in its independence from the Oxford Group for Bill to acknowledge it's early influence while at the same time clearly separating the A.A. program from Oxford Group tenets. In the "Forward to the Second Edition" of the Big Book, Bill wrote:

> … Six months earlier, the broker had been relieved of his drink obsession by a sudden spiritual experience, following a meeting with an alcoholic friend who had been in contact with the Oxford Groups of that day… . Though he could not accept all the tenets of the Oxford Groups, he was convinced of the need for moral inventory, confession of personality, restitution to those harmed, helpfulness to others, and the necessity of belief in and dependence upon God[11].

The reference to the Oxford Group seemed more like an attempt to solidify A.A.'s dissimilarities than to provide credit. Reiterating his disclaimer in the First Edition, Bill went on to say:

> Alcoholics Anonymous is not a religious organization. Neither does A.A. take any particular medical point of view, though we cooperate widely with the men of medicine as well as with the men of religion[12].

Finally, Bill reaffirmed A.A.'s religious flexibility with Appendix V, "The Religious View on A.A." He included endorsements from a Jesuit priest, Father Ed Dowling; a testimonial in the Episcopal magazine, *The Living* Church; and a statement by Dr. Harry Emerson Fosdick, an American pastor and central figure in the Fundamentalist-Modernist controversy within American Protestantism[13].

Religious affiliation was indeed a tough nut to crack, but the difficulty was understandable if not predictable. Again, given Bill's frequent Christian references in the Big Book and in the *Twelve Steps and Twelve Traditions,* it is not surprising that A.A.'s association with religion persists today. It does not take long to find current articles online that declare A.A.'s religiosity. It is useful to scan these critiques for the purposes of a group's self-examination of its conduct and impact on newcomers. As Bill noted, A.A. has a long history of riding out disruptions with minimal harm and such critiques can be helpful to improving the program.

The next tough nut was a self-inflicted difficulty; it was affiliation with a "related facility" in the form of alcohol education.

Alcohol education seemed like a good idea at the time....

Bill's essay in Tradition Six underscored how A.A.'s with wonderful motives quickly were entangled in distracting causes. Bill illustrated the principle of no endorsement using a member's job opportunity that required affiliating A.A. with a liquor company. However, a more difficult and complex entanglement with endorsement occurred between Bill, Dr. Bob, and Marty M[i]. The perilous combination of Marty's ingenuity and Bill's unreserved support for

---
i See Marty M.'s story in the Big Book, "Women Suffer Too."

her ambitions to educate the public about alcoholism propelled the two go-getters toward unexpected upheavals on several fronts for A.A.

Four years sober, Marty attended the Yale School of Alcohol Studies in 1943, which set the course for her future in alcohol education. She focused her efforts on redirecting public attitudes toward alcoholism and recovery. Marty was smart, articulate, and charismatic, all of which thrusted her toward becoming a leader in the field of alcohol education. "She particularly wanted to help women alcoholics, who she felt suffered 'a double stigma[14].'"

With financial support from Yale, Marty created the National Committee on Education on Alcoholism, Inc. (N.C.E.A.) in October 1944. Besides Bill and Dr. Bob, other prominent people and the newly established *Grapevine* magazine enthusiastically applauded her efforts.

When Bill and Dr. Bob allowed their names on Marty's N.C.E.A. letterhead as members of A.A., it must have seemed like a relatively harmless idea to support an alcohol education program. However, as pointed out in *Pass It On*, "N.C.E.A. was not officially affiliated with A.A., but the A.A. co-founders' name on its letterhead gave the impression that the two groups were connected[15]." Unfortunately, rationalizing this support as for the public good only served to open the floodgates for other A.A's to enlist Bill's approval for their own educational and rehabilitative endeavors.

To compound the potential for misunderstandings, Marty had decided that speaking at N.C.E.A. events was a logical venue for her to admit her own addiction to alcohol with warm attribution to A.A. for her recovery, again, for the public good. Furthermore, she broke her anonymity with Yale's strong approval and Bill's encouragement[16].

The real trouble began when, in 1946, N.C.E.A. used its letterhead to send out an appeal to the public for funding. The letter found its way to a few A.A. groups, which prompted Dick S., a Trustee on the Alcoholic Foundation, to warn Bill:

> If this letter should ever go out to the A.A. mailing list quoting A.A. throughout and soliciting funds on a letterhead that carries both your name and [Dr. Bob's] as sponsors, no little hell would be popping[17].

On What Slender Threads

Besides conflating N.C.E.A with A.A. and the anonymity breaks, the appeals letter was seeking its operating funds from outside sources. This was appropriate for Marty's organization, but devastating to A.A.'s principle of not accepting financing from outside entities. Forestalling the inevitable, Bill finally took outraged members' concerns to heart. He was "persuaded that total non-affiliation was the only solution. Within a year, he and Dr. Bob withdrew from N.C.E.A., and Marty discontinued publicly identifying herself as an A.A. member[18]."

Bill shared his difficult lesson when he wrote about the problems with fund raising and affiliation even when they seem beneficial. It is no small wonder that he highlighted first the threat to A.A.'s primary purpose:

> As groups, we cannot endorse, finance or form an alliance with any other cause, however good; we cannot link the A.A. name to other enterprises in the alcohol field to the extent that the public gets the impression we have abandoned our sole aim[19].

And, then he emphasized the threat to A.A.'s unity:

> We must discourage our members and our friends in these fields from stressing the A.A. name in their publicity or appeals for funds. To act otherwise will *certainly imperil our unity, and to maintain our unity is surely our greatest obligation* (emphasis added)[20].

Ironically, N.C.E.A. and Yale eventually diverged on philosophical and practical grounds. Yale decided to no longer sponsor Marty's organization. Marty changed N.C.E.A. to the National Committee on Alcoholism (N.C.A.) in 1949 and renamed it again in 1957 to the National Council on Alcoholism. She struggled for several years to keep the newly independent organization financially viable and after sometime, it did prevail[21].

So goes the hazards of outside affiliations.

The N.C.E.A. debacle was a trifecta of missteps that would inform at least three A.A. Traditions that caution against outside affiliation, anonymity breaks, and financial complications. The decision to break all affiliation with N.C.E.A. did not come easily for Bill given his close relationship with Marty. Bill's lesson about compromising A.A.'s principles for the greater good would affect his decisions on the Fellowship in the future. However, his unavoidable visibility and profile in A.A. would weigh heavily when he abided by principles that could result in the deaths of struggling alcoholics. This dilemma would have its most painful impact on Bill when he practiced the principle of anonymity.

Acknowledging early contributions and avoiding affiliation

Over the years, Bill repeatedly used the story of the $5,000 Rockefeller donation as a high impact metaphor for corporate poverty. Unfortunately, because the Rockefeller donation was a striking story for public consumption, Bill appeared to overlook other contributors whose smaller donations, in effect, made the publishing of the book possible. Whether he did this to minimize the appearance of affiliations with outside agencies or whether these smaller contributions did not make for a flashy story is unknown. Charles Towns was one such faithful donor during the "flying blind" period. Schaberg wrote:

> Mentioning that money was also contributed by Charles Towns would mean having to also explain in some detail who he was and why someone running a drying-out hospital was giving money to A.A. and, even more problematic, why A.A. was accepting money from him[22].

Towns Hospital happened to be where Bill dried out three times and had his spiritual transformation. In addition, after he got sober, Towns Hospital was where he wandered around looking for drunks to help. As soon as the Fellowship started growing in numbers, Towns offered Bill a lay-therapist job. Bill had to reject the offer as it would have professionalized Twelfth Step work. Even though Towns was deeply disappointed, he faithfully continued his support for the Fellowship[23].

When the lion's share of the Rockefeller donation was allocated to Dr. Bob, with Bill's and Hank's full support, Towns generously provided $500 in monthly installments to help Bill and Hank muddle through financially.

He continued to give more later on as the book was reaching the finish line[24]. Schaberg continued:

> Charles B. Towns was not a rich man – certainly not on the order of John D. Rockefeller Jr. and his friends – but his confidence in Bill Wilson and his program of recovery far exceeded the combined faith of all of those men and he demonstrated that faith by writing these all-important monthly checks[25].

There is no doubt that Charles Towns supported Bill because Bill had found an effective solution for alcoholism. This would have positive implications for Towns's recovery hospital whether Bill worked there or not. Nonetheless, he was not concerned with attribution. Schaberg said,

> When talking about the essential help he gave at this decisive point in the story, Charles Towns claimed he had "never sought any credit nor publicity in this matter and I don't care for any[26]."

Nevertheless, as Schaberg justly observed:

> … but it is a sad fact that this man – one of the great unsung heroes in the story of the writing of the Big Book – continues to receive so little credit for his critical role in making it possible for the book to be written[27].

While some early friends of A.A. chastised Bill about their overlooked contributions, Charles B. Towns remained silent.

Tradition Six's overlap with Tradition Eight

In Bill's essay, the liquor trade story raises the issue of affiliation and breaking anonymity in association with a business. In Tradition Eight, we will focus more on A.A.'s working in and being paid for their work in alcohol related fields. This issue was so sticky for early A.A., that it is worthwhile to visit and revisit Bill's careful reminder that echoes his own past mistakes:

Therefore it seems to me that some of us must heed the call from other fields. And those who do need only remember first and last they are A.A.'s; that in their new activities they are individuals only. This means that they will respect the principle of anonymity in the press; that if they do appear before the general public they will not describe themselves as A.A.'s that they will refrain from emphasizing their A. A. status in appeals for money or publicity[28].

Clubs in A.A. evolve to become "related facilities" without A.A. affiliation

Bill's pamphlet, *AA Tradition: How It Developed* provides guidance underscored by the fumbling experiences of the very first club on West 24th Street in New York City. Written in 1947, Bill first referred to problems with leadership, when he said:

> A corporation was formed to take over the club room lease so we then had "officials." Should these "directors" run the club or would it be the A.A. rotating committee?[29]

Bill continued humorously conveying the importance of the Traditions through his own missteps:

> Our first club was known, of course, as an "A.A. clubhouse." The corporation holding its lease was titled "*Alcoholics Anonymous* of New York, Inc." Only later did we realize we had incorporated the whole of New York State, a mistake recently rectified. Of course our incorporation should have covered "24th Street" only[30].

The issue of Clubs in A.A. was so sticky during the forties, Bill devoted much of the Long Form of this Tradition to avoiding those problems. A comparison of the Long Form with the *A.A. Traditions* pamphlet's section on "Clubs in A.A.: Are they with us to Stay" builds a robust picture of the issues during that time along with informed guidance for today's clubs.

The Long Form, part 1:

> Problems of money, property, and authority may easily divert us from our primary spiritual aim[31].

Clubs in A.A.:

> Acceptance of large sums from *any source* to buy, build, or finance clubs almost invariably leads to later headaches. Public solicitation is, of course, extremely dangerous. Complete self-support of clubs and everything else connected with A.A. is becoming our universal practice[32].

The Long Form, part 2:

> We think, therefore, that any considerable property of genuine use to A.A. should be separately incorporated and managed, thus dividing the material from the spiritual. An A.A. group, as such, should never go into business[33].

Clubs in A.A.:

> **This tangle slowly commenced to unravel,** as we began to get the idea that clubs ought to be strictly the business of those individuals who specially want clubs, and who are willing to pay for them. We began to see that club management is a large business proposition which ought to be separately incorporated under another name …[34].

The Long Form, part 3 (Bill could not refrain from expressing an opinion about who should manage clubs):

> Secondary aids to A.A., such as clubs or hospitals which require much property or administration, ought to be incorporated and so set apart that, if necessary, they can be freely discarded by the groups. Hence

such facilities ought not to use the A.A. name. Their management should be the sole responsibility of those people who financially support them. For clubs, A.A. managers are usually preferred. But hospitals, as well as other places of recuperation, ought to be well outside A.A. – and medically supervised[35].

Clubs in A.A.:

… that the "directors" of a club corporation ought to look after club business only; that an A.A. group, as such, should never get into active management of a business project. Hectic experience has since taught us that if an A.A. rotating committee tries to boss the club corporation or if the corporation tries to run the A.A. affairs of those groups who may meet at the club, there is difficulty at once[36].

The Long Form, part 4:

While an A.A. group may cooperate with anyone, such cooperation ought never to go so far as affiliation or endorsement, actual or implied. An A.A. group can bind itself to no one[37].

Clubs in A.A.:

The only way we have found to cure this is *to separate the material from the spiritual.* If an A.A. group wishes to use a given club, let them pay rent or split the meeting take with the club management …[38].

Bill pointed out that, in the early Fellowship, clubs served as a hub for centralizing A.A. activities in a geographical area. As the demand for a "central meeting" of area groups grew, clubs found that they could not sustain such an endeavor. Thus began central or intergroup management of A.A. in larger areas. This portion of the pamphlet, written in 1947, speaks to Bill's prescience with A.A.'s future paid workers and service committees responsible to those they serve per the Eighth and Ninth Traditions.

Every area, sooner or later, realizes that such concerns as intergroup meetings, hospital arrangements, local public relations, a central office for interviews and information, are things in which every A.A. is interested, whether he has any use for clubs or not. These being strictly A.A. matters, a central or intergroup committee has to be elected and financed to look after them[39].

Well-run clubs continue to make recovery possible for many twelve-step programs. Groups can consult the General Service Office guidelines, *Relationship between A.A. and Clubs*[40].

A.A. learns to mind its own business

The principle of attraction rather than promotion bears fruit when it is applied to Tradition Six. In *Alcoholics Anonymous Comes of Age*, Bill wrote that over the years, without affiliating A.A. with outside entities such as medicine, religion and research, those very same entities on their own incorporated ideas from A.A. Additionally, other recovery groups modified the program to suit their concerns, and from that grew twelve-step programs for a wide variety of addictions. Bill claimed that A.A. had even influenced politics and business. In short, Bill said:

> Today we understand and accept this paradox: The more A.A. sticks to its primary purpose, the greater will be its helpful influence everywhere[41].

Coming up: the Seventh Tradition

The more complex issues in Tradition Six are the problems of money, power, and prestige which can surface in a multitude of ways. The old adage that money is the root of all evil certainly contributes to a Tradition solely focused on this topic. A.A. owes a great debt to Hank P. who articulated the need for oversight and accountability. Hank P. acted on his certainty that money would raise suspicions and mistrust within and outside of the Fellowship. Within a few years, that would be exactly what happened.

Thanks for the meeting. Who's picking up the tab?

Tradition 7

> *Every A.A. group ought to be fully self-supporting, declining outside contributions[1].*

The Long Form: *Our A.A. experience has taught us that:*

> The A.A. groups themselves ought to be fully supported by the voluntary contributions of their own members. We think that each group should soon achieve this ideal; that any public solicitation of funds using the name of Alcoholics Anonymous is highly dangerous, whether by groups, clubs, hospitals, or other outside agencies; that acceptance of large gifts from any source, or of contributions carrying any obligation whatever, is unwise. Then, too, we view with much concern those A.A. treasuries which continue, beyond prudent reserves, to accumulate funds for no stated A.A. purpose. Experience has often warned us that nothing can so surely destroy our spiritual heritage as futile disputes over property, money, and authority[2].

Synopsis of Bill's essay in the 12 & 12

Bill humorously opened with alcoholics' predisposition toward entitlement. They should be rewarded because, after all, they stopped drinking! At the same time, while feeling entitled and deserving of support, they clutched their wallets when asked to contribute to expenses at their own meetings. Having laid that groundwork, he used his own flawed experience to characterize how alcoholics have a distorted entanglement with their money and their egos. Bill noted that the opposite problem, large sums of money from grateful families and other bequests, would be hazardous to the Fellowship. Bill concluded that corporate poverty and adherence to a prudent reserve was the Fellowship's only hope for survival. And, of course, alcoholics must be fully self-supporting through their own contributions[3]. (12 & 12, pp. 160 -165)

Problems with money and an unsung A.A. hero, Hank P.

In early March 1938 when Hank P. and Bill realized a donation from Rockefeller was imminent, the two men spent some time discussing the idea of a foundation. However, Hank took the lead in the Fellowship's financial future. He was the first to codify what would be A.A.'s policies on fiscal responsibility.

Hank wrote Rockefeller's representative, Frank Amos, on March 16, 1938 to describe his ideas for what he referred to as The Fund. Expecting a large donation, Hank introduced his thoughts with the caution that careful consideration of handling this money was extremely important as it could serve as a national model for the program's future financial policies. Hank was certainly far-sighted, for this initial letter was the seed that grew to be A.A.'s financial oversight in the form of The Fund, then the Alcoholic Foundation, and finally the current General Service Board[4].

Hank continued his vision with a rationale that became the substance of A.A.'s stance on unpaid Twelfth Step work. The Fund would control the "collection and distribution" of monies for supporting alcohol-recovery related work "while diligently avoiding 'professionalism'" and thus, preserve the Fellowship's principle of members freely sharing the message of recovery to other alcoholics[5].

Hank was barely getting started. He then wrote that only those who benefited from the program would be able to donate to The Fund. However, Hank broadly defined 'those who benefit' as individuals and *businesses*. His inclusion of "companies who enjoyed the result[6]" of the program was based on his assumption that businesses would undoubtedly establish A.A. resource offices in their organizations. Of course, this would mean large-scale purchases of the book! Therefore, such businesses, as direct beneficiaries of the program, could contribute to The Fund.

Hank articulated his aspirations in his chapter, "To Employers," in the Big Book, He referred to his own experience of being fired from a large company because of his alcoholism. Hank's suggestions began with individual employer/employee interventions and extended to training junior executives to aid alcoholic employees. Obviously, the book would be an essential tool for employers to carry out his suggestions[7].

As an aside, Hank had some foresight about the need for businesses to include support for employees struggling with addiction. Many years later, an initiative driven by Fellowship member and Senator, Harold H., resulted in the passing of the Comprehensive Alcohol Abuse and Alcoholism Prevention, Treatment, and Rehabilitation Act of 1970. A very long time coming, the bill created the new federal agency, the National Institute on Alcohol Abuse and Alcoholism. The act also supported grants for periods of three years to state and local governments, nonprofit organizations, and individuals for advancing treatment for alcoholics. This was a high-profile springboard for businesses, and society in general, to reexamine attitudes toward and treatment for alcoholism[8].

In his letter to Amos, Hank added as a qualifier, that there was an immediate need for the Fellowship to accept gifts from outside entities like Rockefeller. However, The Fund would repay such outside contributions as soon as direct beneficiaries were independently able to finance the program. At 18 months of sobriety and struggling to keep his own business afloat, Hank articulated one of A.A.'s most important principles: recovered alcoholics must be self-supporting through their own contributions.

Finally, Hank made it clear that oversight and administration of the Fund must be done by an honest, "disinterested party, who is not an alcoholic" with a significant business background[9]. This last stroke of genius would be the early Fellowship's saving grace and years later, it would be an almost insurmountable barrier against alcoholics gaining full responsibility for the program.

Hank must have been excited at the prospect of a large donation, especially after such careful and painstaking preparation for its administration. He sent the letter to Frank Amos on March 16. The next day, on March 17, Rockefeller confirmed in writing that the Fellowship would receive a one-time donation of $5,000 and that there would be no more money forthcoming.

Discouraging as this must have been, Hank formally established the Alcoholic Fund on March 21, 1938, and asked a non-alcoholic "disinterested party," Frank Amos, to oversee the contribution from Rockefeller. With his Rockefeller associates' blessings, Amos agreed and continued for many years after to be a hard-working friend of the Fellowship[10].

Nevertheless, Hank had not given up on the idea that substantive gifts would be forthcoming.

Over the next few months, providence and a sluggish economic climate dealt Bill and Hank one discouraging blow after another in terms of trying to secure more funding. As a result, their hopes shifted away from the amount of money needed for hospitals and sanitariums and moved toward the more realistic goal of financing completion of the book. Such was the inspiration for Hank's next move in May 1938.

The Fund becomes the Alcoholic Foundation

Hank proposed changing The Fund to a "fully-fledged Foundation" that would be tasked with raising a minimum amount of $15,000 to finance the "writing and publishing of a book for alcoholics[11]."

Not surprisingly, Hank had an ulterior motive. The Foundation's financially savvy and prosperous Trustees, would have better luck raising funds than two newly recovered, broke alcoholics. Furthermore, there would be a need for tax-exempt status with more money pouring in from such dependable sources.

Hank enlisted the help of a non-alcoholic lawyer, John B. Wood, who on August 5, 1938 created the Alcoholic Foundation with the same stipulations as its forebear, The Fund. Mr. Wood assigned oversight of the Foundation to two types of Trustees that is the model A.A. follows today; non-alcoholic Class A Trustees and recovered alcoholic Class B Trustees. The first class A Trustees were John Wood, Frank Amos, and Willard Richardson. The two class B Trustees were Dr. Bob and Bill R., a New York sobered alcoholic[12].

The Alcoholic Foundation included an Advisory Board that gave the appearance of oversight, but in fact, served as a direct channel for its members, Bill, Hank P., and Rockefeller representatives, A. LeRoy Chipman, and Albert Scott, to exert influence over the Trustees' decisions[13].

Hank and Mr. Wood charged the Foundation with multiple objectives that included but was not limited to the "relief and rehabilitation" of alcoholics by supporting "personal work of a religious (but nonsectarian) nature," "places of rest or recuperation for alcoholics," financial assistance to alcoholics, research in alcoholism, and the publication of books and literature related to alcoholism[14].

The Fourth Tradition essay's Rule #62 group apparently emulated this model that, as we know, resulted in a very hard lesson about the importance of sticking to A.A.'s primary purpose[15]. These were only a few of the "duties" assigned to the Trustees! In retrospect, Bill said the Alcoholic Foundation was "charted to do just about anything within the field of alcoholism except lobby for Prohibition[16]."

For Hank and Bill, setting up the Foundation must have engendered the delusion that every alcoholic has: "Now our problems are over!" Bill wrote his first two chapters in the book, "Bill's Story" and "There is a Solution," and then continued to seek funding using those two chapters as an incentive to invest. He was rejected repeatedly and most denials came with the question, "What is the program of recovery?"

Desperate times called for desperate measures

By October 1938, it was apparent that trying to "sell" the first two chapters was not working. Using the Foundation's Advisory Board power, Bill and Hank did a full-court press on Albert Scott to convince the Trustees that they needed to try harder to raise funds. Scott, refusing to approach the Trustees, pushed back insisting that the Fellowship should start to pay its own way. Scott insisted that Bill and Hank would have to convince the membership to start contributing something, no matter how little, before he would go back to Rockefeller or anyone else for donations[17].

Albeit unexpected, Scott's response was very much in line with Rockefeller's philosophy of only providing seed money with the expectation that recipients carry their own weight financially after the initial financial boost. Bill and Hank must have been frustrated, but still, they seriously considered Scott's challenge. After some deliberation, they rejected the idea. Bill and Hank reasoned that recovering alcoholics had a more important priority. Helping other alcoholics was the Fellowship's real safeguard against their deadly disease; not paying dues[18].

Furthermore, Hank and Bill noted that alcoholics' wives and families, who were not yet on their financial feet, would object. Dues would be an encumbrance on an already fragile recovering family. Also, Hank and Bill were wary of a policy that required monitoring payment and non-payment. No one wanted to be the A.A. dues police[19].

The miracle of that measured consideration by Hank and Bill is that today's A.A. principle of "no dues or fees" had been and continues to be the standard for A.A.'s voluntary system of financial contributions from its own members.

Unfortunately, the Trustees continued to do little more than oversee the distribution of Rockefeller's original donation. Hank and Bill, left to their own devices, would have to find other ways to get the money to print the woefully uncompleted book. Disenchanted with the Foundation, they made a decision not to consult with the Trustees about their next plan to raise money.

Hank's next idea: The One Hundred Men Corporation

Hank expanded on his earlier plan, the success of which depended on the Alcoholic Foundation securing enough donations to finance the book. The former plan included creating a "private marketing organization" or "publishing firm" as a separate arm of the Foundation. Furthermore, Hank grandly proposed that if they received more money than needed to publish the book, they would partition and return the excess to the donors. At that time, Hank believed this proposal would help with raising funds, but one obstacle after another resulted in his changing this charitable ideal into a more aggressive and self-serving fund-raising approach[20].

In late October 1938, Hank replaced his former plan with The One Hundred Men Corporation, a stockholder-shared entity. Rather than seeking donations to support the publishing of the book, Hank focused on luring investors with the promise of large returns as the bait. The onus was on Hank to sell as many stocks as needed to get the book published and on Bill to finish the book[21].

On What Slender Threads

While The One Hundred Men Corporation was clearly a philosophical departure from the original plan, a chasm developed with Hank's next steps in setting up the corporation.

Hank purchased blank stock certificates at a stationery story and created stock certificates at a par value of $25. At the top of each blank certificate, Hank signed his name [Henry G. P.], President. Hank "gifted" himself 200 shares, and the author of the incomplete book, Bill, 200 shares. Hank hoped to sell 200 remaining shares giving them the $5,000 they needed to get by financially and to print the book[22].

Bill's and Hank's decision to, in essence, gift themselves $5,000 each and have 2/3 controlling interest in The Hundred Men Corporation would raise eyebrows for many years to come.

Of course, Bill and Hank continued working under the Trustees' radar as they were certain there would be objections. To make matters worse, initial sales of stocks were non-existent for the same reason, as all of Hank and Bill's stalled fund-raising projects – no one wanted to invest in a non-articulated program of recovery[23]. (Would you please just write the book, Bill!)

Thankfully, the cool reception to the stocks prompted Hank to take a more legitimate approach: a detail that is usually not included when people resurrect the old stock scheme story. Hank wrote a fairly well-organized and convincing Prospectus that added more legitimacy and transparency to their efforts. Stocks then started to sell and gained some momentum when he offered a monthly payment plan on each $25 share. By December 1938, the Prospectus and the payment plan contributed to more success in selling stocks and, during that same month, Bill started writing "How It Works[24]."

Finally! It's about time, Bill!

According to Schaberg:

> A total of forty-four recovered alcoholics, friends, relatives and business relations purchased one-hundred-seventy-nine shares of stock over the next six or seven months, producing an adequate, but uneven income stream for Hank that eventually totaled $4,475 and thereby

moved his dream of making The One Hundred Men Corporation a successful publishing enterprise one step closer to reality[25].

Incidentally, *Pass It On*, listed the number of paying subscribers as forty-nine, with Hank, Bill, and Ruth listed as gifted subscribers[26]. Only ten of the paying subscribers were alcoholics. Additionally, The One Hundred Men Corporation was renamed Works Publishing but the exact date of that change is unknown. Based on Bill's recollection, he and Hank changed the name some time before February 1939[27].

The fall-out from the stock scheme begins

It is unclear whether Bill and Hank had discussed with others their proportion of control when they first formulated the stock idea. However, considering that many stock owned companies start with one or two controlling owners, at least some of the investors had to be aware of and accepted Bill's and Hank's majority holdings. Given they were the ones who dedicated virtually all of their time and energy to writing the Big Book and trying to find funds for its publication, their expectation for controlling the publishing company with commiserate compensation was certainly reasonable. Similarly, Ruth Hock received free shares for her extraordinary services rendered during the "flying blind" period.

Probably without realizing it, this compensation for work done to make the program possible laid the foundation for the second part of Tradition Eight, *but our service centers may employ special workers*[28]. Nonetheless, this event continues to cast a long shadow on A.A.'s history. Some early members believed that all work done for the Fellowship must be without compensation. That included not selling, but giving away the book. Of course, they were not giving up their livelihoods to do the work!

In a decision that would have unforetold consequences, Dr. Bob reluctantly approved the stock idea, but deliberately withheld the scheme from the Akron/Cleveland groups. Clarence S. and the Cleveland group did not find out about the stocks until the prepublication manuscript came out[29]. This caused such dissension within the Fellowship, that some members were seriously considering breaking away to form their own program[30].

Compounding withholding the stock venture from the Trustees and the Akron/Cleveland groups was the obvious potential for two members to make a substantial profit on a book that was attributed to the Fellowship. It is this last point that probably gave the stock scheme story an enduring life of its own.

Some years later, when challenged about Hank's stock scheme, Bill claimed that he protested these irregularities, but Hank convinced him they had no time to waste. Nevertheless, as Schaberg so eloquently says:

> ... characterizing [Hank] as "the serpent in the garden" of this selfless new recovery movement is just too convenient; completely ignoring the fact that Bill undeniably accepted the apple Hank offered him and took a bite[31].

About four months after the book was published and before sales started to gain momentum, Hank drank. Unfortunately, in his anger and bitterness, he ignored Bill's and others' pleas to come back to the Fellowship.

Ending the stock scheme does not end A.A.'s troubles

By early 1940, it was clear sales of the Big Book were gaining momentum and the growth was surprisingly rapid after such a sluggish start. Having learned about the stock venture, the Trustees decided, and Bill agreed, that the Big Book and Works Publishing should belong to the A.A. Fellowship and not to the stock subscribers; especially not to Bill and Hank. Bill was willing to donate his 200 shares and the Foundation planned to buy back the other subscribers' shares.

However, there was one very important holdout. Hank resisted all pleas to turn over his one-third controlling interest in Works Publishing. A few months later, he showed up at Bill's office broke and shaky. In a crisis, Hank wanted Bill to buy his Honors Dealers furniture, which prompted Bill to make a counterproposal. If Hank gave his shares to the Alcoholic Foundation, Bill would purchase the furniture[32].

Schaberg referred to the stock scheme as a complete disaster in spite of the fact that from November through April, it sustained Hank and his promotional efforts. Nevertheless, along with help from the printing company and from Charles B. Towns, the stock scheme was instrumental in getting the book to press. Hank's own misfortunes turned into what would eventually be a bargain for the Alcoholic Foundation. In May 1940, Bill and Hank signed over all of their shares. With a 1942 loan from John D. Rockefeller, Jr., the Alcoholic Foundation bought back the remaining $25 shares at face value. Thus, the Foundation "thereby assumed ownership of both the publishing company and the book[33]."

It is important to note that Bill and Hank signed over stocks that had the potential, in theory, to be worth $5,000 each. They could have argued for some payment given their two years of dedicated efforts during the "flying blind" period and financially dismal months that followed publishing the book. Nonetheless, both men donated their shares to the Alcoholic Foundation[34], which was a considerable financial sacrifice. Hank was an unwilling donor. Bill was willing but added a self-less condition for signing over his shares; "… that Dr. Bob and Anne receive royalties for the rest of their lives[35]."

Later, Bill too received royalties, which added fuel to the burning resentments Hank already had. Hank's drinking further alienated him from the Fellowship, resulting in many members becoming supportive of Bill getting royalties. While the income was modest at first, eventually it provided Bill and Lois with a substantial income. Sadly, according to Hank's son, Hank would always feel Bill and the Fellowship treated him badly[36].

For Hank, so goes the consequences of drinking, consequences of which many alcoholics are familiar.

Providentially, the royalties kept Bill at Headquarters during turbulent times for the Fellowship. While the membership and groups were increasing in numbers, Bill was steering the Alcoholic Foundation and Headquarters through the storms of many groups' collapses. Furthermore, A.A.'s budding unity was starting to disintegrate due to discord within the Fellowship.

And, unfortunately, consequences of the stock scheme would still be forthcoming for Bill and Dr. Bob.

It only got worse

Harkening back to his first letter to Frank Amos written March 16, 1938 about financial oversight of the Fellowship, Hank made an eerie prediction when he recommended The Fund have "a definite procedure for handling money that would **be above reproach should hostile parties later make any investigations into their affairs**[37]." [Bold Mine]

Hank also cautioned that the distribution of these funds needed to be fair and impartial, avoiding paid professionalism while at the same time **forestalling all "jealousies and political possibilities**[38]." [Bold Mine]

Ironically, Hank laid the groundwork for A.A.'s corporate poverty, self-support and fiscal responsibility that would, a few years later, ultimately save Bill and Dr. Bob from the man who would accuse them of financial improprieties – Hank P.

The relinquishing of the stocks to the Alcoholic Foundation probably gave Bill some hope that the dust would settle so he could resume devoting his full attention to the escalating number of inquiries that were pouring into Headquarters. Unfortunately, Hank was on a mission to roil the already discontented members of the Fellowship. He found a convenient sympathizer in Clarence S. who continued to stew over Bill's national profile, the storm caused by the stock venture, and the "commercialization" of the Big Book. As it was, when Hank arrived at Clarence's doorstep, the Cleveland groups were seriously considering breaking away from Bill's brand of A.A[39].

Unaware of any trouble brewing, Bill and Dr. Bob accepted an invitation to speak at a dinner in Cleveland. Both noticed attendance was small and there was a palpable chill in the room. After dinner and their talks, the chairs of the various groups escorted Bill and Dr. Bob to a separate room. In the presence of an attorney and a certified public accountant, the distressed chairs claimed a Trustee at the Foundation shared awful stories about the withholding of incredible profits from the Big Book. Along with a list of other accusations, they claimed Bill and Dr. Bob received $64,000 in the past year[40].

One can only imagine the devastation Bill and Dr. Bob felt as they listened to men who had been their earliest and dearest friends in the Fellowship. As Bill said in *Alcoholics Anonymous Comes of Age*, "This incredible but more than half-believed fantasy hit Dr. Bob and me quite hard."

Bill must have known tensions were bubbling out west, because then he said, "Fortunately, I happened to have with me a certified audit of all of our affairs from the beginning[41]." Apparently, the rumors had already reached Headquarters and Bill was prepared. After the attorney and the accountant confirmed the veracity of the audit, Bill said,

> The committee was crestfallen and we received an apology. The committee's chairman explained that the meeting had been called to set the record straight; that few of the committee members had actually believed the stories[42].

Even though the chastened chairs promised to stop the rumors, Bill unhappily acknowledged that "they never quite succeeded; the racket talk went on for years in that region[43]."

As it is with rumors, the story of the stock scheme continues well beyond the region today.

Lessons and principles come from tremendous pain

Over the years, Bill tempered his sadness about this event by defending his accusers; that not all of them were disgruntled malcontents or politically ambitious. He believed that some of the people were "strong and serious" and "were genuinely distressed by what they regarded as an attempt to commercialize A.A[44]." In such a case, it was fair and important to be able to 'set the record straight' and verify the Foundation's handling of A.A.'s money.

After this experience, Bill applied a rigorous standard to his personal financial affairs by maintaining the same policy of transparency and candor[45].

As wounding as this event was to both Dr. Bob and Bill, Bill underscored his and A.A.'s lesson in the pamphlet, *A.A. Tradition: How It Developed*:

> That the use of money in A.A. is a matter of the gravest importance. Where its use ends and its misuse begins is the point we should vigilantly watch[46].

As an abrasive and argumentative member of early A.A., Clarence S. would present multiple opportunities for Bill to practice spiritual principles. Nonetheless, Bill graciously thanked Clarence for all of his contributions to early A.A. in a very generous 1943 letter. Over twenty years later, at the 1965 International Convention, Clarence and Bill reminisced companionably about the early days as two old friends would do[47].

Unfortunately, Hank disappeared in the background of early A.A. history. At the end of the day, setting aside his money-making schemes and ambitious visions for large profits, it was Hank who articulated so many of A.A.'s most important policies with regard to money, including oversight, transparency, and self-support. While Hank did not successfully forestall "all jealousies and political possibilities," A.A. owes a tremendous debt for all of his dedicated efforts to place the Fellowship above financial reproach and for doggedly working with Bill to finish the book.

Tradition Seven and property – the original Big Book manuscript

A.A. still needs to be vigilant when dealing with matters of property and money as evidenced by the recent discovery of a printer's copy of the First Edition manuscript.

In 1978, Lois gave Barry L. the original manuscript of the First Edition of *Alcoholics Anonymous* as a gesture of friendship and appreciation. Barry said that he wrote in his will that the manuscript belonged to A.A. in its archives but that he was keeping it until he died[48].

According to Gillian Brockell in an article for *The Washington Post*, A.A. World Services lost track of this arrangement sometime between 1979 and 1985 when Barry died. Barry's brother said that Barry left no property of any value. The location of the manuscript remained unknown until 2004 when it resurfaced at an auction house. It sold for $1.5 million, and then auctioned again for $992,000 in 2007.

The General Service Board Trustees discovered in 2017 that the manuscript was going up for auction yet again. On the advice of a lawyer, the Trustees sued to stop the sale claiming A.A. as the rightful owner. All attempts for the Board to reach a settlement proved futile given the prospective value of the document. A.A. decided to withdraw its claim. The settlement required that A.A. compensate the auction house and lawyers, while at the same time waiving the right to the manuscript[49].

Upon its release, the manuscript sold at auction for $2.4 million to billionaire Indianapolis Colts owner Jim I., who now makes it available at the G.S.O. archives for several months each year.

The General Service Conference Delegates and A.A. members were divided in their opinions of whether or not A.A. should have pursued the sale. Some members believed that it was paramount for A.A. own this piece of history in order to preserve its integrity. Given the costly stalemate, perhaps the General Service Board acknowledged the manuscript as a property of such great value, that its purchase and ownership would compromise A.A.'s philosophy of corporate poverty.

So goes the problems with money and property.

A.A. treasurers, good group practices, and transparency

However much or however little is contributed to the group, it is important for the Treasurer to be transparent and report regularly to the members. Our *A.A. Group Pamphlet* provides clear guidelines:

> Treasurers generally maintain clear records (a ledger is helpful) and keep their groups informed about how much money is taken and how it is spent. They may make periodic reports to the group and post financial statements quarterly. Problems can be avoided by keeping group funds in a separate group bank account that requires two signatures on each check. The flyer "The A.A. Group Treasurer" offers many other helpful suggestions.
>
> A.A. experience clearly shows that it is not a good idea for a group to accumulate large funds in excess of what is needed for rent and other expenses. It is wise, though, to keep a prudent reserve in case an unforeseen need arises (an amount to be determined by the group conscience). Group troubles also may arise when extra-large donations – in money, goods or services – are accepted from one member[50].

In practical terms, groups might consider establishing a policy of receipts for everything that contributes to their functioning. Related to the issue of keeping track of expenses, in general, groups should discourage members' providing supplies or online platforms in lieu of donations. It is important for groups to have an accurate reporting of its costs so that when positions rotate, unexpected expenses will not catch the succeeding trusted servants and the group by surprise.

> On a personal note: *For example, I have purchased cups, coffee, and other supplies for a group. I declined reimbursement as I considered it a donation to the group. While my motive was to be helpful to the group, it was still an ego-feeding proposition in which I deprived all other members of my group the responsibility for sharing all of its expenses; that is, I deprived my group of the responsibility to be fully self-supporting. By making the group reliant on my own individual "contribution," I also introduced an element of unpredictability in terms of operating expenses for the group.*

Financial transparency begins with our groups and continues through our District Meetings, our Area Assemblies, and finally our General Service Office. The General Service Office models transparency by posting a summary of financials four times a year. See General Service Office Quarterly Report (accessed 01/21/2023): https://www.aa.org/quarterly-reports-from-gso[51].

A full financial report can be obtained through the Area's Delegate.

A.A. members' contributions and our primary purpose

On a lighter note, Bill's reminds us that groups should strive to get "the least possible money needed to do the job well[52]." He reflected that alcoholics' peculiar entanglement with money and ego is a mixed blessing when he said:

> Nevertheless, we still balk a bit when it comes to paying A.A.'s very reasonable service bills. Sometimes I think this may be all to the good. There is not the slightest danger that A.A. is ever going to get too rich from the voluntary contributions of its own members[53]!

Given Bill's missteps and heartache, his lesson unsurprisingly reminds us never to be diverted from our primary purpose. The essence of Traditions Six and Seven is to "divide the spiritual from the material…[54]."

> …we don't need money. The core of our A.A. procedure is one alcoholic talking to another, whether that be sitting on a curbstone, in a home, or at a meeting. It's the message, not the place; it's the talk, not the alms[55].

Coming up: the Eighth Tradition

In Tradition Eight, we will see how money continued to plague A.A. well after the "flying blind" period. Bill referred to this next period as A.A.'s biggest test for unity of the Fellowship. Could there be an Alcoholics Anonymous World Services if A.A. did not appropriately compensate its members and others to make Twelfth Step work possible?

You get what you pay for!

Tradition 8

Alcoholics Anonymous should remain forever nonprofessional, but our service centers may emply special workers[1].

The Long Form: *Our A.A. experience has taught us that:*

Alcoholics Anonymous should remain forever non-professional. We define professionalism as the occupation of counseling alcoholics for fees or hire. But we may employ alcoholics where they are going to perform those services for which we might otherwise have to engage nonalcoholics. Such special services may be well recompensed. But our usual A.A. Twelfth Step work is never to be paid for[2].

Synopsis of Bill's essay in the 12 & 12

In this Tradition's essay, Bill stressed the importance of Twelfth Step work freely given. However, some members of the early Fellowship defined "work freely given" too broadly. He described their cries of opportunism when caretakers wanted compensation for their labor and when A.A.s started working in fields closely associated with alcohol recovery. It is sad to note the ill treatment by members of the Fellowship toward A.A.s who were paid, not for Twelfth Step work, but for making Twelfth Step work possible. These tensions created heated dissension in the Fellowship that necessitated three clear principles:

1. Those who labor in service for A.A. are worthy of their hire,
2. A.A.'s who pursue alcohol related professions are not in violation of

pursuing this work so long as they don't break the principles of anonymity, and
3. All Twelfth Step work is non-professional and therefore offered not just for free, but without any expectations[3].

Introduction

Typically, A.A. members fully embrace the leading phrase of the Eighth Tradition, "Alcoholics Anonymous shall remain forever nonprofessional." After all, Twelfth Step work freely given is the hallmark of the A.A. program! However, it is the second clause of the Eighth Tradition that is the cornerstone for carrying the message beyond the groups: "but our service centers may employ special workers."

Some of A.A.'s earliest members believed that carrying the message by word-of-mouth was the only way to share their solution. Still, Bill was not satisfied with only reaching alcoholics who could come to Akron or New York. He worried about the millions of sufferers who would die of alcoholism simply because they did not know there was a solution that worked for so many. Thus, he wrote the Big Book to carry the message in a way that extended beyond his geographical confines. Through writing the Big Book, Bill was a paid service worker and his efforts reached millions of sufferers.

Similarly, today's A.A. paid workers provide a lifeline that connects suffering alcoholics to members who have a solution. With the expertise of those workers, groups have access to resources and additional opportunities to carry the message that extend beyond the walls of their meetings.

Bill's essay on this Tradition primarily focused on groups' paid workers that made Twelfth Step work possible in their immediate proximity, such as clubs. That included maintenance of facilities, answering phones and written queries, and other supporting tasks. Furthermore, Headquarters needed paid workers so that they could answer the countless pleas for help from all across the country. Over time, Headquarters evolved to become the General Service Office (G.S.O.) and Alcoholics Anonymous World Services, Inc. (A.A.W.S.).

In this discussion, we will divide the Long Form into four parts to discuss early A.A.'s first "paid service workers" and we will survey other related controversies. That is, we will track what Bill referred to as the anvils of experience that led to hammering out A.A.'s Eighth Tradition. Understanding our struggles with paid staff and professionals during the "flying blind" period and during the subsequent period of the "great test of A.A.'s unity" underscores the Eighth Tradition's impact on the Fellowships' ability to carry out its primary purpose. With that in mind, we will conclude by exploring the multitude of services today's paid workers provide to make Twelfth Step work possible close to home and around the world.

Part I of the Long Form:

Alcoholics Anonymous should remain forever non-professional.

The hallmark of the early Fellowship: working with others for free

The first part of this Tradition is rooted in A.A.'s earliest beginnings when members of the Fellowship suggested that their prospects work with other struggling alcoholics in order to stay sober. That they did so voluntarily is what attracted attention to the Fellowship. From "The Doctor's Opinion:"

> The unselfishness of these men as we have come to know them, the entire absence of profit motive, and their community spirit, is indeed inspiring to one who has labored long and wearily in this alcoholic field[4].

Even with A.A.'s rapid growth, *most* members honored the spiritual principle of freely giving back what was given to them. Approximately ten years after the publication of the Big Book, Bill wrote in the *Twelve Steps and Twelve Traditions*:

> Even the newest of newcomers finds undreamed rewards as he tries to help his brother alcoholic, the one who is even blinder than he. This is indeed the kind of giving that actually demands nothing. He does not expect his brother sufferer to pay him, or even to love him[5].

A.A.'s who practice the Traditions understand that carrying the message for free is essential to their sobriety and to A.A.'s unity and common welfare.

Unfortunately, A.A., as an unquestionably successful program, has attracted and will continue to attract opportunism that surfaces in the form of paid Step sponsors or for-a-fee spin-offs. To paraphrase a conversation between spies, 'Trust takes years to build, but only a few minutes to buy[6].' Of course, we will see in Tradition Ten, A.A. has no opinion on these entrepreneurial endeavors.

The "flying blind" period uncovered the hazards of early alcoholics' expectations that included the belief that Fellowship members should work with others for free *and* voluntarily do the nitty-gritty and time-consuming labors that expanded the program's reach. This unrealistic expectation would result in a hard-fought battle between the economic survival of its early members and the survival of A.A. itself.

The first "paid professional" was Dr. Bob

From June 1935 until March 1938, Bill and Dr. Bob devoted most of their time to carrying the message. Bill had a few odd jobs with brokerage firms, but none of his attempts at regular work produced any substantial income. Dr. Bob was financially behind due to his drinking and struggled to rebuild his practice while working with drunks. While the Rockefeller donation was a disappointment in terms of their larger plans for the Fellowship, it did provide some sorely needed support for Dr. Bob. In all likelihood, however, Dr. Bob did not share openly with the Akron squad that he was receiving money to continue working with alcoholics. As Schaberg said:

Taking money "for the work" was still a taboo subject in Ohio[7].

In March 1938, Frank Amos wrote the first check to Dr. Bob for $500 from the Alcoholic Fund[8]. When the Fund became the Alcoholic Foundation, the Trustees allocated $200 a month to Dr. Bob from September 1938 to April 1939 to carry on his work in Akron. For that time, it was enough support for him to reduce his debts and keep his practice operational[9].

Unfortunately, when the Foundation Trustees realized funds were needed to get the book printed, they assigned to Bill the unpleasant task of telling Dr. Bob his monthly payments would be reduced to $50 for several months. To put it mildly, Dr. Bob was upset. He appealed to the Foundation for more money, but never received a reply[10]. Undoubtedly, this was a surprising and radical reduction in income for Dr. Bob. Nonetheless, it speaks to the perils of relying on outside support for one's livelihood.

During the period that Dr. Bob was receiving financial support, Bill, Hank, and Fitz M. scrambled to find more funding while they continued to craft future policies for A.A and work on the book. In short, Dr. Bob was paid to do what was eventually called Twelfth Step work, while Bill, Hank, and Fitz frantically sought support to make Twelfth Step work possible. Quite the reverse of the Eighth Tradition!

Part II of the Long Form:

> *We define professionalism as the occupation of counseling alcoholics for fees or hire.*

Bill's first struggle with professionalism

When Bill told the story of Charles Towns' job offer, it was understandable for Bill to consider taking the position especially given the Alcoholic Foundation was paying Dr. Bob for his work. Hank, via the group conscience, helped Bill to see the ramifications of this very difficult decision. As Schaberg rightfully pointed out, "This job offer is one of the more fateful turning points in A.A.'s history. Who knows what might have happened if [Bill] had actually become a lay therapist[11]."

In that particular group conscience, if the members even knew about Dr. Bob's compensation, they probably still would have discouraged Bill from taking Dr. Towns' offer. The obvious problem with the lay therapist job was that Bill's results would have benefited and been credited to Towns Hospital. In contrast, Dr. Bob's pay originated from a donation given to the Fellowship for developing the program. That is, Dr. Bob's work directly helped the Fellowship by growing the number of recovered alcoholics, which in turn provided for the book more evidence that the program worked. The distinctions were in the motive for support and the source of income.

Even though he was disappointed, Charles Towns continued to keep Bill, Hank and Fitz on their feet financially without any obligation to the hospital.

In short, the three men received pay for helping Bill get the book across the finish line.

Part III of the Long Form:

> *But we may employ alcoholics where they are going to perform those services for which we might otherwise have to engage nonalcoholics. Such special services may be well recompensed.*

Tensions surface over control of the book's sales

As of April 1939, Bill, Hank, and forty-six share-holders controlled Works Publishing – and, in effect, owned the newly published book. In the first six months, sales were sluggish and all of the early co-founders were struggling financially[12]. Bill and Ruth Hock were continuing to work on behalf of the Fellowship in Hank's Honors Dealers[i] office in New Jersey. Discouragingly, work at that time generally consisted of going to the mailbox to see only a trickle of queries about the book. In the meantime, Hank started drinking.

With some publicity in September and October, the trickle of inquiries became a flood of calls and correspondence. Bill and Ruth answered everything that came into the office but quickly found they needed help. With no money to pay for staff, Bill wanted to move the A.A. office to Manhattan where there were more volunteers available to help.

Hank was understandably upset as he probably could feel his lifeline of control slipping away. He wrote a disjointed letter in late 1939 to Bill that reverberated with active alcoholism. Hank's argument to keep the potentially lucrative Works Publishing separate from the Alcoholic Foundation was a conflation of reasonable questions and distracting platitudes. His plausible questions included "Would money that would be spent on an office be better spent for traveling expenses for people spreading the good news?" and "Would an office tend to take away the endearing amateurism of this work and tend to

---

i According to Schaberg, Honors Dealers was a business venture Hank started with financing arranged by Bill W. It was intended to bypass larger industries' supply lines in automobile parts. It was never productive enough to provide any form of financial security. See page 32, *Writing the Big Book*.

professionalize it?" Certainly reasonable questions, but scattered before, in between and after were rambling detractors among which included, "Did Jesus Christ have an office?" and "Will there be a Grand Pooh-bah of A.A.[13]?" After a few more befuddling comments, Hank got to the heart of his concerns:

> I honestly believe a tide is rising on the book. You and I are going to profit from it if it rises high enough. If and when the time came, I think we would find it the subject of less criticism if the book company be the giver, not the receiver...[14].

That is, Hank wanted to keep their two-thirds ownership of Works Publishing and thus, two-thirds of the profits. As it was, Bill knew that the Fellowship was already starting to fall apart over the stock deal. Hank's suggestion definitely would have resulted in more criticism if not a full-scale revolt.

Hank continued with an additional reason to keep the publishing company at Honors Dealers:

> Another point – essentially, Works Publishing Company, if successful, must be a business organization. Does this mix with humanitarian and charitable work?
> ..... In other words, how can you successfully operate what might be a large business organization when everyone naturally feels a proprietary interest in it[15]?

Here, Hank's point was very important in that Works Publishing eventually would have to incorporate to adhere to business laws for the state of New York. Such an entity would require employees and professional management, which in turn would incur additional expenses. However, Hank failed to see that incorporation did not preclude oversight by the Foundation.

Of course, Hank could never have predicted the solution would be in the *Twelve Traditions* and *Twelve Concepts*.

Bill's reply to Hank made it clear that their days of making freewheeling business decisions on behalf of the Fellowship had come to an end. Bill seemed to sense that there would never be unity in A.A. unless he consistently consulted and mostly complied with the Fellowships' group consciences and he said as much in his reply to Hank. Furthermore, he committed the book to the Fellowship by saying, "The gang's money have gone into the venture; they have contributed material for half of the book; and the book and the work are unavoidably tied together[16]."

On a conciliatory note, Bill then acknowledged indirectly that Hank had been right about tempering the book with fewer Christian references among his other good contributions.

> When the book was written, I know I found it sometimes hard to accept suggestions and ideas from you when they really should have been accepted[17].

Nevertheless, he added a "but" that could well have been a reference to the stock venture:

> And then it comes to the business end of our deal. I think you have always had the same difficulty in considering my advice[18].

Finally, Bill pointed to the crux of Hank's inability to weigh in on any decisions regarding the future of the Fellowship:

> Another point – the gang would like you to come back with us very much. It would be helpful to you, to them, and most helpful to me. Even with respect to the book, it is difficult to sell your suggestions and ideas to people who sometimes feel that you are no longer one of them[19].

This debate between Bill and Hank began with moving Works Publishing to Manhattan so that Bill could get more help from volunteers. The substance of the debate revealed the many complexities facing the Fellowship on the cusp of seeing success through the sales of a book that essentially belonged to Bill and Hank.

On What Slender Threads

First, the Trustees and Bill had to figure out how to buy back all of the shares of stock and put the book under the purview of The Alcoholic Foundation. Then Bill and the Foundation would have to unravel the tangled web of compensation for A.A.'s early co-founders. Finally, they had to reckon with the rapid growth of the Fellowship resulting in the need for paid assistance to make Twelfth Step work possible.

No doubt, these were all consequences of Bill and Hank "flying blind".

Paid A.A. workers? Where does it begin and where does it end?

On the heels of publishing the book, Bill and Dr. Bob continued to struggle with finding financial relief for their families while continuing their work with the Fellowship. In 1940, shortly, after his written exchange with Hank, Bill wrote, "From the beginning, we have wrestled with the question of the paid alcoholic worker. He seemed an absolute necessity and probably was that until recently[20]."

Bill was referring to the compensation provided to members of the Fellowship, i.e., Dr. Bob, Hank, Fitz, and himself, before and shortly after the publication of the book. He acknowledged that such compensation was essential to getting the book published but that it had to end for the sake of not professionalizing Twelfth Step work.

As a result, the co-founders carried the burden of starting a life-saving program that was growing beyond comprehension and, at the same time, was taxing their ability to survive and support their families. This sticky problem would take a very long time to resolve through "the very careful wording of the A.A. Eighth Tradition[21]."

Furthermore, the Big Book itself was a complex issue that contributed to the problem.

Did the Big Book professionalize Twelfth Step work?

After the Foundation secured ownership of the Big Book, the Trustees awarded Dr. Bob royalties, in part to compensate for the loss of income he had suffered in order to get the book printed[22]. Shortly after, it was clear that the Foundation would have to find some compensation for Bill as he was giving his full attention to scores of individuals and groups' entreaties for guidance. There was no one better suited for the job.

The obvious solution was to award Bill royalties for the book. Some of the early Fellowship members objected and resurrecting their mantra that the Big Book was a written form of Twelfth Step work. After all, wouldn't royalties from the sales of the book be considered paid Twelfth Step work? Therefore, they believed it should not be sold; rather, it should be given away free of charge.

Bill believed that while the members' intentions were sincere, they did not take the future of A.A. into account. As much as he was trying to encourage unity by respecting the group consciences, in this instance, he insisted that the Foundation should sell the book. In later years, he could point to this particular decision to override the group conscience as one that was pivotal to A.A.'s future success:

> Our history proves that the sometimes idealistic majority of that day was seriously mistaken. Had there been no book earnings for the Headquarters and no royalties for Dr. Bob and me, A.A. would have taken a very different and probably disastrous course[23].

Easier to see in retrospect, Bill continued to paint a vivid picture of the disasters that would have followed, including no Traditions and no General Service Conference.

Awarding Bill royalties wasn't setting a precedent, particularly with Dr. Bob already receiving them. As the very first A.A. members and as earliest contributors to the growth of the movement, Dr. Bob and Bill more than earned their right to royalties from the sales of the book. Dr. Bob provided evidence that the program worked through his tireless efforts carrying the message. And, Bill wrote the book. About Bill in particular, *Pass It On* posited:

> The book royalties he received were not payment for Twelfth Step work; they were payment for special services; but the money nonetheless freed his time to do the Twelfth Step work that he unceasingly

did. Tradition Eight also made acceptable the proper compensation, in years to come of other special workers[24].

Part IV of the Long Form:

But our usual A.A. Twelfth Step work is never to be paid for.

A.A. members in alcohol recovery related fields

In the *AA Tradition* pamphlet, Bill distinguished between professionalization of A.A. Step work and A.A.'s who enter professionally related fields, which he considered logical and valuable. Bill only asked that A.A.s in professionally related fields avoid breaking their anonymity and, in particular, not use their affiliation with A.A. to raise money for or attract attention to their organization.

In short, they should enjoy their jobs. Outside of their jobs, they should do Twelfth Step work for their own sobriety and for free.

Certainly, Bill must have thought about the Towns Hospital offer when he said:

> … that A.A.'s going into alcohol therapy should never trade on their A.A. connection; that there is not, and can never be, any such thing as an "A.A. therapist[25]."

Today, Bill would probably add "or a paid A.A. Step sponsor." As discussed earlier, this unfortunate departure from A.A.'s spiritual principle of Twelfth Step work freely given currently does occur. However, two people are complicit: the one who is charging the fee and the one who is paying the fee.

Good old Tom, the fireman

A more salient and humorous telling of the club manager and cook story in this Tradition's essay is detailed in *Alcoholics Anonymous Comes of Age*. 'Good old Tom, the Fireman' clearly had an innate understanding of Tradition Eight before it was written. Tom was a newly recovered codger who had the sense not to let anyone sucker him into being an unpaid janitor for the clubhouse on Twenty-Fourth Street in New York. Bill's folksy narrative recounts that the clubhouse problems would be solved if the "trusted servants" could just con Tom into living there "for free." Tom, of course, was on to them. He responded:

> "What you guys want is a janitor."
> "All right," we said, "sure, we want a janitor."
> "Well," said Tom, "ain't you going to pay me nothing?"
> "Oh, no," we said, "that would make you a professional. This is Alcoholics Anonymous. We must not mix money with spirituality[26]."

With Bill's story-telling flair, the response from Tom was the Eighth Tradition in its purist form:

> "Okay," said Tom, "no money, no work. I'm doing my Twelfth Step work free, but if you're going to have me here as a janitor, you're going to pay me, see[27]?"

Bill ended the story humorously, but with a lingering sense of those desperate times for the Fellowship:

> Lots of us were working at that time and earning money. But believe it or not, we actually haggled with that old man to get him down to the last cent we could for doing that grubby job[28]!

This story exemplifies the struggles A.A. had trying to fulfill their need for paid workers as inexpensively as possible. As the Fellowship's needs for accomplishing Twelfth Step work became more complex, using cheap labor to support those needs was clearly not the answer.

Which brings us to today's paid service workers in A.A.

When studying this Tradition, it is essential to explore the broad scope of tasks for today's A.A. paid service workers. Area intergroup or central offices usually fulfill the needs of groups working in partnership in a

On What Slender Threads

specified geographic location. These offices rely on volunteers, but may be large enough to employ one or two special workers. Among their multitude of tasks, they purchase literature, chips, and other materials, answer phones, refer new prospects to members, and facilitate committees' activities including local outreach[29]. Generally, per Tradition Nine, a committee of A.A. volunteers manage or have oversight over these important offices and staff.

While paid service workers in intergroup or central offices and other A.A. service entities are possible by the Eighth Tradition, we will focus on paid service workers at the General Service Office (G.S.O.) and Alcoholics Anonymous World Services (A.A.W.S.). The *A.A. Service Manual* recommends thinking of A.A.W.S. as the people and G.S.O. as the place[30].

G.S.O. makes available a wealth of information to help groups operate effectively within and beyond their meetings. G.S.O.'s standing offices support the common needs and interests of most intergroup or central offices, Area Service committees, groups, and other service entities. The names of some of G.S.O's offices should strike a familiar chord with A.A. members who have served on committees in their local areas. These offices are Literature, Corrections, Public Information (PI), Cooperation with the Professional Community (CPC), Accessibilities and Treatment, Group Services, and Archives. There also are offices that support Area Delegates' annual Conferences, Regional Forums, and International Conferences. Finally, there are administrative offices essential for running a business operation such as IT Services, and Digital Media.

Much like Bill, Dr. Bob, and others' in the Headquarters of A.A.'s early days, G.S.O. staff and staff assistants handle correspondence and databases and assist with presentations and conferences. Twelve staff, who are also members of A.A., rotate their positions every two years. These important paid staff use their valuable experiences to help with:

> ... group problems through extensive correspondence, emails and telephone calls with members sharing G.S.O.'s store of accumulated A.A. experience, archival information, A.A. literature, *Box 4-5-9* articles and other Fellowship resources[31].

With the help of staff assistants, who are not required to be A.A. members, the twelve alcoholic staff members serve around 70,000 groups or 1.4 million members. They also serve an additional 1,500 groups or 38,000 members in corrections facilities[32]. A brief description of the offices and duties for the alcoholic A.A. staff is below.

G.S.O. A.A. Staff Rotating Assignments and *Very Brief* Description[33]	
Accessibilities & Remote Communities	Accessibility projects and Loners Internationalists Meeting bulletin for remote or culturally constrained members
Conference	Logistics and Planning for annual General Service Conference (U.S. and Canada)
Cooperation with the Professional Community (C.P.C.)/Treatment	Communications, outreach, and exhibits between A.A. groups and the professional community
Corrections	Logistics and outreach for A.A. in corrections facilities
Group Services	Serves groups' representatives and liaises with intergroup/central offices
International	Serves General Service Offices in other countries and coordinates World Services meeting every two years
International Convention	Coordinates International Convention which occurs every five years
Regional Forums	Coordinates four Regional forums for areas around the U.S. and Canada to improve communication at all levels of A.A.

Literature	Serves with Publishing Department to work on Conference approved literature, G.S.O. Bulletin and *Box 4-5-9*	
Nominating	Assists Trustees to ensure all vacancies are properly filled	
Public Information	Public service announcements, public relations/media communications	
Staff Coordinator	Staff, review bequests made to A.A. and serves A.A.W.S. board and on General Service Board	

Alcoholics Anonymous World Services, Inc.

A.A.W.S.'s purview is over all services, publishing, finance, and archives[34]. According to the *A.A. Service Manual*, G.S.O. means the entire operation and the staff. In that capacity, A.A.W.S. employs G.S.O. personnel, directs G.S.O. services, and is responsible for A.A.'s website and broad publishing efforts[35]. Staff are responsible for the production of literature in various formats and translations. This includes braille and media in American Sign Language. To get a sense of the span of literature made available by the Publishing office, peruse the A.A. Literature Catalogue. In the back portion, there is a list of translations of A.A. literature covering the globe including specific dialects within regions[36]. It tells a powerful story about how our paid staff help with A.A's primary purpose.

Among other assignments, staff coordinate and facilitate a Loners-Internationalists Meeting bulletin for members who are in remote areas or are culturally restricted from participating in A.A. events[37]. The International Office staff serve as a liaison to general service offices in other countries and respond to queries from outside the U.S. and Canada.

The table below provides the offices and brief corresponding administrative and service roles that support all A.A. activities including G.S.O for the U.S. and Canada.

Other A.A.W.S. Administrative and Support Services[38]	
Operations	Member services: handles communications with members and groups related to records, literature orders, and contributions. Manages group database and mail lists
Finance/Accounting	G.S.O.'s bills, accounts payable, contributions departments, independent auditors, financial statements, and financing International Convention
Technology Services	Technical infrastructure/governance, information security, and G.S.O. business applications
Contributions	All incoming contributions for U.S. and Canada
Human Resources	Employment management, compensation, compliance, and wellness
Communication Services	Website, YouTube, Meeting Guide and other apps, digital media projects. Responsible for all communications from G.S.O. entities
Meetings, Events, and Travel Services (METS)	Travel and accommodations, event planning particularly General Service Conference, Regional Forums, and World Services Meeting
Mail and Shipping	Mailing and shipping for all A.A.W.S. and Grapevine/La Viña
Publishing	Creates and publishes all literature. Includes handling translations of literature to other languages
Finance	Accounting, budgeting, financial statements, Reserve Fund management and retirement plans for A.A.W.S. and Grapevine/La Viña
Archives	A.A. history repository, preservation, conservation, and exhibits

There are over 49,000 groups or almost 500,000 members outside of the U.S. and Canada, Thus, in total, A.A.W.S. serves over 120,000 groups or almost 2 million members worldwide[39]. There is A.A. activity in an estimated 180 countries, including 66 autonomous general service offices outside of the U.S. and Canada[40].

Conference planning and reporting

The annual General Service Conference of Delegates meets every year to discuss and decide on A.A policy, literature, and other current issues. The Delegates and Trustees are volunteers who fully discuss all issues and then put forward final decisions or recommendations. Besides planning the Conference, the paid staff prepare all necessary background information, support the committees' meetings, and write their reports. A.A. members may more fully appreciate the scope of this work by reading a final report on the Conference usually posted on the Delegate's page of an Area's website. An online search can produce other Area Delegates' reports.

A.A. World Services Meeting

Every two years, the International Office in G.S.O. organizes and provides the report for A.A.'s World Service Meeting. The meeting is an unincorporated association of service structures of Alcoholics Anonymous in various countries. Information about the meeting is in the pamphlet, *Your AA General Service Office*.

> The World Service Meeting (WSM), started in 1969 and now biennial, is held alternately in New York and an overseas country. The staff member handles correspondence with members and groups in countries without a structure, works with the Publishing Department on translations of A.A. literature, coordinates the WSM and is responsible for the *World Service Meeting Report*[41].

The link to the *2020 World Services Report* is available online. The report includes in the Table of Contents a list of General Service Offices located across the world. It is a must-read for all A.A. members to appreciate

A.A.W.S.'s efforts to make recovery possible everywhere. For example, the report from Turkey is an inspirational account of the lengths A.A.s in Turkey have gone through to get meetings into hospitals and prisons[42].

And still, these are only a few of the services A.A.'s paid workers provide to make carrying the message possible.

Those who labor in service for us are worthy of their hire

Clearly, A.A. members and groups would want paid professionals to oversee A.A.'s web sites and other information technology resources. Pamphlets and publications require good writers and editors. Digital media, translations of our literature, and rigor in keeping A.A.'s archives require professionals in those fields. Finally, managing an effective workforce is a special talent. A.A.'s paid workers are worthy of their hire!

The A.A. Group pamphlet, provides an explanation of how A.A. pays for service to struggling alcoholics around the world.

> Like the expenses of other A.A. activities, those of the General Service Office are met generally by group and individual contributions. Since these contributions do not completely cover the cost of A.A.'s world services, publishing income is used to help offset the deficit[43].

It seems Bill's choice to over-ride the group conscience about giving the Big Book away may have been a good decision.

Business portions of A.A. are "special workers" on a large scale and are necessarily incorporated

Hank P. thought that A.A. should separate the spiritual from the material by keeping the publishing company separate from the Foundation. It turns out that A.A. has separated the material, but has retained spiritual accountability through its volunteers and paid staff. The chart below lists A.A.'s history of incorporating the portions of its efforts in order to adhere to state and federal requirements. Then, addressing Hank P.'s concerns, this chart is followed by a discussion on how A.A. keeps the material separate from the spiritual.

A.A. History of Incorporation[44]

Year	Entity	Description
1938	The Alcoholic Foundation	Formed as an unincorporated entity
1938	Works Publishing Company (The One Hundred Men Corporation)	Formed as an unincorporated entity
1940	Works Publishing Company, Inc.	Incorporated as a business corporation under the Stock Corporation Law of the State of New York. It takes over the assets of the former company and is wholly owned by The Alcoholic Foundation.
1943	The Alcoholic Foundation, Inc.	Incorporated as a non-profit corporation under the Membership Corporation Law of the State of New York.
1944	Grapevine Magazine	(June) First Edition
1946	The Alcoholics Anonymous Grapevine, Inc.	Incorporated as a business corporation under the Stock Corporation Law of the State of New York and is wholly owned by The Alcoholic Foundation
1953	Alcoholics Anonymous Publishing, Inc.	Works Publishing, Inc. is renamed Alcoholics Anonymous Publishing, Inc.
1954	General Service Board of Alcoholics Anonymous, Inc.	The Alcoholic Foundation, Inc. is renamed General Service Board of Alcoholics Anonymous, Inc.
1959	A.A. World Services, Inc.	Name of A.A. Publishing, Inc. officially changed to A.A. World Services, Inc.

1962	Alcoholics Anonymous World Services, Inc.	Incorporated as a non-profit corporation under the Membership Corporation Law of the State of New York. Takes over assets and functions of A.A.W.S., Inc., which is subsequently dissolved.
1971	Alcoholics Anonymous Grapevine, Inc.	Incorporated as a not-for-profit corporation under the Not-For-Profit Law of the State of New York. It takes over the assets and functions of The Alcoholics Anonymous Grapevine, Inc., the stock corporation then known as A.A. Grapevine, Inc., which is subsequently dissolved.

Separating the spiritual from the material

The Delegates adopted *The Twelve Concepts* at the 12th Conference on April 26, 1962. Bill defined the Concepts as the "twelve principles of service that have emerged from A.A.'s service accomplishments and mistakes since its beginning[45]." Portions of the Concepts are relevant to the oversight of A.A.'s corporate structures, A.A. World Services, Inc. and A.A. Grapevine, Inc.:

> The General Service Board has custodial oversight over both of these corporations, which it exercises by electing the directors of each. While the General Service Board does not interfere with the daily operation of either corporation, it does have the ultimate responsibility for seeing that both operate in the best interest of the Fellowship as a whole.
>
> The makeup of the two boards of directors, one for A.A.W.S. and the other for Grapevine, is a good example of the application of the Concept IV right of participation, which has resulted in *well-informed and highly unified boards of directors, and ruled out authoritarian and institutional operation styles that would conflict with A.A. principles* (emphasis added)[46].

Hank could not imagine a system that would separate the material from the spiritual. Bill created that system through A.A.'s service structure and the *Twelve Traditions* and *Twelve Concepts*.

The Eighth Tradition is the foundation for freely given Twelfth Step work while separating the material from the spiritual so that this altruistic service is possible for anyone anywhere. The Eighth and the Ninth Traditions make possible a service structure that allows A.A.'s around the world to share the solution to their common problem, alcoholism.

Coming up: the Ninth Tradition

Next, we will explore the structure of A.A.'s volunteer service committees. There are inextricable connections between Tradition Eight and Tradition Nine. Those connections ensure our unity and common welfare worldwide.

Children of chaos choose orderly chaos

Tradition 9

A.A., as such, ought never be organized; but we may create service boards or committees directly responsible to those they serve[1].

The Long Form: *Our A.A. experience has taught us that:*

Each A.A. Group needs the least possible organization. Rotating leadership is the best. The small group may elect its secretary, the large group its rotating committee, and the groups of a large metropolitan area their central or intergroup committee, which often employs a full-time secretary. The trustees of the General Service Board are, in effect, our A.A. General Service Committee. They are the custodians of our A.A. Tradition and the receivers of voluntary A.A. contributions by which we maintain our A.A. General Service Office in New York. They are authorized by the groups to handle our overall public relations and they guarantee the integrity of our principal newspaper, the A.A. Grapevine. All such representatives are to be guided in the spirit of service, for true leaders in A.A. are but trusted and experienced servants of the whole. They derive no real authority from their titles; they do not govern. Universal respect is the key to their usefulness[2].

Lyn S.

Synopsis of Bill's essay in the 12 & 12

Bill raised the seeming contradiction that A.A. is not organized, yet A.A. has service boards and committees aplenty. He explained the inconsistency by associating organization with a governing hierarchy. He reminded us that alcoholics rebel against authority, thus an organized hierarchy would never work for A.A. Bill argued that as long as our service and our committees focused on helping alcoholics and as long as such entities were accountable to their groups, A.A. would succeed. Bill mimicked naysayers who claimed alcoholics would fail because they are "defiant brats." In closing, Bill emphasized that A.A.'s Trustees are *directly* accountable to the *groups*[3].

How is service defined?

In *Alcoholics Anonymous Comes of Age*, Bill gave an overview of service that is timeless in its application. He said:

> And just how much territory does 'service action' take in?
>
> The answer is simple. An A.A. service is anything whatever that legitimately helps us to reach fellow sufferers. As we have seen, the Twelfth Step call is the greatest of A.A.'s services[4].

Bill went on to provide the long list of volunteer services that made Twelfth Step work possible, from fixing coffee to participation on committees, or working as a trusted servant to the General Service Conference. Then Bill provided the litmus test for any service that groups are considering:

> Regarding any particular service, we need to ask only one question: "Is this or that service *really needed?*" If it is not, then let it be eliminated. But if it *is* needed, then maintain it we must or fail in *our mission* (emphasis added) to those who want and seek A.A.[5]

In this study, Tradition Eight provides an overview of the tasks A.A. paid service workers carry out to make Twelfth Step work possible. However, there would be no work for paid staff without A.A. groups whose members serve as volunteers to help decide *how to make Twelfth Step work possible*. If A.A.

members' volunteer services are the heartbeat of Tradition Nine, A.A.'s service committees are its circulatory system. Both are needed to succeed in what Bill referred to as *our mission*.

It is important to note that Bill's discussion in Tradition Nine culminated in holding the Trustees of the Alcoholic Foundation directly accountable to the groups. The General Service Conference had not yet completed its experimental five-year trial! Essentially, Bill heralded the General Service structure for Alcoholics Anonymous when he said:

> It is clear now that we ought never to name boards to govern us, … It is in this spirit of service that we elect the A.A. group's informal rotating committee, the intergroup association for the area, and the General Service Conferences of Alcoholics Anonymous *for A.A. as a whole* (emphasis added).[6]

In this study, we will first examine the criteria for service positions needed to run an A.A. meeting and for carrying the message beyond the A.A. group. Evolving from over seventy years of A.A.'s experience, strength, and hope, we will discuss service "committees" that help make Twelfth Step work possible followed by "service boards" that provide conduits for decision-making and other activities in A.A. in the United States and Canada. We will conclude with an overview of the long-standing and final battle Bill fought on behalf of the Fellowship. Relevant to this, Bill wrote in his essay on the Ninth Tradition, "He [a churchman] is joined by a psychiatrist who says, "Defiant brats! They won't grow up and conform to social usage[7]!" Bill was indirectly referring to some of A.A.'s nonalcoholic Trustees, who firmly believed members of the Fellowship would never be able to suit up and show up for the voluntary service needed to run A.A. Bill persevered in a years-long struggle to convince not only those Trustees, but also the Delegates in the embryonic Conference, that alcoholics could be fully responsible for A.A.

Long Form Part 1: The essentials for individual groups

The Long Form of this Tradition first addresses basic fundamentals for A.A.'s service positions.

1. Each A.A. Group needs the least possible organization.
2. Rotating leadership is the best.
3. The small group may elect its secretary, the large group its rotating committee[8].

The G.S.O. pamphlet, *The A.A. Group*, is an essential resource for all A.A. members who are considering starting a regular meeting or modifying an existing meeting. The pamphlet provides guidelines for open and closed meetings along with suggested meeting formats and possible topics if appropriate. Usually a Chair, Treasurer, and Secretary are helpful for facilitating A.A. groups' meetings. *The A.A. Group* pamphlet provides a description for each of these positions along with a snapshot of other typical service positions needed for running an A.A. meeting[9].

According to *The A.A. Group* pamphlet, some members choose only to gather at a set time and place for an *A.A. meeting*[10]. Bill's essay on the Fourth Tradition assures members that, "Any two or three alcoholics gathered together for sobriety may call themselves an A.A. group provided that as a group they have no other affiliation[11]."

Nonetheless, the pamphlet distinguishes *A.A. groups* from *A.A. meetings*. *A.A. groups* continue "to exist outside the prescribed meeting hours, ready to provide Twelfth Step help[12]." Groups that want to carry the message beyond their own meetings will want to consider service activities or special positions that are specifically for such outreach. More information about these activities are in *The A.A. Group* pamphlet particularly under "How Can Newcomers Be Reached and Helped[13]?"

The *AA Group* pamphlet explains that groups with larger numbers of members may find it convenient to form a *representative* steering committee. Usually, the groups or entities that the steering committee serves should define the committee's role and approve their representatives. The trusted servants of such a committee are "directly responsible to those they serve." As a subset of the group, the committee can streamline the amount of work involved in addressing issues and then bring their recommendations to the group for a decision[14].

A.A. groups today can "create service boards or committees" if they choose to do so. However, since it has been over seventy years since Bill wrote this Tradition, the service boards or committees most helpful to groups may already be easily accessible. There are six service committees that are supported by standing offices at the General Service Office (see Tradition Eight in this study). These committees have proven to be effective modes for systemic outreach when established and maintained by groups:

- Public Information committee members carry the message locally using a range of methods that are suitable for letting struggling alcoholics know where meetings and groups are located[15].
- Archives committee members generate an historical timeline of A.A. in their area and catalogue local groups' histories.
- Treatment Facilities/Corrections committee members serve as liaisons to area treatment and corrections facilities organizing on-site meetings and transition assistance (Bridging the Gap)[16].
- Literature and Grapevine/La Viña are usually two separate committees whose members are resources for procuring and distributing their publications to the groups and individual members[17].
- Cooperation with the Professional Community committee members focus on cooperation, not affiliation, by sending A.A. members' to provide information about the Fellowship at professional organizations' conventions and at other professional venues[18].

Groups or combined groups may want to create special events for reasons they believe will help with Twelve Step work. *A.A. Guidelines* provides a specific publication on how to organize "Conferences, Conventions and Roundups." Based on the shared experience of A.A. members in various service areas, these guidelines are an invaluable resource for planning anything from special open meetings to conventions[19].

An A.A. group working in cooperation with other A.A. groups can work collaboratively in the six aforementioned committees and other service committees that makes outreach broader and more visible for struggling alcoholics. The next part of the Long Form of this Tradition presents a model for organizing such intergroup cooperation.

Long Form Part 2: The essentials for groups' combined efforts: service in Central or Intergroup Committee

> And the groups of a large metropolitan area [may have a] central or intergroup committee, which often employs a full-time secretary[20].

Groups in more sparsely populated areas may have intergroup or central committees as well. If there is an intergroup or central office that serves in an A.A. group's locale, an A.A. group can choose to have an Intergroup (or Central Office) Representative. This member would serve on an Intergroup Committee with representatives from other groups. As indicated in the Long Form of Tradition Eight, these offices sometimes have one or two paid staff who maintain groups' location and contact information, and accrue literature and other materials for easy access by the groups they serve. However, the office relies on oversight by the Intergroup or Central Committee. One of the many advantages of this cooperation among groups is that it is easier to populate with members from these combined groups' any outreach service committees deemed suitable for carrying the message. Some intergroups allow members of the groups who are not Intergroup Representatives to serve on their committees[21].

Not all A.A. groups are in regions that can sustain an intergroup or central office. However, all A.A. groups in the United States and Canada that have a General Service Office group number are associated with one of ninety-three Area Committees. Such groups can elect to have a General Service Representative (G.S.R.), who serves as the group's liaison to the Area Committee. The A.A. group's G.S.R. is an essential part of the communication channel to the General Service Conference and, ultimately, to the General Service Board[22]. Besides other service committees, the Area Committee usually has the aforementioned six service committees. Some Areas allow members who are not G.S.R.s to serve on their outreach committees.

All of this is to say that opportunities abound for any group member who wishes to participate in outreach service.

When a group examines how it would like to expand its service beyond the confines of the meeting, it will help to think about the impact of the service on carrying the message. The chart below illustrates the breadth of outreach possible at different levels of already existing service boards or committees.

The Ripple Effect of Carrying the Message through Service

Local Outreach
Meeting Service
Group Activities
(e.g. Hospitality, Workshops, Socials, Twelfth Step Work)

Regional Outreach
Intergroup Representative
Intergroup Officer
Intergroup Service Committees

National/International Outreach
General Service Representative
District Committee Member
Area Officer
Area Service Committees
Delegate

The following chart provides a more detailed overview of the service positions that could be available to group members:

Service Positions Available to Group Members
Local Outreach **Group** **Positions** Chair Treasurer Secretary Other as the group requires (See *A.A. Group* pamphlet)

> **Regional Outreach**
> **Intergroup/Central Office Positions**
> Intergroup Representative
> Intergroup Officer
> Public Information
> Cooperation w/ Professional Community
> Treatment/Corrections
> Literature
> Grapevine/La Viña
> *and others*
>
> **National/International Outreach**
> **Area Committee Positions**
> General Service Representative
> District Committee Member
> Area Officer
> Public Information
> Cooperation w/ Professional Community
> Treatment/Corrections
> Literature
> Grapevine/La Viña
> *and others*

Before completing the last portions of the Long Form of the Ninth Tradition, we will reflect on the phrase in the short form, "*we may create service boards or committees directly responsible to those they serve*[23]." A.A.'s general service structure is an application of this Tradition that allows A.A. groups to participate in issues related to A.A. particularly in the United States and Canada, but also worldwide.

The G.S.R. connects the A.A. group to the General Service Conference

The General Service Conference is an annual meeting of Delegates from the aforementioned ninety-three designated A.A. Areas across the United

States and Canada. The General Service Representative is the voice of the A.A. group through the Area's Delegate in the Conference. The *A.A. Service Manual* says:

> It might be helpful to think of general service as a kind of dialogue or communication between the groups, the trusted servants working on their behalf, and the General Service Office and General Service Board as they all manage the Fellowship's affairs[24].

Each A.A. group can contribute to the General Service Conference by forming "a group conscience on proposed changes or actions on matters relating to A.A. as a whole[25]." The graphic, "Structure of the Conference *U.S. and Canada*[26]," in *The A.A. Group* pamphlet, purposefully places A.A. groups at the top of an upside-down triangle. It is a representation of the chain of responsibility in A.A.'s general service structure. It illustrates how each group communicates its recommendations starting with each individual group through its G.S.R.

1. The group's G.S.R. shares the recommendations of the group conscience with the District Committee. (Some Areas may not have District Committees. In that case, G.S.R.s take their recommendations to the Area's pre-General Service Conference meetings.)
2. The District Committee is a service committee of G.S.R.s from the groups in an assigned District. The District's G.S.R.s select a representative, District Committee Member (D.C.M.), who shares with the Area Committee the sense of the groups in the District.
3. The Area Committee holds a special meeting to discuss the agenda for the upcoming General Service Conference. The Delegate, elected by the Area Assembly, listens to the discussion at the Area's pre-General Service Conference meeting.
4. The Delegate attends the General Service Conference[27] and participates in discussing and voting on matters that affect A.A.
5. The Trustees implement the decisions and recommendations of the Conference

Then, working back from the bottom of the diagram to the top:

1. The Trustees report to the Delegates.
2. The Delegate reports the results of the Conference to the D.C.M.s (or G.S.R.s) in the Area.
3. D.C.M.s report back to their District's G.S.R.s
4. G.S.R.s report back to their groups.

In essence, the channel of communications is dependent on the A.A. groups' participation and is only possible through the efforts of trusted servants at each level.

The most important point is that the General Service Board and General Service Conference are accountable to the A.A. groups who participate through their G.S.R.s.

The General Service Conference is held every year in April attended by half of the Delegates serving their first term and the other half continuing their second term[28]. In advance of the meeting, Delegates are assigned to service committees, each with its own list of tasks, issues, and proposals to consider during the conference. Delegates discuss proposed changes to the literature or policies related to theirs and other committees.

Traditions Eight and Nine at Work		
G.S.O. A.A. Staff Offices	**General Conference** *Secondary Conference Committees*	**Corresponding Trustees' Committees**
Accessibilities & Remote Communities	Treatment and Accessibilities	
Conference	Agenda	General Service Conference

Cooperation with the Professional Community (C.P.C.)/ Treatment	Cooperation with the Professional Community	Cooperation with the Professional Community (C.P.C.)/Treatment and Accessibilities
Corrections	Corrections	Corrections
International International Convention Regional Forums	International Conventions/ Regional Forums*	International Conventions/Regional Forums
Literature	Literature	Literature
Nominating	Trustees	Nominating
Public Information	Public Information	Public Information
	Grapevine/LaViña	Meets with members of the Grapevine Corporate Board
	Archives*	Archives
	Policy/Admissions	
	Report and Charter	
	Finance	Finance and Budgetary

The center column is a list of the annual General Service Conference committees. The right column lists the Trustees' committees that work in tandem with the Delegates committees. The left column demonstrates how paid workers per the Eighth Tradition support volunteers per the Ninth Tradition by listing A.A.'s offices whose staff assist with the preparation, discussion, and recommendations of the Conference committees.

Echoing the discussion on the Eighth Tradition, the Delegates and Trustees fully deliberate all issues and then put forward advisory actions or recommendations. The paid staff prepare all necessary background information, support the committees' meetings, and write their reports. With Tradition Eight, paid service workers carry out the tasks for the Delegates and Trustees that make Twelfth Step work possible. However, as indicated earlier, through its service structure channel, A.A. groups decide through the General Service Conference *how to make Twelfth Step work possible.*

In the Eighth Tradition, the discussion included the invitation to seek out Delegates' reports on the Conference from the standpoint of the support that paid staff provide. It helps now to look at the same report from the standpoint of the scope of Delegates' work. To learn more about A.A.'s General Service structure and the Conference, see *The A.A. Service Manual.*

Long Form Part 3: The essentials for our General Service Board

> The trustees of the General Service Board are, in effect, our A.A. General Service Committee. They are the custodians of our A.A. Tradition and the receivers of voluntary A.A. contributions by which we maintain our A.A. General Service Office [in] New York. They are authorized by the groups to handle our overall public relations and they guarantee the integrity of our principal newspaper, the A.A. Grapevine[29].

The Trustees of the General Service Board are unpaid trusted servants answerable to A.A. groups. They are also voting members of the Conference along with 6 nontrustee directors from A.A.W.S. and Grapevine and 15 A.A. staff at G.S,O. There is a correspondence between the Trustees' committees and the Delegates' service committees. Trustees review the Conference Advisory Actions and refer them to the appropriate committees for implementation. They provide quarterly reports of their activities. With their fiduciary responsibilities, Trustees oversee A.A.'s two corporate entities, The Grapevine and A.A.W.S.[30]

Hearkening back to the last paragraph in Bill's essay on the Ninth Tradition, one can see his determination to reinforce the future Conference's strength when he said, "Even our Foundation, once an independent board, is today directly accountable to our Fellowship. Its trustees are the caretakers and expediters of our world services[31]."

Whew! And yet, Bill claimed A.A. was not organized? How and why was that? It helps to go back to the years before the Conference when all decisions for A.A.'s future were made by Headquarters (Bill and Dr. Bob) and the Alcoholic Foundation's Trustees, the majority of whom were non-alcoholic. We will then conclude with the remaining portion of the Long Form of the Ninth Tradition.

In it's early beginnings, A.A. was organized

In 1938, Hank P. and Bill understood very well the skepticism and distrust that an organization managed solely by alcoholics would engender from prospective donors. In reality, the early founders themselves recognized their own limitations and potential for misconduct. The Alcoholic Foundation, with its majority of nonalcoholic Trustees, was the gift that would overcome such skepticism and help launch A.A. as a worldwide phenomenon.

Less than ten years later, after inconceivable growth and success, Bill fretted about A.A.'s survival with non-alcoholics comprising a majority of the Board. The *Twelve Points* that eventually became the *Twelve Traditions* was only a small step in reversing that framework. Bill would not rest peacefully until he could be sure Alcoholics Anonymous belonged to alcoholics. Describing his fears, Bill predicted that the disconnect between the Fellowship and the Board would only grow when he said:

> …The main link between our world services and A.A. itself had been Dr. Bob, our secretarial staff, and me. To our world-wide fellowship

its devoted Board of Trustees was scarcely known at all. Not one A.A. in a thousand could name even half of them[32].

Then Bill implicitly acknowledged the danger inherent in his and Dr. Bob's inescapable association as A.A.'s leaders.

> When death or disability finally took us few old-timers out of the picture, where would that leave the Trustees and the Headquarters[33]?

Bill continued to paint a picture of the doom he believed was inevitable. He predicted the Trustees and whoever managed Headquarters would make a devastating mistake that would result in A.A. groups' "failure of confidence." Ultimately, Headquarters and A.A. would collapse. Finally, Bill struck the final blow to the status quo by saying:

> It was evident that here was a world-wide movement that had no direct access to its own principal service affairs. The Trustees had authority over our services; A.A. itself had no authority. The simple trusteeship had been the ideal guardian for our infancy and adolescence, but how in future years could it possibly go on functioning as it had[34]?

From those fears grew Bill's idea for the Conference. He proposed that, at the very least, the Trustees and Headquarters' decision-making processes must include input from representatives of A.A. groups from across the United States and Canada.

The Conference laid the groundwork for earning Trustees' trust

As we learned in this study on the Second Tradition, the Trustees initially objected to the proposed Conference. Bill's response was nothing short of a temper tantrum, but thankfully, A.A.'s nonalcoholic friends weathered this and other ill-tempered fits by Bill. With the help of a compromise between Trustees Bernard Smith and Leonard Harrison, an annual Conference of Delegates from the groups began a five-year trial in 1951[35].

However, Dr. Harry Tiebout was not at all convinced that alcoholics would ever be mature enough to handle the responsibilities of A.A.'s global outreach, especially with those crazy Traditions that encouraged anarchy and discouraged leadership. When raising the issue of the chronic immaturity of alcoholics, Tiebout's first case in point was usually Bill.

After reading Bill's report of the first 1951 experimental Conference, Tiebout, in a fury, sent Bill a letter, "pointing out the dangers of historical distortion, egotism, and damaging ingratitude[36]." Tiebout fumed that Bill had snubbed all of the non-alcoholics who saved Works Publishing from falling apart. This neglect particularly peeved Tiebout as he was "an open-pursed purchaser of the apparently worthless stock[37]."

Bill agreed that his telling of A.A.'s early history lacked clarity but went on to deny vigorously any intentional "historical distortion" that resulted in the early Fellowship appearing "self-sufficient" or mature. Bill then continued resentfully that he had been giving credit to many of the Fellowship's non-alcoholic friends including Tiebout[38].

The experimental Conference had met only once, and Bill was already on the defensive with Tiebout, who would become a Class A Trustee in 1957!

Bill's defensiveness only served to reinforce Tiebout's argument about the immaturity of alcoholics, especially Bill. As Tiebout pointed out, alcoholics claim that they have an obsessively compulsive inclination to addictive dependency, and they declare that self-reliance is dangerous to their recovery! How can such impaired individuals ever say, at the same time, that they are mature? Was that contradiction not the best proof of "*immaturity* – the denial of the reality of dependence[39]?"

Bill took Tiebout's points to heart and spent the next four years searching for answers to this conundrum. Kurtz pointed out that Bill's search was reflected in the themes of the succeeding experimental Conferences.

1952 – *Progress*: Clearly, Bill had a supporter of the *Traditions* in Bernard Smith, non-alcoholic Trustee chair, who set the tone with,

"We here must dedicate ourselves to insure that there is never any government in the hearts of Alcoholics Anonymous[40]."

The next Conference's theme was hopeful, but Bill's frustration in trying to find answers to Teibout's challenge was evident.

1953 – *We Are Standing on the Threshold of Maturity*: Ironically, in the Final Report, Bill admitted, "No one can say in truth that we are really mature yet. The process of maturing will go on as long as we last[41]."

Threshold, indeed!

The following Conference's theme was contradictory, given Bill believed his prediction about alcoholics losing confidence in A.A. was starting to come true.

1954 – *Confidence and Responsibility*: Following the conference, Bill vented his frustration in a letter to a member by enumerating "... some examples of "plain irresponsibility" that had arisen from the members' sense of separation from the Trustees of the Alcoholic Foundation[42]."

Driven by his own lack of confidence in the Trustees, Bill propelled the October 1954 name change of the Alcoholic Foundation to the General Service Board of Alcoholics Anonymous. As Kurtz pointed out, it was minimal progress in that non-alcoholics retained a majority of the Board, "and selection continued to be essentially from within, although the elective process was slightly opened and formalized[43]."

Bill declared the last experimental Conference to be a pivotal moment in alcoholics' responsibility for A.A. and it most certainly was monumental. But, in Bill's view, it was not enough.

1955 – *Coming of Age*: The annual Conference's successful five-year trial resulted in "... a formal handing over to the membership, as represented by the General Service Conference, of the "Three Legacies of Alcoholics Anonymous … Recovery, Unity, and Service[44]."

In that five-year period, alcoholic Delegates demonstrated that A.A. members could not only suit up and show up, but also provide valuable perspectives to solving some of A.A.'s problems. While the newly endorsed Conference gave Delegates a vote on matters that related to A.A. as a whole, the Fellowship did not control the Board. Thus, alcoholics did not yet have full responsibility for the complexities and fiscal obligations of their own worldwide organization.

Bill would not let go of his obsession that alcoholics' majority representation on the Board was essential to A.A.'s long-term survival. He was concerned that many people who suffered from the disease would not be attracted to a program that perpetuated the idea that alcoholics could never recover enough to be responsible for their own program[45]. His problem in achieving that outcome was two-fold after the Conference completed its successful trial. Bill not only needed to sway the Trustees, he needed to convince the Delegates. Both were skeptical.

By the time of the *Coming of Age* Conference, Bill was exhausted and keenly aware that in order for the Conference to be successful in the future, he had to distance himself from his leadership role in A.A. After the Trustees' official approval of the Conference, Bill hoped the Delegates would continue his fight[46].

Unfortunately, each year from 1956 through 1962, the Delegates advised retaining the non-alcoholic majority on the Board. From their perspective, everything seemed to be working[47]. During that time, Bill continued to hold back on advocating for ratio change. Nevertheless, he was smoldering when he said, "At the forthcoming Conference I am having nothing to say whatever about the Trustee ratio…I really did quit at St. Louis and meant to[48]."

It was not long before Bill started using his abrasive tactics again on the heels of writing:

> Nobody wishes to quit the "papa" business any more eagerly than I do. A.A. needs to stand on its own feet, that's the primary thing… What am I supposed to do? Am I supposed to transfer the remainder

of my leadership to a Board in which I cannot have full confidence? …I am fully fed up with it… [But at St. Louis] I … agreed to turn over full responsibility to the groups… So, when they still refuse to name a majority of their own membership to run their own affairs, I wonder if they are really doing this. It looks to me rather that they were consulting their fears rather than their trust…[49].

In 1961, spurred by the inactive stance of the Delegates, Bill submitted his own list of Class B nominees stressing the responsibilities of "Responsibility" itself. The predictable, if not annoying, Tiebout, now a Trustee, promised to vote against the change. He wrote to Bill:

Most [A.A.'s] are not impressed by the need to grow up…
I am not very much moved by the emphasis on growing up. Most adolescents are very conscious of having grown up. The trouble is that they do not know that they still have a lot to learn[50]."

Between the Delegates and the Trustees, Bill could not win! Nevertheless, he continued sporadically and sometimes angrily to argue not only with Tiebout, but also with other Trustees and with the Delegates.

In the meantime, Bill wrote the *Twelve Concepts for World Service*. The *Concepts* outlined the "why" of A.A.'s service structure, with substantive components that meticulously described "how" A.A.'s service structure works. Key to this discussion, Bill said that one of the ideas prevalent throughout *The Concepts* is, "No group or individual should be set in unqualified authority over another[51]."

The Delegates accepted *The Concepts*, but continued to support the non-alcoholic majority representation on the Board in 1962.

Almost ten years after the *A.A. Comes of Age* conference, Tiebout came around through Bill's insistence that while alcoholics may be chronically immature, that did not mean they could not be responsible. It is hard to believe that *The Concepts* were not a factor in Teibout's change of heart. *The Traditions* spoke to how groups avoid irresponsibility, while *The Concepts* spoke directly to how groups assume responsibility. Dr. Tiebout agreed to vote for the ratio change in late 1964[52].

On What Slender Threads

Sensing that the needle was finally moving, Bill continued to stress to the Trustees and Delegates the importance of alcoholics taking responsibility for their own program. His constant exertion of this theme culminated in A.A.'s 30th Anniversary International Convention's acceptance of "The Declaration" as its keynote." With 10,000 A.A. members and others in attendance, Bill and Lois closed the convention with attendees holding hands and reciting[53]:

> I am responsible. When anyone, anywhere, reaches out for help, I want the hand of A.A. always to be there. And for that: I am responsible[54].

As emotional and moving as that moment must have been, there was still a bit of work to do to overcome Bill's heavy-handed tactics. Dr. Jack Norris had to remind the Board that the alcoholic Trustees had been up-standing and solid contributors. Dr. Jack recalled what he said that swayed the reluctant Trustees:

> At the time the majority was set up, nobody had more than three years' sobriety in A.A., and they didn't trust themselves in the money department. I said, 'Give it a try. If it doesn't work, we can change it.' And it was that easy[55].

Surely, Bill would have vigorously disputed the "And it was that easy!" part!

The Conference recommended and the Board approved the two-thirds alcoholic majority representation in 1966. From that point on, A.A.'s future belonged to alcoholics. And for that, A.A. members are responsible.

Currently, there are fourteen alcoholic Class B Trustees and seven Class A Trustees. The Class B Trustees are in three categories: eight regional Trustees (six from the U.S. and two from Canada), four General Service Trustees (two from Alcoholics Anonymous World Services and two from Grapevine), and two Trustees-at-Large (one from the U.S. and one from Canada)[56].

Lyn S.

Long Form Part 4: We are not organized

> All such representatives are to be guided in the spirit of service, for true leaders in A.A. are but trusted and experienced servants of the whole. They derive no real authority from their titles; they do not govern. Universal respect is the key to their usefulness[57].

In short, as codified by the *Traditions* and *The Concepts*, there is no governing heirarchy in Alcoholics Anonymous. As underscored by this last portion of the Long Form of the Tradition, A.A.'s Trustees are trusted servants to the A.A. groups. Ultimately, A.A. groups are responsible for A.A.

As a result of this discussion, hopefully groups will contact their Area Committee for facilitating an exploration of, or even a brief overview of *The A.A. Service Manual Combined with the Twelve Concepts for World Service*. And, if not done already, groups will elect a volunteer for the critical "A.A. communications channel" position of G.S.R.!

Caution against confusing service with leadership/ownership

In this final cautionary observation, Bill emphasized the spiritual principle of A.A.'s service committees and service boards. He said:

> While A.A. has to function, it must at the same time avoid wealth, prestige, and power, three great dangers which necessarily tempt nearly all human societies. Though Tradition Nine at first sight seems to deal with purely practical matters, it embodies a deep spirituality in its actual operation. A.A. is a *society without organization, animated only by the spirit of service – a true fellowship* (emphasis added)[58].

Bill emphasized the role of *trusted servants* – no matter what the service position is. Indeed, active Delegates, Area Representatives, District Representatives, General Service Representatives, and Intergroup Representatives do a substantial amount of heavy lifting in their roles. However, Bill makes it clear that service for inside the meeting and for outreach are equally important.

There is no higher echelon of service.

Coming up: the Tenth Tradition

One would think that with all of Bill's trials in establishing the service structure for A.A., he would be the staunchest defender of the *Traditions*. When we explore Tradition Ten, we'll learn how the Trustees, Headquarters, and Bill occasionally faltered under the pressures of outside issues.

Outside opinions contaminate the solution

Tradition 10

> *Alcoholics Anonymous has no opinion on outside issues; hence the A.A. name ought never be drawn into public controversy*[1].

The Long Form: *Our A.A. experience has taught us that:*

> No A.A. group or member should ever, in such a way as to implicate A.A., express any opinion on outside controversial issues – particularly those of politics, alcohol reform, or sectarian religion. The Alcoholics Anonymous groups oppose no one. Concerning such matters they can express no views whatever[2].

Synopsis of Bill's essay in the 12 & 12

Bill began this essay by quoting an old-timer who said, "Practically never have I heard a heated religious, political, or reform argument among A.A. members." Bill emphasized that even if the cause is worthy, A.A.s must never *publicly* take sides in any fight. He pointed to the Fellowship's principle of humility and reminded A.A. members this was not a "special virtue." It was a matter of A.A.'s survival. Wryly, he corrected the misapprehension that A.A. was one big happy family and hearkened to the time when A.A. was "one prodigious squabble." In conclusion, Bill reminded members of the fate of the Washingtonians; one he hoped A.A. would avoid[3].

Lyn S.

The Long Form's explicit charge to A.A. members

The Sixth Tradition states *A.A. ought never endorse, finance, or lend the A.A. name to any related facility or outside enterprise, lest problems of money, property, and prestige divert us from our primary purpose*[4].

The Tenth Tradition states *Alcoholics Anonymous has no opinion on outside issues; hence the A.A. name ought never be drawn into public controversy*[5].

Similar in spirit, both Traditions ask A.A. groups and individual members to avoid using the name of A.A. in association with supporting or not supporting outside entities or causes. However, the Long Form of the Tenth Tradition reminds members that there are more nuanced ways of associating A.A. with outside causes: *No A.A. group or member should ever, in such a way as to implicate A.A., express any opinion on outside controversial issues*[6]. The phrase, "as to implicate A.A.," requires members to be sensitive to *where and when* they are expressing their personal opinions on politics, religion, medicine, addiction treatment, or any subject that might deter a newcomer or divert the group from carrying the message. Even when A.A. is, at best praised or, at worst maligned, the practice of this Tradition is to have no opinion on outside opinions of A.A.

Perhaps a more positive approach to practicing Tradition Ten is to ask, when in the A.A. Fellowship, *"When I am speaking, am I carrying the message of recovery to **all** alcoholics who still struggle?"*

As with all the Traditions, the road to the Tenth Tradition was paved with mistakes made by early members, the Trustees, and Bill, himself. This study will begin with early A.A. and the always controversial topic of war. It will continue with the minefields of opinions on medicine, religion, drug addiction, and A.A. itself as the subject of legal disagreements. The study will then explore how the Conference weilded the spiritual sword of the Traditions to protect A.A. from its own protectors and conclude with a Tenth Tradition list of what A.A. does not do. In short, the Tenth Tradition kept and continues to keep A.A. out of the battlefield of controversies.

A.A. members had an opinion on World War II

Barely two years after the publication of the Big Book, membership surged from less than 100 to 2,000, which necessitated a second printing in March 1941. Nine months later, in December 1941, the Japanese Imperial Fleet attacked Pearl Harbor thrusting the formerly isolationist United States into war. By that time, the membership had mushroomed to 8,000 members. Bill said, with that remarkable growth, the Fellowship entered into "a period of awful uncertainty[7]." Thus, the United States was at war when, what Bill called, the "big test of A.A.'s unity began in earnest[8]." Involvement in World War II also tested unity in the United States and, as with any war, not everyone supported that cause.

With his brief experience as a soldier near the end of World War I, it seems that Bill never considered that his support for World War II would be problematic. After the Army repeatedly denied his attempts to enlist and rejected his overtures to serve as an alcoholic counseling resource, Bill had no alternative but to focus on the newly evolving Headquarters and continue his work with alcoholics at home. In that effort, Bill and Dr. Bob, successfully petitioned the government for gas rations so that they could transport struggling alcoholics to meetings[9].

Bill also continued doing whatever he could to help alcoholics who went to war. With less than one or two years in recovery, alcoholic members in the military were reaching out to Headquarters seeking guidance for starting groups. Bobbie B., then office manager, was devoted to answering these queries, providing moral support, and helping members to connect with other alcoholics where they were stationed[10]. With Bill's support, six New York A.A. members started the *Grapevine* to share news and stories from home. The Alcoholic Foundation's publishing company shifted to a cheaper stock of paper for reprints of the book. And wherever Bill spoke, he told groups that they "needed to be prepared for a bumper crop of drunks" when the war was over[11].

Other than Bill's attempt to establish what was tantamount to an A.A. Office in the U.S. Army, his and Bobbie's efforts were reasonably aligned with Twelfth Step work or, at least, making Twelfth Step work possible. A more obvious overreach occurred through several groups' distribution of "An AA's Pledge for National Defense and Self Preservation." As a gesture of supporting the nation at war, members were encouraged to take this pledge affirming their loyalty to the United States with a promise to be productive citizens actively engaged in politics. Of course, this loyalty initiative prompted various newspapers to report, "Alcoholics Anonymous pledged its support for the duration of the war[12]."

According to *Pass It On*, A.A.s who served in the armed forces numbered about 300 by 1944. Those members proved they could stay sober under the horrors and stress of military action[13]. Bill dedicated a paragraph to these recovered alcoholic soldiers in his essay on the Third Step, identifying their perseverance as the first major test of that Step's spiritual principle[14].

Thus, when World War II began, there were no Traditions that emphasized the importance of unity and there was no General Service Conference to debate A.A.'s degree of involvement at that difficult time in U.S. history. Certainly, there is no doubt that recovered soldiers carried the A.A. program to struggling alcoholics worldwide. Nevertheless, A.A. avoided a formal stance in favor of World War II in spite of Bill's and other members' overt support.

Levels of practicing Tradition Ten

Bill chose to have two separate Traditions on Anonymity. Eleven addressed A.A.'s policy of anonymity at the public level and Twelve spoke to the spiritual principle of anonymity at a personal level. To understand Tradition Ten, it helps to examine opinions on outside issues at the same two levels, the public level and the personal level.

At the personal level: opinions are a dubious luxury

While Bill never meant the beginning of "There is a Solution" to have a cautionary tone, members might keep the following in mind before broaching outside issues in an A.A. meeting:

> ... All sections of this country and many of its occupations are represented, as well as many political, economic, social, and religious backgrounds. We are people who normally would not mix[15].

By itself, that observation is a compelling reason for why members should not discuss their personal opinions on outside issues when they gather as a Fellowship. A restatement of the Tradition might be, "We don't agree on much, but we do agree that we have a common solution to the problem of alcoholism."

In the Big Book, the Fourth Step reminded alcoholics of their limitations, which they might consider before voicing outside opinions in meetings:

> The first thing apparent was that this world and its people were often quite wrong. To conclude that others were wrong was as far as most of us ever got… But the more we fought and tried to have our own way, the worse matters got. As in war, the victor only *seemed* to win. Our moments of triumph were short-lived[16].

Bill anticipated alcoholics' rebellious nature particularly with respect to personal opinions when he wrote of A. A. in his essay on the First Tradition:

> … surely there is none which more jealously guards the individual's right to think, talk, and act as he wishes[17].

However, when members and groups avoid outside issues, they stand a better chance of successfully carrying the message of recovery to many sufferers. Thus, Bill went on to gently remind alcoholics that A.A.'s unity and the Fellowship's common welfare depended on members' acceptance that they are "but a small part of a great whole; that no personal sacrifice is too great for preservation of the Fellowship[18]." In the First Tradition, alcoholics learn that "the clamors of desires and ambitions within [them] *must be silenced* (emphasis added) whenever these could damage the group[19]."

Finally, A.A.'s primary purpose, to carry the message, is the most important reason to adhere to the Tenth Tradition, so that all who enter are assured of a place that addresses only problems as they relate to alcohol.

Bill tried to avoid outside issues when writing the book

To avoid any controversy that would hinder acceptance of the book, Bill made a concerted effort not to offend religion, medicine, and other professions when he wrote the Big Book. In "There is a Solution," he wrote:

> Of necessity there will have to be discussion of matters medical, psychiatric, social, and religious. We are aware that these matters are, from their very nature, controversial. Nothing would please us so much as to write a book which would contain no basis for contention or argument. We shall do our utmost to achieve that ideal[20].

One could say that Bill was moderately successful in the medical field, but not very successful in the area of religion. Let's start with medicine.

At the public level: medical opinions about alcoholism

The undoing of the Emmanual Approach was partly a function of disagreements between medical professionals. Dr. Elwood Worcester, a nonalcoholic chaplain, started the movement in 1909 to treat assorted forms of nervousness. Courtney Baylor, a nonalcoholic therapist, expanded the approach to treat alcoholics in 1913. Worcester and Baylor achieved some success using techniques that included hypnosis and alcoholics sharing their experiences with each other. Sigmund Freud publically expressed some disdain for their techniques, which partially contributed to the demise of the Emmanuel Approach. Though Worcester had supporters who were medical professionals, the movement could not withstand the fallout from Freud's and other doctors' competing views within the medical profession[21].

In the First Edition of the Big Book, Dr. Silkworth wrote a glowing endorsement of the program, but he did not sign his name for fear of censure from his colleagues. His professionally protective instincts were borne out by the less than lukewarm AMA review in October 1939 that said that the only good thing about the book was "the recognition of the seriousness of addiction to alcohol," and that the book "had no scientific merit or interest[22]."

With the help of Dr. Harry Tiebout, an early and avid proponent of A.A., the medical profession did eventually acknowledge the substantive merit of A.A. as early as 1943[23]. Bill received multiple invitations to speak at medical societies in Baltimore, New York, and at Yale[24]. Bill had the medical profession's attention with the astounding success of the Big Book, and he professed no credentials except that of being a recovered alcoholic.

Thus, Dr. Silkworth did witness the uneven but progressive acceptance of A.A. by his own profession. Unfortunately, he died five months before A.A. received the Lasker Award presented in October 1951 by the American Public Health Association[25]. Four years later, the late Dr. Silkworth's name appeared at the end of "The Doctor's Opinion" in the First Printing of the Second Edition in 1955.

Conscientiously avoiding conflict with the medical field, Bill did not attempt to provide a clinical definition of alcoholism. For example, he avoided the use of the word "disease" given its meaning evoked disagreement in the medical community during that time. As Kurtz pointed out, medical terms were irrelevant because they are "outside issues." Thus, when biochemists and psychiatrists eliminated the use of "physical allergy" and "mental obsession," this had no effect on the efficacy of a book 'written by alcoholics' who posed no medical theories about alcoholism[26].

Bill skirted opinions on the medical view of alcoholism by eloquently describing the manifestations of alcoholism as informed by his own experience and by the experiences of other early members. Bill also used some examples from a 1931 publication, *The Common Sense of Drinking* by Richard Peabody, a former patient of Baylor and the Emmanuel Approach[27]. As Kurtz pointed out, "Alcoholics Anonymous thus offered a concept of the alcoholic rather than an understanding of *alcoholism*[28]."

Avoiding outside issues did not result in immediate benefits, but over time, it saved Alcoholics Anonymous from *wholesale* censure from the medical community. Such is the reward when A.A. members avoid opinions on medically related topics.

Medical opinions at the personal level: don't practice medicine

In *The A.A. Group* pamphlet, the section "What A.A. Does *Not* Do," provides a reminder that A.A. members do not 'Make medical or psychological diagnoses or prognoses[29].'

Other helpful pamphlets include *The A.A. Member – Medications & Other*

Drugs[30], and *A.A. for Alcoholics with Mental Health Issues – and their Sponsors*[31]. Both contain the reminder:

> No A.A. member should "play doctor"; all medical advice and treatment should come from a qualified physician.

Unfortunately, uninformed diagnoses by A.A. members have resulted in tragic consequences. Members can avoid contributing to such harm by carefully following A.A.'s Tenth Tradition with respect to opinions in the area of medicine.

At the public level: opinions about A.A. and religion

Given A.A.'s complex and interlaced history with religion, members who wish to practice the Tenth Tradition might reflect with special care on how to share their own spiritual journey to recovery. It is helpful to consider A.A.'s own difficult history in this area.

In the Sixth Tradition, we reviewed how problematic it was for A.A. to separate itself from religion particularly given the numerous religious overtones in the Big Book. Fortunately, Bill wrote several disclaimers akin to "We have no desire to convince anyone that there is only one way by which faith can be acquired[32]," hoping to convince wary alcoholics that the program offered a generically spiritual solution.

Almost as soon as Bill published the Big Book, it was clear that claiming non-association with religion was not convincing. The first Akron meetings and Bill's repeated religious references probably contributed to the aforementioned tepid AMA review that also likened the program to the godlike guidance of the Oxford Group[33]. Furthermore, the Fellowship's own supporter, Dr. Tiebout, reinforced A.A.'s religiosity when he described A.A. as "a therapeutic program which includes a definite religious element…[34]" in his 1944 paper in *The American Journal of Psychiatry*. Finally, Bill's religious leanings continued to be evident when he wrote the *Twelve Steps and Twelve Traditions*.

As a result, A.A.'s early history, its basic literature, and public opinions about the religiosity of A.A. contributed to the misperception that it was a religious organization. This misapprehension persists today with the added element of some A.A. members and groups promoting their own religion in meetings. Thus, public opinions about the religiosity of A.A., particularly on the internet or social media, continue to vary wildly.

Court rulings across the United States provide an interesting illustration of differing opinions. Two such cases are *Griffin v. Coughlin* in New York and *Stafford v. Harrison* in Kansas. A New York State of Appeals court concluded in *Griffin v. Coughlin* that A.A. "engages in religious activity and religious proselytization." The judges focused on the multiple Christian references throughout the Big Book and the *Twelve Steps and Twelve Traditions* and ruled that state prison officials could not force prisoners to attend its meetings[35].

In contrast, the *Stafford v. Harrison* case resulted in the court concluding that A.A. could not be designated as a religion:

> It was noted that the definition of a "Higher Power" is expressly left to the individual in AA texts and that the terms "spiritual experience" and "spiritual awakening" are broadly defined to include a spectrum of experiences that transform individual behavior[36].

The *Griffin v. Coughlin* decision prevailed after an appeal. According to an article in *The New York Times*, the judge who wrote on behalf of the majority acknowledged that they had not intended to:

> … denigrate the Alcoholics Anonymous approach to fighting addiction. Nor, the decision said, should the prison system scrap drug- and alcohol-abuse treatment programs if they are offered voluntarily[37].

As happens when such controversies occur, reporters sought comments from A.A. Even though the *Griffin v. Coughlin* decision, in effect, classified A.A. as a religious organization in its home office state of New York, the *New York Times* reporter wrote:

> Alcoholics Anonymous would not say whether it saw itself as a religious organization. A spokeswoman in Manhattan, who insisted that

her name not be printed because she is also an A.A. member, said the group "has always refrained from commenting on outside issues[38]."

At the end of the day, A.A.'s literature is subject to interpretation and A.A.'s Big Book and *Twelve Steps and Twelve Traditions* provide fertile ground for a wide range of opinions and judgments about A.A.'s affiliation or non-affiliation with religion.

Per the Tenth Tradition, A.A. has no opinion on these opinions.

However, judges, reporters, and all others who are confused might refer to one of A.A.'s many written resources such as the pamphlet, *The "God" Word: Agnostic and Atheist Members in A.A.*, that clearly states that it is not a religious organization[39].

At the personal level: opinions about religion within A.A.

A.A. groups are autonomous according to Bill's essay on the Fourth Tradition. However, Bill went on to say that a group "ought not affiliate itself with anything or anybody else[40]" and used religion as a specific example:

> There would be real danger should we commence to call some groups … "Catholic" or "Protestant[41]."

The Tenth Tradition reminds individual members to share only their own spiritual experience without implicating A.A. by including any opinions, positive, negative, or denigratingly humorous, about religious or nonreligious beliefs.

Alcoholics Anonymous grapples with personal opinions about drugs

With some early members' stories about drug use in the First Edition of the Big Book and with no clear policy established on chemical substances, it was not surprising that A.A. would have to face the "Pill Problem." In autumn of 1945, Bill's concern increased when *The A.A. Grapevine* published two stories, "Evidence on the Sleeping Pill Menace" and "Those 'Goof Balls."

At that time, as Kurtz described, there was a growing sentiment inside and outside the Fellowship to include chemical substances in its program and expand the Fellowship to take in all who were addicted to those substances[42]. By that time, Bill was formulating the *Twelve Points* and had enough experience to know that other addictions would only dilute the program's primary purpose. Kurtz wrote:

> … Alcoholics Anonymous itself, faithful to its traditions, remained aloof. Generously, the fellowship shared its ideas and literature with any who found them helpful. More cautiously, it declined to accept responsibility for other ideas and literature that reached further than the precise problem of alcoholism[43].

A.A. could not be the solution for all of society's ills. The resolution was in A.A. freely sharing with others the formula followed by its own members. By the 1960s these chemical dependency issues and many other issues were addressed by forming separate fellowships that modified the Twelve Steps to their particular needs[44].

Public and personal opinions were the undoing of the Washingtonians

Bill had learned about the Washingtonians shortly before he formulated the *Twelve Points*. He offered his first thoughts about the group in the August 1945 issue of *The Grapevine*. Kurtz wrote:

> His pointed lament was "that today the influence of this good work has so completely disappeared that few of us had ever heard of it[45];"
>
> [Bill] concluded his article with the exhortation: "May we always be willing to learn from experience[46]!"

Kurtz noted the irony of this statement since it was clear that over the following twenty-five years, "A.A.'s ability to learn from the experience of others as well as from its own development was tested …[47]."

While the members of the Fellowship experienced some stumbles with the Tenth Tradition, the Trustees, Headquarters, and Bill also put it to the test.

Publicly protecting A.A.'s reputation became an outside issue

In the early 1950s, the Traditions, while not yet formally adopted by A.A., were presumed to be a model for A.A.'s conduct. After all, Bill had already spent almost four years selling them to the groups. However, Bill did not mind sharing when, for his part, the application of that model was uneven.

In *Alcoholics Anonymous Comes of Age*, Bill reflected on a period in A.A. when outside entities were using its name in controversial, moneymaking enterprises. The fear of how these endeavors could negatively affect A.A. prompted the Trustees to seek legal recourse. However, the "mass of technicalities, red tape, and charters[48]" quickly disrupted their plans.

Later, the Trustees found out about an upcoming film called *Mr. and Miss Anonymous* that they felt was in very poor taste. Mild protestations produced only a change in the title but not much else. Headquarters then threatened an injunction, which caused the company to revise its script. The film was distributed as *Something to Live For* with Joan Fontaine, Ray Milland, and Teresa Wright[49].

In retrospect, Bill acknowledged that the Trustees and Headquarters were overly distressed about the movie. So much so, they failed to recognize A.A.'s action went against their own principle of avoiding public controversy[50]. That issue underscored Bill's concern that the Trustees and Headquarters by themselves could cause significant harm which would alienate the membership. He believed if groups were accountable for A.A.s decisions, then the Fellowship would be responsible for its stumbles and successes. United in this effort, groups could participate in ushering A.A. through any difficulties of relating to the world outside and to each other. This proved true when the very name of Alcoholics Anonymous was threatened.

The Delegate's group conscience protects A.A. from public incorporation

In the cause to save A.A.'s name from misuse, Bernard Smith came up with the idea of obtaining a Congressional Charter for Alcoholics Anonymous, which would put it on par with the Red Cross. It seemed like the "legal bludgeon" needed to deter exploitation of the A.A. name and as Bill says, "It looked like a grand idea and we at the Headquarters were all for it[51]."

The resulting Conference Advisory Actions, in 1953, shines a bright light on the spirit of the Tenth Tradition with an itemized rationale of A.A.'s principles that is essential reading for all members.

1. The evils which caused the question to arise have largely abated.
2. A Congressional incorporation would create by law a power to govern which would be contrary to, and violative of, our Traditions.
3. *It would implement the spiritual force of A.A. with a legal power, which we believe would tend to weaken its spiritual strength* (emphasis added).
4. When we ask for legal rights, enforceable in Courts of law, we by the same act subject ourselves to possible legal regulation.
5. We might well become endlessly entangled in litigation which, together with the incidental expense and publicity, could seriously threaten our very existence.
6. Incorporation of A.A. could conceivably become the opening wedge that might engender politics and a struggle for power within our own ranks.
7. Continuously since its beginning, and today, A.A. has been a fellowship and not an organization. Incorporation necessarily makes it an organization.
8. *We believe that "spiritual faith" and a "way of life" cannot be incorporated* (emphasis added).
9. *A.A. can and will survive so long as it remains a spiritual faith and a way of life open to all men and women who suffer from alcoholism* (emphasis added)[52].

For Bill, this was a perfect example of why the Conference structure was essential to A.A.'s survival:

> The Conference thought we ought to forget about the questionable advantages of legality and controversy and rely upon group and

public opinion for our ultimate protection. After long debate, we at the Headquarters saw that the conscience of Alcoholics Anonymous, acting through the delegates, was wiser than we were[53].

It was through the wisdom of the Conference that attraction prevailed over force.

At the personal level, Bill's opinions on outside issues

Having succeeded in securing majority representation for alcoholics on the Board, Bill was free to pursue other interests. Kurtz wrote:

> ... [Bill's] main efforts outside A.A. in the final fifteen years of his life were attempts to remove the mental or psychological and physical obstacles that impeded some persons from openness to the spiritual[54].

Among Bill's many pursuits were three that generated some historical distortions in their telling and retelling: spiritualism, LSD, and vitamins B-3 and niacin.

Bill's personal opinions on spiritualism

Bill's slowly growing awareness of the importance of A.A.'s non-association with religion may have informed his reticence to share with others what he was experiencing when he started exploring spiritualism. Kurtz writes:

> [His] conviction that he had incontrovertible personal evidence of individual human conscious life lasting beyond physical death profoundly influenced Bill's adult faith, at least from the mid 1940s...
>
> [Bill] experimented with and eventually claimed some power over spiritualistic phenomena...[55].

Bill believed he had evidence of the existence of a Higher Power, yet he deliberately avoided sharing his conviction with the Fellowship, much to the relief of the Trustees. Bill only "guardedly" shared his insights with a few close friends, believing "that the faith required for salvation from alcoholism had to be just that –faith...[56]."

Bill's personal opinion on LSD

In 1954, two English psychiatrists, Drs. Hoffer and Osmond, contacted Bill claiming their work with LSD and schizophrenia might help alcoholics with delirium tremens. Bill was not enthusiastic at first, but after substantial research indicated positive results, he took the drug under the guidance and presence of a psychiatrist at the Los Angeles Veterans Administration Hospital in August 1956. Bill, driven by his belief in spiritualism and by a desire to find similar experiences that would help struggling alcoholics find a God of their own understanding, asked some of his closest associates to try the drug, including Father Ed Dowling and Lois[57].

Predictably, when word reached the Fellowship, there was substantial opposition. Bill firmly believed LSD could be helpful to alcoholics and he bitterly resented being told by the Fellowship how to live his life when he was making every effort to back away from the leadership of A.A[58].

The LSD experiment's ensuing controversy overlapped with Bill's ongoing argument with Tiebout about his own immaturity. He reluctantly withdrew from the LSD experiments in 1959, acknowledging that he could never escape his status as a founder of A.A. Soon after his withdrawal from the experiment, the government terminated the research, shortly after which LSD was declared illegal. As Kurtz pointed out:

> Whatever its effects upon him, there is no evidence that he ever thought his alcoholism "cured" in the sense that he could again drink alcohol safely. His main interest was in the possible usefulness of the LSD experience as an aid for those who otherwise could not "get the [A.A.] program[59]."

Bill shared his personal opinions on B-3 and niacin

When Bill tried vitamins B-3 and niacin he was convinced they were a breakthrough treatment for depression, particularly his own. Believing the vitamins could help alcoholics dually diagnosed with alcoholism and depression, he enthusiastically began working with researchers in that field. Bill started writing about B-3 and niacin using A.A. letterhead in the General Service Office. To make matters worse, he started freely sharing the vitamins with the staff in G.S.O. and with alcoholics in meetings[60].

A.A. members who were devoted to Bill quickly followed suit. *Pass It On* described the impact on meetings with camps forming with Bill and against Bill.

> Some of the opinions were about the merits or [non-merits] of niacin; most were about Bill's behavior… Almost everyone agreed on one thing: Bill was in direct violation of two of his own Traditions [Six and Ten][61].

Bill was certainly entitled to engage in this research, but the Trustees decided to take measures to stop him from pursuing this interest under the auspices of A.A. At the very start of its transition to a majority of alcoholic Trustees, the Board issued a report that included a recommendation that Bill separate his non-A.A. matters from A.A. by using his own letterhead and his own address rather than that of the G.S.O. Furthermore, the Board recommended that he not to involve G.S.O. employees in activities not related to A.A. The 1967 Conference supported the Board's recommendation and Bill complied. However, he did continue his research and writing on B-3 and niacin up until shortly before he died[62].

Oddly, Bill broke his own Traditions, but the Traditions and his hard-fought-for Conference and General Service structure saved A.A. from Bill. Whether or not he appreciated it at the time, his dream was a working reality.

Fortunately, all of these personal experiences with the Tenth Tradition occurred before Congress called on Bill to report on Alcoholics Anonymous. He went into that intoxicating arena having more practice with restraining his own personal opinions.

At a very public level: Congressional testimony by A.A.s

Committees of the United States' Congress called A.A. on two occasions to present at hearings. Such public and heady environments by nature could be tempting for grandstanding alcoholics to "hold forth." Fortunately, the committee reports from these two sessions provide a model on how A.A.s' trusted servants practiced restraint and honored the Tenth Tradition.

Referred to throughout the proceedings as Bill W., Bill spoke about the

On What Slender Threads

history of A.A. before the U.S. Senate Special Subcommittee on Alcoholism and Narcotics of the Committee on Labor and Public Welfare in July 1969[63]. In 1988, nonalcoholic Trustee, Dr. Joan Jackson, testified before the Committee on Governmental Affairs. Dr. Jackson was "asked to discuss the AA philosophy of the treatment of alcohol abuse and to describe the AA program[64]." After her testimony, the Committee asked a number of questions. A snapshot of Dr. Jackson's responses demonstrates the simple practice of the Tenth Tradition:

- We do not take a position on this question[65].
- AA would not consider it to be appropriate for it to comment on the studies cited by [doctor's name][66].
- As stated above, Alcoholics Anonymous does not have an opinion on other forms of treatment for alcoholism or about their effectiveness[67].

Fortunately, it was the Tenth Tradition that allowed A.A. to keep to its primary purpose by avoiding controversy no matter what the venue, whether it is on the web, in print media, social media, in the courtroom, or in Congress. Staying out of the fray caused by outside issues, even those that involved A.A., helped the Fellowship to survive.

What A.A. does not do

The A. A. Group pamphlet offers guidelines for the Tenth Tradition in "What AA does not do."

1. Recruit members or furnish initial motivation for alcoholics to recover.
2. Keep membership records or case histories.
3. Follow up or try to control its members.
4. Make medical or psychological diagnoses or prognoses.
5. Provide hospitalization, drugs, or medical or psychiatric treatment.
6. Provide housing, food, clothing, jobs, money or other such services.
7. Provide domestic or vocational counseling.
8. Engage in or sponsor research.
9. Affiliate with social agencies (though many members and service offices do cooperate with them).

10. Offer religious services.
11. Engage in any controversy about alcohol or other matters.
12. Accept money for its services or contributions from non-A.A. sources.
13. Provide letters of reference to parole boards, attorneys, court officials, schools, businesses, social agencies, or any other institution[68].

In summary

Bill referred to A.A.'s experiences with outside opinions as only short-term disruptions that in essence had nothing to do one alcoholic talking to another alcoholic. Thus, at this point in our study of the Traditions, it may seem outright laughable that Bill wrote in his essay on the Tenth Tradition,

> Never since it began has Alcoholics Anonymous been divided by a major controversial issue[69].

Every Tradition was born out of controversy within the Fellowship, mostly of its own making, and always accompanied by the roar of angry members! But as Bill said,

> Despite their din, our puny rows never did A.A. a particle of harm. They were just part and parcel of learning to work and live together[70].
>
> I hope that this journey through the Traditions has demonstrated that what Bill said is true:
>
> … that they were almost always concerned with ways to make A.A. more effective, how to do the most good for the most alcoholics[71].

Coming up: the Eleventh Tradition

Given that we see the importance of avoiding public controversy, it is no small wonder that the next Tradition discusses anonymity at the level of press, radio, and film.

Alcoholics Anonymous: where actions speak louder than names

Tradition 11

Our public relations policy is based on attraction rather than promotion; we need always maintain personal anonymity at the level of press, radio, and films[1].

The Long Form: *Our A.A. experience has taught us that:*

Our relations with the general public should be characterized by personal anonymity. We think A.A. ought to avoid sensational advertising. Our names and pictures as A.A. members ought not be broadcast, filmed, or publicly printed. Our public relations should be guided by the principle of attraction rather than promotion. There is never need to praise ourselves. We feel it better to let our friends recommend us[2].

Synopsis of Bill's essay in the 12 & 12

In this Tradition's essay, Bill emphasized how various forms of public media were instrumental in bringing struggling alcoholics to A.A. The early Fellowship learned that *attraction rather than promotion* was A.A.'s best form of publicity. A.A.'s media friends were better press agents than members who broke their anonymity. The press appreciated a society that publicized its principles rather than its individual members. Bill reminded members, "personal ambition has no place in A.A.[3]"

Anonymity and the Fellowship's early inconsistencies

At first, Bill naively underestimated the potential damage to the Fellowship caused by members' publicly breaking their anonymity. After all, high profile breaks might serve to bring in more alcoholics. It took time for Bill to learn that those same anonymity breaks might turn struggling alcoholics away. Moreover, once there was a leak in the dam, a flood of anonymity breaks was bound to follow.

Then, what would the name, Alcoholics Anonymous mean?

Trial by fire revealed that anonymity meant far more than the withholding of surnames. As the Fellowship matured, anonymity evolved to become a fundamental spiritual principle.

In the beginning, the name Alcoholics Anonymous guaranteed safety during an era of overarching and gross misunderstandings about alcoholism. There was no policy on anonymity beyond Bill's admonishment in the Foreword to the First Edition Big Book, in which he spoke first to members of the Fellowship and then to the press:

> When writing or speaking publicly about alcoholism, we urge each of our Fellowship to omit his personal name, designating himself instead as "a member of Alcoholics Anonymous."
>
> Very earnestly, we ask the press also, to observe this request, for otherwise we shall be greatly handicapped[4].

Predictably, given alcoholics' egos, members at best, followed those guidelines inconsistently. At worst, they were blatantly ignored. The unpredicted result was an unraveling of the essence of the program's identity: humility and self-sacrifice. Therefore, it is not surprising that Bill wrote two separate Traditions on anonymity, maintaining anonymity at the public level and practicing anonymity as a spiritual principle.

Bill spoke to *how* members practice the principle of anonymity in Tradition

Eleven. He spoke to *why* the principle is essential to members' recovery and to A.A.'s survival in Tradition Twelve. To understand both, it helps to remember what it was like.

The first publicity stumble

According to Kurtz, there were two areas of absolute rigidity in the early days of the Fellowship. The first was "Don't drink!" The second was in the Fellowship's very own name, "Anonymous," which was a two-faceted principle. One was protection against economic consequences associated with public exposure as an alcoholic and the other was protection against members who simply could not stay sober[5]. Such was the motivation for Bill's aforementioned caution in the Foreword to the First Edition.

Surprisingly, the first public anonymity breach would not come from Akron or New York, but from Cleveland. Dorothy S. was grateful for the miracle A.A. had performed on her husband, Clarence. In early 1939, she asked a local preacher to spread the word about this miraculous program. First Unitarian Rev. Dr. Dilworth Lupton initially resisted because he believed the Fellowship was part of the Oxford Group, which was partly true in Akron.

Later, in the summer of 1939, Dorothy gave a copy of the Big Book to the Rev. Lupton and pointed out that in Cleveland there was no association of the Fellowship with the Oxford Group. As proof, she said there were two Catholics attending the Stillman Avenue group. This astonishing news prompted Rev. Lupton to read the book after which he urged Dorothy to tell their local newspaper, *The Cleveland Plain Dealer*, that he was going to preach on A.A[6].

Years later, Cleveland A.A. would rightfully recall these articles as contributing to a rapid escalation in the number of A.A. groups. The growth of A.A. groups in Cleveland was so outstanding compared to Akron and New York that many people thought Cleveland was where A.A. began.

But there was more to the story.

In the weeks that passed after *The Plain Dealer* series, one group split into three smaller groups. While this split, indeed, increased the number of groups in Cleveland, its cause was not as much an issue of burgeoning numbers as it was a disagreement amongst the Cleveland members and Clarence over the unwelcomed publicity. Clearly, there was contention within the Fellowship about the framework for anonymity[7].

Notwithstanding Cleveland A.A.'s disapproval, the news in print began to spread and A.A. rapidly stretched out into the Lake Erie metropolis of Chicago. The issue of anonymity at the public level would only intensify.

The first high-profile anonymity break

In early 1940, the American economy struggled with high unemployment and constricted spending. This, along with the country's disposition to avoid the war in Europe, required a national distraction. Professional baseball served that purpose better than any other sport.

In 1939, Rollie H. was a Cleveland Indians star catcher whose behavior and performance, due to alcoholism, was becoming alarmingly visible. An early member of the Akron squad, Bob E., said that the team's owner, Alva Bradley, witnessed Dr. Bob's work with hopeless drunks through another member of the squad. That member had sobered up and "moved from the gutters of Cleveland to an executive position" rapidly in Bradley's firm. Hoping for similar results, Bradley offered two hundred thousand dollars to Dr. Bob if he could get Rollie sober[8].

Of course, Dr. Bob refused the money but promised to try to help. Dr. Bob picked Bob E. and five others from the squad to work with Rollie. Bob E. said, "Somehow [Rollie] got the program. He became one of the staunchest members we ever had, [setting] a terrific example for the children all over the country[9]."

When Dr. Bob broke off from the Oxford Group meetings at T. Henry Williams' home, most of the alcoholics followed. However, some alcoholics, including Rollie, continued attending the Oxford Group meetings for a few more months before finally joining Dr. Bob's group. This probably contributed to rumors that the Oxford Group got Rollie sober[10].

In spite of the Big Book's plea for members to maintain their anonymity and for the press to support that plea, Rollie decided to do otherwise. On April 16, 1940, he publicly announced in a news conference in Chicago that his erratic behavior had been due to "booze," and that he had been dry for a year "with the help of and through Alcoholics Anonymous[11]." While Rollie may have wanted to set the record straight about how he got sober, it is more likely that with his immense gratitude for the program, he meant only to show his appreciation for and raise awareness about A.A.

In the meantime, American baseball lovers became particularly enchanted with a gangly eighteen-year-old Cleveland pitcher named Robert Feller who could throw a baseball at speeds approaching one hundred miles an hour. Still, Feller was naïve and inexperienced but so valuable a player that Bradley asked Rollie to take Feller under his wing. In the spotlight of an attentive press, Feller modestly pointed to ex-alcoholic Rollie as indispensable to his success. This further strengthened Rollie's already public reputation as a shining example of sober members in A.A.[12]

Rollie's anonymity breaks continued to gain public approval when his untiring Twelfth Step work "contributed to the sobering of the father of a strategically located and respected Catholic priest." This in turn gave the Fellowship entry into at least one local Catholic Hospital[13].

Rollie was on a roll!

With such glowing press and attention, anxieties about anonymity breaks like Rollie's started to wane. As a result, there was very little concern when Bill allowed the picture-oriented *Saturday Evening Post* to include photos of alcoholics with Jack Alexander's story, a concession that was required by the magazine.

A perfect storm was roiling, for these very same events paved the way for "the next occasion on which Alcoholics Anonymous would face the necessity of re-thinking its understanding of its name[14]."

That occasion would be Marty M.'s anonymity break.

Bill's struggle with Marty M.'s anonymity break

Marty M.'s contributions to alcoholism education can never be overstated. Her creation of the National Committee for Education on Alcoholism and its succeeding entities broke barriers for alcoholism in policy and research for years and her groundbreaking work continues today. The timing of her recovery from alcoholism through to her work launching NCEA overlapped with Rollie's recovery and subsequent anonymity breaks. Combined, these events appeared to benefit the Fellowship by attracting more alcoholics to the program[15].

Marty was beautiful and intelligent and thus, her vivacity and her promotion of NCEA resulted in newspaper stories and a Time Magazine article with full-faced pictures and references to her recovery in Alcoholics Anonymous[16]. As a result, Marty was a high-impact 'domino' that led to a succession of other alcoholic 'dominoes' seeking the same privilege of breaking their anonymity "for the common good." Stubbornly, Bill continued to maintain his support for Marty. He said:

> I still feel that it was right for [Marty] to do exactly as she did. Though the risk of a precedent for other A.A.'s to drop their anonymity was serious, and may still be, the gains to A.A. and to the cause of education have apparently outweighted this consideration by far[17].

However, the weight started to shift too heavily in the other direction. Bill found out subsequently that if one alcoholic could break anonymity to promote a special cause, many others would follow. For example, an alcoholic member published a Prohibition magazine and used the A.A. name to "attack the evils of whiskey." The member claimed that: "… he too was an 'educator,' and that his brand of education was the 'right kind[18].'"

Other members' proposals started to flood Headquarters, until Bill declared *mea culpa* as evident in a 1948 letter to a Florida member:

> [In] this particular matter, I confess a great deal of fault myself. Several years ago, we did not realize the protective value of anonymity *to the A.A. movement as a whole* (emphasis added). When, for educational purposes, Marty broke hers, I consented to it. In the light of later events, that has proved to be a mistake[19].

In what hereinafter could be referred to as a "Marty Moment" for all A.A.s who follow her example, Marty stopped breaking her anonymity. She continued to fight ceaselessly for alcohol education. In his January 1955 Grapevine article, *Why Alcoholics Anonymous is Anonymous*, Bill paid tribute to her difficult path:

> Seeing what happened, my friend, wonderful member that she is, tried to resume her anonymity. Because she had been so thoroughly publicized this has been a hard job. It has taken her years. But she has made the sacrifice, and I here want to record my deep thanks on behalf of us all[20].

Marty's sacrifice was at great cost. She relapsed after twenty years and denied herself A.A.'s help when she needed it most. Such is a weight that no member of A.A. should have to bear alone.

Early A.A.'s heavy hand on anonymity breaks

Once the importance of anonymity started to register, Headquarters struggled with trying to reverse its erosion within the Fellowship. In *Alcoholics Anonymous Comes of Age*, Bill recounted a story in which Headquarters answered a difficult public relations problem with a heavy hand. During the early adolescence of A.A., members were frequently putting their own personal spin on the recovery program.

One early member started a radio program called the "Twelve Lectures and Alcoholics Anonymous" that blended the program with his own religious beliefs. When the program aired with modest success, he created his own group and found a prominent life insurance company to provide him an income and fund his radio program with his name. Headquarters protested and received the following response: "To hell with the trustees, the world is waiting for my message. I've got the right of free speech and I'm going on the air whether you like it or not[21]

Headquarters and the Trustees then threatened to recruit members to write the insurance company strongly worded protests and proffered consequences that would be to the company's detriment. This aggressive approach worked and the broadcast never went on the air.

During this time of A.A.'s early adolescence, the Trustees and Headquarters were in the unpleasant parental position of having to use severe tactics to try to reverse similar trends in which "promotion, professionalism, and anonymity-breaking [were] all in one package[22]." With no Conference, it was up to the Trustees to protect A.A. According to Bill, their experiences contributed to an important component of the Eleventh Tradition:

> A.A.'s Trustees were empowered to conduct our over-all public relations, and the principle of attraction rather than promotion became established as the key to our relation with the world about us[23].

Still, convincing members and groups of the importance of anonymity as a principle of attraction rather than promotion had a rough road ahead.

Bill's 1948 anonymity apology

While Bill was traveling and peddling the *Twelve Principles*, some newspapers published his full name as the face of Alcoholics Anonymous. Bill had mistakenly relaxed his formerly proactive stance of anonymity with the press and the result was an important lesson for the Fellowship. A.A. members must always vigilantly remind the press of the Fellowship's policy on anonymity. In the December 1948 issue of the Grapevine, Bill acknowledged his lapse in *A Request and an Apology* and cautioned:

> Everywhere the press has been uniformly cooperative on anonymity when it is explained as a vital protection to the Alcoholics Anonymous movement. May I therefore urgently request all AA groups to carefully cover my anonymity on any future appearances and I shall, of course, try to take far greater care myself.
>
> Let us never let go of this vital principle[24].

Anonymity breaks continued

In less than 10 years after the publication of the Big Book, A.A. had become a household word. While Bill was writing the Traditions, the press reviews were uniformly positive about the program and it was becoming fashionable to declare one's recovery as attributable to Alcoholics Anonymous.

On What Slender Threads

After breaking her anonymity in 1946 and 1947, a celebrity wrote her autobiography in 1954 and had a movie made in 1955, both of which included her A.A. story. Afterwards, on the heels of drinking, she sought support from the Fellowship by hiring a lawyer, also an A.A. member, to restore what she perceived to be her tattered reputation. Bill wrote:

> [The lawyer and the star] assumed that both the public and A.A. would be rightfully angry if the facts were known. Soon several newspapers headlined how Alcoholics Anonymous was rooting for one of its lady members, named full, of course to win her suit for libel[25].

During that same period, a well-known radio personality broke his anonymity on the air and in the press to an estimated twelve million listeners. Bill's comment about this incident in a letter to Jack Alexander reflected his altered and more mature view of the importance of anonymity to A.A. as a whole.

> Of course, this looks like wonderful publicity to folks outside A.A. But to 99 A.A.'s out of 100, it is a danger signal. Most of us deeply realize that enough repetition of such blasts could alter the whole character of our Society…[26].

Then drawing upon his own lesson from the Marty M. and NCEA debacle:

> And more seriously, we would enable all those who choose to break anonymity at the general public level to hire out in other fields of work and draw the A.A. implied endorsement along with them[27].

Poignantly, Bill ended with:

> [The radio announcer] hasn't the slightest idea that he is busting the best protective gadget our Fellowship will ever have. As to the immense spiritual implications of anonymity, poor old [name] just doesn't know[28]."

Bill looked at these breaks with compassion and understanding. No one better than he, could express alcoholics' struggles with ego as he did in *The Grapevine*:

> ... we alcoholics are the biggest rationalizers in the world, and ... fortified with the excuse that we are doing great things for A.A., we can, through broken anonymity, resume our old and disastrous pursuit of personal power and prestige, public honors, and money – the same implacable urges that when frustrated once caused us to drink, the same forces that are today ripping the globe apart at its seams[29].

Bill's quandary: save lives or compromise the principles of A.A.

Can one individual's anonymity break save more lives than the whole Fellowship of Alcoholics Anonymous? For Bill, the answer was *NO* but that answer did not come without heartache. *Time Magazine* offered Bill the "Man of the Year" honor with the inducement that the cover page picture would show only the back of his head[30]. Bill's rationale for turning down the article is a study on the unimaginable pain he bore in maintaining his own anonymity. He wrote:

> ... when I turned that article down, I denied recovery to an awful lot of alcoholics – some of these may already be dead. And practically all the rest of them, we may suppose are still sick and suffering. Therefore, in a sense, my action has pronounced the death sentence on some drunks and condemned others to a much longer period of illness.
>
> But I went well over on the conservative side, because the requirements of the piece would have tended to create a clear and colorful public image of me as a person. This would have created for the future, I am sure, a temptation in our power-driving people to get like pieces – presently with full names and pictures. For this reason, I estimated that it would be better for some to die and others to suffer,

rather than to set such a perilous precedent. Therefore, I declined the publicity, and I must confess it wasn't easy[31].

Was Bill being overly dramatic? In light of the multitude of very public anonymity breaks today, probably not.

How can the A.A. group help? One way is to study this tradition regularly.

The Long Form of this Tradition offers explicit guidance with the first point setting the overall tenor of anonymity for all members of A.A.

- Our relations with the general public should be characterized by personal anonymity[32].

"Characterized by personal anonymity" means that the general public should be accustomed to and comfortable with A.A. members not revealing their surnames. The next two points are more specific.

- We think A.A. ought to avoid sensational advertising.
- Our names and pictures as A.A. members ought not be broadcast, filmed, or publicly printed[33].

The remaining two points provide a bridge to the Twelfth Tradition, the spiritual principle of anonymity.

- Our public relations should be guided by the principle of attraction rather than promotion.
- There is never need to praise ourselves. We feel it better to let our friends recommend us[34].

As clear as these guidelines are, the General Service Conference has responded with additional suggestions to address changes in communications and media since the 1950s.

Lyn S.

Understanding Anonymity pamphlet

A.A.'s General Service Office offers a wonderful, must-have pamphlet for all members, *Understanding Anonymity*. As it applies to the Eleventh Tradition, one point is counter to the myth that when A.A. members die, it is permissable to use their last names:

> A.A. members generally think it unwise to break the anonymity of the member even after his or her death, but in each situation, the final decision must rest with the family. A.A. members, though, are in agreement that the anonymity of still living A.A. members should be respected in obituaries or in any type of printed remembrance or death notice[35].

A second point relates to anonymity in the digital world.

Personal anonymity online

Obviously, the Eleventh Tradition reflects the media of the late-1940s in its phrase, "*personal anonymity at the level of press, radio, and films.*" Although already invented and available, televisions were not in general use. Less than a decade later, the TV became a common household appliance, but the spirit of anonymity at the level of public media still held. Now media has become interactive, rapid, and public in ways that even users do not fully understand.

As it has responded to so many other societal issues and changes, the General Service Conference discussed and approved language that would clarify anonymity in digital media in the *Understanding Anonymity* pamphlet.

> When using digital media, A.A. members are responsible for their own anonymity and that of others. When we post, text, or blog, we should assume that we are publishing at the public level. When we break our anonymity in these forums, we may inadvertently break the anonymity of others[36].

Anonymity Online and Digital Media is a valuable service material resource provided by the General Service Office. This publication is easily available online and touches on multiple aspects of digital media and anonymity. They include A.A. websites, social networking websites, email, internet, and videos and audios[37].

The pandemic of 2020 ushered in a new arena for issues in anonymity. With the rapid proliferation of online meetings, the Continental European Region of Alcoholics Anonymous responded with guidelines that include:

> "Anonymity is so fragile, you can break it with one finger[38]." The site can be accessed at https://alcoholics-anonymous.eu/anonymity-online-2019/
>
> The second site, *Online Anonymity and Meeting Safety*[39] includes links to additional resources. That site, with the additional resources are: https://alcoholics-anonymous.eu/online-meeting-safety-and-anonymity/. See also Online Zoom Meeting Hosting Guidelines and Good practice for listing online meetings.

Bill's caution

All should consider carefully Bill's caution from the *AA Tradition: How it Developed*.

> **Any who would drop their anonymity** must reflect that they may set a precedent which could eventually destroy a valuable principle. We must never let any immediate advantage shake us in our determination to keep intact such a really vital tradition[40].

That is, we should always remember when we think it is a good idea to break our anonymity at the public level, *perhaps there is a better way*.

Coming up: the Twelfth Tradition

Public anonymity breaks cause harm to A.A.'s public relations. But there is a more compelling reason for anonymity. It is a fundamental spiritual principle. In terms of anonymity, the Eleventh Tradition tells A.A. members *what not to do*, while the Twelfth Tradition tells A.A. members *what to do*.

Equality, vulnerability, and freedom in the spiritual principle of anonymity

Tradition 12

Anonymity is the spiritual foundation of all our traditions, ever reminding us to place principles before personalities[1].

The Long Form: *Our A.A. experience has taught us that:*

And finally, we of Alcoholics Anonymous believe that the principle of anonymity has an immense spiritual significance. It reminds us that we are to place principles before personalities; that we are actually to practice a genuine humility. This to the end that our great blessings may never spoil us; that we shall forever live in thankful contemplation of Him who presides over us all[2].

Synopsis of Bill's essay in the 12 & 12

Bill began this essay with "The spiritual substance of anonymity is sacrifice." He gave a picture of how anonymity was at first a fear-driven necessity. In that vein, Bill reminded members to protect the anonymity of others, especially newcomers. He described the surprising result of achieving respect from the press through members' adherence to the principles of anonymity. Members who practiced the humility and self-sacrifice, that is inherent in anonymity, were the best messengers of hope for other alcoholics[3].

Appropriate and inappropriate anonymity breaks

The Long Form of the Eleventh Tradition is stated in the negative in that it tells A.A. members what *not to do* when practicing the principle of anonymity. "Our names and pictures as A.A. members ought not be broadcast, filmed, or publicly printed[4]." As one who struggled with his own ego, Bill reminded members that they *never* need to praise themselves.

The Long Form of the Twelfth Tradition, thankfully, is stated in the positive. It tells A.A. members what *to do* when practicing the principle of anonymity. "We are to place principles before personalities; that we are actually to practice a genuine humility[5]."

Bill clearly defined "inappropriate" anonymity breaks in the Eleventh Tradition. So what are "appropriate" anonymity breaks?

The A.A. Group pamphlet indicates that *at the group level*, it is appropriate for members to use their last names as long as they respect others' anonymity according to their own wishes[6]. Implicit in this suggestion, is the need for members to inventory their practices on anonymity with their group ideally through an *informed* group conscience. To be informed, studying the Traditions with the group is a good start. Including General Service Office literature is essential to this study. Adding the historical background behind the Traditions is even better. While the practice of anonymity is up to each individual, this particular group inventory provides an opportunity for A.A. members to be better *informed* before making any decisions about their personal anonymity.

Anonymity is frequently associated with the oft-heard mantra in meetings, "Who you see here, what you hear here, let it stay here." While this is certainly vital, the principle of anonymity has a spiritual depth that only surfaced after A.A.'s early days. Today's A.A. members are fortunate to be able to draw on the experience of the early Fellowship. Spiritual principles were not foremost in early A.A. members' minds when guarding their anonymity.

The origin of the name Alcoholics Anonymous

According to Kurtz, early A.A.'s were not enthusiastic about the evangelistic, thus non-anonymous, practices encouraged by their Oxford Group

On What Slender Threads

guides. Active alcoholics were indifferent to, if not resentful of, religious pressure and sober alcoholics were not eager to declare their alcoholism publicly[7]. By necessity, the principles of *attraction and anonymity* were a solution for both the A.A. member and the prospect.

Pinning down the origin of the name "Alcoholics Anonymous" was difficult requiring researchers to sift through faulty recollections and A.A. lore. Bill couldn't remember who had suggested "Alcoholics Anonymous," which at the very least ruled him out as the one who coined the name. Jim B. had attributed the name to a man named Joe W. However, Joe W. didn't join the Fellowship until later in December 1938, well after the name was already in use[8].

Schaberg's research revealed that around June of 1938, while Bill was working on his first draft of "There is a Solution," Hank P. drafted out a title page for the book. On Hank's hand-written page are the first use of the words "Alcoholics Anonymous" with notes that the name would also apply to the Fellowship and the foundation that would be publishing that book[9].

One can surely surmise that Bill, Hank, and others had previously batted the name around informally, but Hank at least was the first to put "Alcoholics Anonymous" on paper.

However, the Fellowship's debate as to what to name the book continued into early 1939 when they ran out of time and had to make a decision. Their considerations gravitated toward *The Way Out* and other titles. Fitz M. visited the Library of Congress whereupon his research eliminated most of the proposed ideas including *The Way Out* as there were 25 books with that same title. On the other hand, there were no books entitled *Alcoholics Anonymous*. Thus, the debate was over[10].

As beautifully stated in *Pass It On*, in light of A.A.'s history and in the title of the Big Book, the term

> "Alcoholics Anonymous" had always referred to the members, never to the message ...[11].

While the early Fellowship embraced the practicality of anonymity, its largest success with convincing a skeptical public was through attraction.

Lyn S.

Jack Alexander sets out to expose A.A.

The Big Book was barely two years old, when Judge Curtis Bok, owner of the *Saturday Evening Post*, recruited the talented and cynical journalist, Jack Alexander. Bok had good friends who were raving about the promising A.A. Fellowship and he wanted someone to scrutinize this rapidly growing phenomenon. Since Alexander had recently exposed the New Jersey rackets, the judge hoped he would be able to sniff out improprieties amongst a group of drunks. When Alexander learned of the Fellowship's connections with religion and Rockefeller money, he was, at once, curious and suspicious.

Alexander attended A.A. meetings in Philadelphia and found the members to be intelligent but frustratingly opaque saying only, "The Big Book says …" The members also extracted his promise to keep their anonymity unless he had no other possible means to continue his research. Their reverence toward Bill W. prompted Alexander to go to New York[12].

He probably thought he was closing in on the leader of the cult!

Given his reputation for ferreting out frauds, Alexander was surprised that Bill warmly welcomed him. However, Alexander's experience with con artists who could confidently maintain their ruse, motivated him that much more to unveil the "real" man behind Alcoholics Anonymous.

Upon meeting Bill, Kurtz writes that he "struck Alexander as either incredibly naïve or a bit stupid[13]." Bill readily told Alexander about his problems with alcohol and ongoing struggles with grandiosity. He admitted the group welcomed publicity, but urged Alexander to go to Akron to meet Dr. Bob and then continue to Cleveland to see other A.A.'s at work. To Alexander's amazement, Bill minimized his role and drew attention toward other members of the Fellowship.

In short, Bill's honesty and humility won over the hardened skeptic. The writer who sought to expose Alcoholics Anonymous wrote a glowing overview in the March 1, 1941 issue of the *Saturday Evening Post*, resulting in an increase in the Fellowship from 2000 to 8000 members in eight months. Alcoholics Anonymous became a household name. Alexander remained close friends with Bill for the rest of his life, and allowed Bill the ability to edit his future articles about A.A.; a privilege he never allowed anyone else[14]. The cynical journalist eventually became one of A.A.'s Trustees.

Jack Alexander and Bill's long friendship bears out the rewards of attraction. From that relationship, the principle of anonymity, still in the embryonic stage, started to evolve. However, without well-articulated guidelines on anonymity, it was painfully slow to mature.

Undoing damage already done

Almost a year before the *Saturday Evening Post* article, Rollie H. had already broken his anonymity. Perhaps it was considered a minor problem given there weren't many alcoholic star athletes anxious to do the same. In contrast, Marty M.'s anonymity break was associated with advancing her National Committee for Education on Alcoholism. As a result, many alcoholics followed her lead labeling their interests just as educational as Marty's. With a rapidly growing number of egregious breaks, the intrinsic value of anonymity started to surface.

Headquarters and the Trustees were in the unenviable position of having to reverse this rapidly growing tide of departures from A.A.'s principles. As fretful as those efforts must have been, out of the ashes of multiple missteps grew an understanding of *attraction and anonymity*. To illustrate that the message was getting out there, Bill included a favorite story in *Alcoholics Anonymous Comes of Age* that spoke volumes in its simplicity and elegance.

A.A. is no one's song and dance routine

Bill knew a popular performer from Texas who got sober under the program. Her account, according to Bill, was a clearly stated view on anonymity as shown by her first point:

Alcoholics Anonymous has a principle called anonymity – no public big shots allowed[15].

She directed her second point to A.A. as a whole:

We know that A.A. can't be run like show business, no matter what the short-term benefits may be[16].

Her boundless gratitude and obligation to A.A. was her third point:

A.A. saved my life and my career. Therefore, the future welfare of Alcoholics

Anonymous is more important to me than any publicity that I could get as an A.A. member[17].

Finally, her fourth and most important point speaks to avoiding the temptation breaking anonymity for the sake of short-term results:

You know, Bill, I often see drunks in my audience and wonder how I can help them. If only I could tell them from the stage that I am in A.A. But that would only be temporary, wouldn't it? In the long run, we'd all be ruined if everybody did it[18].

As promising as that story was, there was an earlier hallmark moment for the practice of anonymity. It came in the form of a request Bill made on behalf of himself and Dr. Bob and A.A. members often ignored it.

Bill and Dr. Bob's plea as members of A.A.: Can't we be like everybody else?

In the October 1947 issue of the *Grapevine*, Bill and Dr. Bob expressed a desire to be recognized only as members of A.A.

> Dr. Bob and I are now going to confess a deep yearning. As private citizens of AA, we shall often wish to come and go among you like other people, without any special attention. And while we would like always to keep the wonderful satisfaction of having been among the originators, we hope you will begin to *think of us as early AAs only, not as "founders* (emphasis added)."

So, can't we join AA, too[19]?

Given their unprecedented roles in A.A.'s origins, there was no doubt about the extraordinarily visible profiles of Bill and Dr. Bob. Most A.A.s knew Bill and Dr. Bob's last names, what they looked like, and where they lived. Regardless, both men had one other request made in the spirit of anonymity. And the request was made in Bill's usual self-effacing way.

After we're gone, can't we be like everybody else?

Bill said of Dr. Bob:

Dr. Bob was essentially a far more humble person than I. In some ways he was a sort of spiritual "natural," and this anonymity business came rather easily to him. He could not understand why some people should want so much publicity. In the years before he died, his personal example respecting anonymity did much to help me keep my own lid on.

... some of his friends suggested that there should be a suitable monument or mausoleum erected in honor of him and his wife Anne – something befitting a founder and his lady.

Telling me about this, Dr. Bob grinned broadly and said, "God bless 'em. They mean well. But for heaven's sake, Bill, let's you and I get buried just like other folks[20].

There is no indication of their contributions to A.A. carved on the tombstones of Bill, Lois, Dr. Bob, and Anne. Nonetheless, their graves are easy to find. Grateful A.A.s from around the world leave their sobriety tokens and other items at the sites. It is the only evidence that shows that these two men and their wives were a pivotal part of the movement that changed the world for suffering alcoholics.

Today, some members of the Fellowship continue to respect Bill and Dr. Bob's wishes. The staff and volunteers at the General Service Office try never to use Bill and Dr. Bob's last names. Perhaps, in their honor and according to their wishes, A.A. members should do the same.

The Long Form of Tradition Twelve: In Seven Parts

The Long Form of Traditions Two and Twelve are significantly different from the other Traditions in that they are not as instructive in terms of practice as they are spiritually ethereal. Both Tradition's Long Forms call for a reflective intention to practice their principles.

The seven phrases in the Long Form of the Twelfth Tradition below contain my own reflections and, of course, include some of Bill's writings. I hope readers will pursue this or a similar exercise of their own creation. One can easily meditate on the Long Form alone, but it is far more rewarding with another person or a group.

Part 1: *We of Alcoholics Anonymous believe ...*

In the *Twelve Steps and Twelve Traditions*, the Third Step ends with:

God, grant *me* the serenity to accept the things *I* cannot change, courage to change the things *I* can, and wisdom to know the difference[21].

While the Twelfth Step ends with:

God, grant *us* the serenity to accept the things *we* cannot change, courage to change the things *we* can, and wisdom to know the difference[22].

Whether Bill did this intentionally or not, it is sublime that Bill ended his essays on the Steps with the "*We*" form of the Serenity Prayer and began the Traditions with "*Unity*." Such is the spirit of the Long Form of the Twelfth Tradition, when it says "We of Alcoholics Anonymous believe…."

However, that does not mean A.A. members agree on how to practice anonymity. In the January 1946 issue of the *Grapevine*, Bill detailed the evolution of anonymity in *A Tradition Born of Our Anonymity*. Still relevant today, he described the range of individual stances on anonymity within the Fellowship, from one who is "extremely sensitive" about it to one who "declares that anonymity is a lot of childish nonsense." Bill goes on to say, "In between these extremes, the shades of opinion are legion[23]." Then as now, Bill's 1946 conclusion on the individual member's responsibility applies:

> Each individual will then have to decide where he ought to draw the line – how far he ought to carry the principle in his own affairs, how far he may go in dropping his own anonymity *without injury to Alcoholics Anonymous as a whole* (emphasis added)[24].

"Injury to Alcoholics Anonymous as a whole" reflects the practice of the First Tradition. A.A. members learn that the clamor of desires and ambitions within must be silenced whenever these could damage the group[25].

Part 2: *The principle of anonymity has an immense spiritual significance –*

In his writings, Bill repeatedly referred to sacrifice as the spiritual substance of anonymity[26]. Each Tradition echoes the need for setting aside individual desires for the common good. Thus, reflecting on each Tradition in the context of self-sacrifice is of itself a good exercise for members of A.A. Based on my own brief reflection, self-sacrifice and humility are spiritual principles in:

- Tradition 1 when members set aside self for unity and common welfare.
- Tradition 2 when members defer to, and accept the decision of the group conscience; acknowledging that there are no leaders; only trusted servants.
- Tradition 3 when members welcome *all* who have a desire to stop drinking.
- Tradition 4 when autonomy of the group, not the individual, serves only to improve how it serves struggling alcoholics.
- Tradition 5 when members focus only on carrying the message.
- Tradition 6 when members and groups decline outside affiliation, even of personal interest, thus avoiding problems with money, property, and prestige.
- Tradition 7 when self-support is by the group, and not by the individual,
- Tradition 8 when members avoid paid Twelfth Step work but strive to fairly compensate workers who make Twelfth Step work possible.
- Tradition 9 when members volunteer their services to make A.A. Twelfth Step work possible.
- Tradition 10 when members do not discuss outside issues within the Fellowship to avoid implicating A.A. in public controversies.
- Tradition 11 when members maintain anonymity at the level of public media.
- Tradition 12 when members set aside personalities to practice the spiritual principle of anonymity.

Bill summarized the spiritual foundation of all A.A.'s Traditions as "really an expression of the deflation that each of us has to take, of the sacrifice that we shall all have to make in order to live and work together[27]."

Part 3: *We are to place principles before personalities* –

Early A.A.'s quickly learned that there was a causal relationship between receiving public adulation and reinflation of the ego. A.A.'s continue to learn this hard lesson even today.

Lyn S.

Anonymity breaks are easily found on the web, on audio, and on other media. They are posted by professional athletes, television and film celebrities, artists, business leaders, and more. Many of these sources are positive testimonials to A.A. while others are less than complimentary. Some are public confessions of relapse and subsequent recovery with A.A.'s help, while others express disappointment and disenchantment with the Fellowship and the program. As Bill said in 1946, it was up to each individual to decide "where to draw the line." The same holds true for today.

All in all, pronouncements such as these are easily at everyone's virtual fingertips today and they are probably no worse or no better than any that have occurred since A.A.'s early years.

A.A. members frequently apply "principles before personalities" to other program-work-family scenarios, which certainly is all to the good. Nevertheless, it is important for A.A. members to remember that Bill originally penned "principles before personalities" to the Twelfth Tradition. Thus, while useful in other aspects of sober living, principles before personalities is rooted in the spiritual practice of anonymity.

However, personality definitely trumps principle when an A.A. breaks another member's anonymity. A.A.'s who have celebrity status probably have suffered from this presumption more than any other group in the Fellowship. Whether the breach involves a celebrity or a non-celebrity, the principle of anonymity requires the practice of restraint.

> On a personal note: *As a result of this study, I conducted my own self-examination with respect to this principle. In my workshops, I cited sources where individuals broke their anonymity in public venues such as the web and other readily available media. Being one of the great rationalizers of this program, I reasoned that this information was already public and could be used as an "educational" example. Then I had a "Marty moment" – a moment like Marty M.'s recommitment to anonymity – and realized that perhaps there is a better way. Therefore, my amends was and is not to perpetuate any anonymity break no matter who started it. I decided to let it end with me.*

Bill usually tried to emphasize the importance of the Traditions by illustrating his own foibles. For example, in *Pass It On*, after the furor over Rollie's anonymity break, Bill said,

> For two or three years I guess I was A.A.'s number one anonymity breaker... What a bang it gave me when I read those two-column spreads about 'Bill the Broker,' full name and picture, the guy who was saving drunks by the thousands[28]!

Even though Bill's actual anonymity breaks occurred a few years later, he never hesitated to portray himself as the errant child when he thought it would serve to underscore a principle. According to *Pass It On*, Bill tried to "illustrate how baser human emotions such as competitiveness and envy can be disguised as motives of altruism and desire for the highest good[29]."

Pass It On beautifully summarized Bill's concerns for A.A. members who break their anonymity:

> Early on, Bill had realized that the limelight – something that most A.A. members, himself included, craved – was an experience that most had little tolerance for. To lose one's bid for the limelight could be as disastrous as to win it... It was much better, then, to rely on principles and ideas, which were constant, stable, and dependable, than on the unstable and quixotic ups and downs of personal relationships[30].

Fortunately, there is a solution when members want to change their own behavior with respect to anonymity. Oddly enough, the Sixth Step is somewhat parallel to the Eleventh Tradition in that members examine what not to do particularly when driven by lesser motives. The Twelfth Tradition is parallel to the Seventh Step in that it is on a spiritual foundation of humility, that members choose to practice principles before personalities.

Part 4: *We are actually to practice a genuine humility* –

In January 1946, Bill wrote in *A Tradition Born of Our Anonymity* "... that our movement not only preaches, but actually practices a truly humble modesty[31]."

Bill exhibited this practice when he turned down six honorary degrees, the most difficult being Yale's offer to bestow an honorary Doctorate of Laws. Bill's 1954 letter of refusal to the Yale nominating committee was, according to *Pass It On*, "a masterpiece of humility, tact, and intelligence." After expressing his gratitude, Bill explained why he had to deny "an opportunity of this dimension" indicating the Traditions were the Fellowship's only means of self-government and, thus, essential to A.A.'s survival[32].

Bill maintained that unlike alcoholics, people who are more balanced would have no difficulty humbly accepting distinguished service awards. In contrast, if A.A.s accepted such awards, they would compromise the principles of sacrifice and service freely given and in turn jeopardize their own recovery.

Bill provided his own example of how the pursuit of alcohol-fueled glory led to self-destruction. His important concluding point was:

> Though I survived that grim misadventure, I well understand that the dread neurotic germ of the power contagion has survived in me also. It is only dormant, and it can again multiply and rend me – and A.A., too. Tens of thousands of my fellow A.A.'s are temperamentally just like me. Fortunately, they know it, and I know it[33].

The Yale committee members were so moved by Bill's heartfelt letter, that their response included the following:

> After hearing your magnificent letter, [the committee members] all wish more than ever they could award you the degree – though it probably in our opinion isn't half good enough for you …[34].

In a moving testimony to Bill's pursuit of humility, Lois wrote:

> Bill felt very strongly that of all things, he should not set himself up as superior in any way to other alcoholics. So to emphasize this, he took every opportunity reasonable to exaggerate his own defects. He was a tremendous egotist. But he recognized this, and I believe that the triumph of his life was his victory over himself and his becoming truly humble[35].

On What Slender Threads

Part 5: *That our great blessings may never spoil us* –

In the *AA Tradition* pamphlet, Bill made four points on anonymity that can also remind members to enjoy their blessings but to never forget what it was like.

- Bill's first point is the blessing of empathy toward newcomers and their families through anonymity. Members show them through their actions "that the alcoholic skeleton in the family closet will not wander in the streets[36]."
- Bill's second point is that A.A. members are gifted with learning to be trusted servants, not leaders[37].
- Bill's third point is that A.A. members are blessed with anonymity as a principle of sincerity and service that wins the respect of the press, ergo the public[38].
- Bill's last point speaks to the gifts A.A. members share with everyone when practicing these principles as a way of life. Non-A.A.'s are "refreshed by our quietness, modesty and anonymity… Influenced by our spiritual transformation, they sense that something new could come into their own lives[39]."

That seems to be what happened when Jack Alexander met Bill.

Part 6: *That we shall forever live in thankful contemplation*

Bill's own awakening about the gifts of the Traditions was at the end of the 1950 International Convention in Cleveland:

> On Sunday morning – the last day of the Convention – I found those Twelve Traditions still on my mind. Each of them I saw is an exercise in humility that can guard us in everyday A.A. affairs and protect us from ourselves[40].

Bill continued to write about the multitude of protections the Traditions provide and emphasized the importance of A.A.'s keeping their egos in check. He went on to say, "It really means personal and group sacrifice for the benefit of all A.A.[41]"

Then, in a surprising comment from the author of the Traditions, Bill fervently declared:

> Right then I resolved to learn our Twelve Traditions by heart, just as I had learned the Twelve Steps. If every A.A. did the SAME and really soaked up these principles we drunks could hang together forever[42].

Part 7: ... *of Him who presides over us all.*

Of course, when Bill wrote the *Twelve Steps and Twelve Traditions*, he still believed that members who worked the program would eventually come to believe in a higher power similar to his own understanding. Some years later, Bill finally acknowledged that non-traditional members were getting and staying sober through their own very personal spiritual journeys.

For purposes of this last phrase in the Long Form, as Bill suggested in the Big Book, members can also meditate on what his spiritual terms mean to them. In my own interpretation and in the context of this study of the Twelve Traditions, *of Him who presides over us all* is an expression of the Second Tradition. "For our group purpose there is but one ultimate authority – a loving God as he may express Himself in our group conscience[43]."

After all, it is a "We" program.

General Service Office pamphlets and statements on anonymity

The A.A. Group pamphlet reminds members that personal anonymity is an assurance to vulnerable newcomers that all members of A.A. will guard their privacy[44]. This important point is reinforced in the *Understanding Anonymity* pamphlet:

> Over the years, anonymity has proved one of the greatest gifts that A.A. offers the suffering alcoholic. Without it, many would never attend their first meeting[45].

Following the *A.A. Group* pamphlet's suggestion, it is appropriate to share last names with A.A. group members. In the January 1955 *Grapevine*, Bill expanded the non-anonymity arena by saying:

> Nor is there any special danger when we speak at group or semi-public AA meetings, provided press reports reveal first names only[46].

If members choose to be non-anonymous in any semi-public venue where there are newcomers, visitors, or even seasoned A.A.s who may not be fully informed about the principle of anonymity, consider adding two reminders:

1. In keeping with the Eleventh Tradition, A.A. asks members to maintain their anonymity at the general public level, and
2. The name Alcoholics Anonymous means that individual members' anonymity is safe and protected according to their own wishes.

But let's not close this important Tradition with A.A.'s own experience, strength, and hope. Bill had pointed out that the impact of A.A.'s principle of anonymity had the added benefit of attracting those outside of the program. The next and last portion of this study is a stellar example.

Anonymity – equality, vulnerability, and freedom

There is no better insight into the freedom an alcoholic experiences from practicing the principle of anonymity than that provided by Ernest Kurtz in *Not-God*. Kurtz's laudatory praise of the principle of anonymity parallels the first three Steps of the program.

Kurtz started:

> Within Alcoholics Anonymous, the promise of anonymity made possible the acceptance of oneself as limited.
>
> Mutual honesty about shared vulnerability followed from acceptance of self and others as other-than-perfect...[47].

Lyn S.

Step One: *We admitted that we were powerless over alcohol – that our lives had become unmanageable.*

Kurtz went on to say:

> From this sense of sharing, this sense of participation in ultimate reality in and through others, sprang a profound realization of alcoholic equality.
> And from this awareness of equality flowed a liberating sense of true freedom[48].

Step Two: *Came to believe that a power greater than ourselves could restore us to sanity.*

Kurtz continued:

> Among others who openly acknowledged their not-God-ness, there was neither need nor inclination for any alcoholic to play God[49].

Step Three: *Made a decision to turn our will and our lives over to the care of God as we understood him.*

Kurtz concluded:

> Anonymity testified to this shared equality and its consequent freedom.
> Those outside the fellowship, the culture in general, saw in anonymity only a witness to the weakness of shame and fear.
> The members of Alcoholics Anonymous, however, saw beyond that. In testifying to their acceptance of equality in vulnerability, anonymity reminded them of their freedom to be themselves[50].

Tradition Twelve: *Anonymity is the spiritual foundation of all our traditions, ever reminding us to place principles before personalities.*

Has A.A. achieved unity?
In the *A.A. Service Manual*, there is the A.A. Declaration of Unity:

> This we owe to A.A.'s future; to place our common welfare first; to keep our Fellowship united. For on A.A. unity depend our lives, and the lives of those to come[51].

A.A.'s best hope for unity and common welfare is in groups' active participation in the General Service Conference. From the *A.A. Service Manual*:

Why Do We Need a Conference?
The late Bernard B. Smith, nonalcoholic, then chairperson of the board of trustees, and one of the architects of the Conference structure, answered that question superbly in his opening talk at the 1954 meeting: "We may not need a General Service Conference to ensure our own recovery. We do need it to ensure the recovery of the alcoholic who still stumbles in the darkness one short block from this room. We need it to ensure the recovery of a child being born tonight, destined for alcoholism. We need it to provide, in keeping with our Twelfth Step, a permanent haven for all alcoholics who, in the ages ahead, can find in A.A. that rebirth that brought us back to life.

"We need it because we, more than all others, are conscious of the devastating effect of the human urge for power and prestige which we must ensure can never invade A.A. We need it to ensure A.A. against government, while insulating it against anarchy; we need it to protect A.A. against disintegration while preventing overintegration. We need it so that Alcoholics Anonymous, and Alcoholics Anonymous alone, is the ultimate repository of its Twelve Steps, its Twelve Traditions, and all its services.

"We need it to ensure that changes within A.A. come only as a response to the needs and the wants of all A.A., and not of any few. We need it to ensure that the doors of the halls of A.A. never have locks on them, so that all people for all time who have an alcoholic problem may enter these halls unasked and feel welcome. We need it to ensure that Alcoholics Anonymous never asks of anyone who needs us what his or her race is, what his or her creed is, what his or her social position is[52]."

We are responsible.

Epilogue: Keep coming back!

THIS STUDY EXPLORED MANY EXAMPLES of recovered alcoholics who, like the Big Book's metaphorical tornado, roared through A.A.'s principles and then, looked back at the wreckage and said "Ain't it grand the wind stopped blowing!"

On a personal note: *After working on this study, I changed.*

> *My former superficial appreciation of and very provincial approach to the Traditions were old ideas that I decided to discard. I became a General Service Representative and served on the Budget and Finance Committee for my group's area committee. As this goes to press, I am now a District Committee Member. Currently, I continue to learn so much more in Service Manual and Concepts studies.*
>
> *As a result of this study, I am truly enjoying the ordered chaos of general service.*

Lack of familiarity with the Traditions contributes to so many group problems even today. Each member's action or inaction affects their group and A.A. as a whole. The impact of a member's misapplication of the Traditions may be minor; nothing more than a very subtle ripple that influences a newcomer or another program member. However, this study has shown that, as it goes with ripples, the ramifications of not practicing the Traditions affects A.A. as a whole.

My hope is that this study will spur A.A. members to have their own "Marty Moments" and recommit to understanding and embracing the Traditions. A positive ripple effect can help to preserve A.A. for years to come and most of all, make possible carrying the message for all who still suffer from alcoholism.

From the *A.A. Group* pamphlet P-16 pp 31, we know there is *always* a solution:

> Almost every group problem can be solved through the process of an informed group conscience, A.A. principles, and our Twelve Traditions[1].

And don't forget Rule 62!

> For all involved, a good sense of humor, cooling-off periods, patience, courtesy, willingness to listen and to wait – plus a sense of fairness and trust in a "Power greater than ourselves" – have been found far more effective than legalistic arguments or personal accusations[2].

This idea of this book began as an attempt to better understand the Traditions through the lens of A.A.'s history. It evolved to a better understanding of the general service structure and the indispensable role each A.A. group can play in protecting A.A.'s future.

I hope we can keep trudging this road to Happy Destiny!

For questions and comments about this study, contact Lyn at whatslenderthreads@gmail.com.

Sources

Introduction Sources

1. The A. A. Grapevine, Inc. 1988. *The Language of the Heart: Bill W.'s Grapevine Writings.* New York: The A. A. Grapevine, Inc.
2. A.A. General Service Office. 1957. *Alcoholics Anonymous Comes of Age: A Brief History of A. A.* New York: Alcoholics Anonymous World Services, Inc.
3. A.A. General Service Office. 1984. *'Pass It On': The Story of Bill Wilson and How the A.A. Message Reached the World.* New York City: Alcoholics Anonymous World Services, Inc.
4. Kurtz, Ernest. 1979. *Not-God: A History of Alcoholics Anonymous.* Expanded Edition 1991. Center City, MN: Hazelden.
5. Schaberg, William H. 2019. *Writing the Big Book: The Creation of A.A.* Las Vegas, NV: Central Recovery Press.
6. Brown, Sally, and David R. Brown. 2001. *A Biography of Mrs. Marty Mann: The First Lady of Alcoholics Anonymous.* Center City, MN: Hazelden.
7. Borden, Audrey. 2007. *The History of Gay People in Alcoholics Anonymous: From the Beginning.* Binghamton, New York: The Haworth Press, Inc.
8. A.A. General Service Office. 1952. *Twelve Steps and Twelve Traditions.* 1991. New York City: Alcoholics Anonymous World Services, Inc., 112.
9. Kurtz, Ernest. *Not-God: A History of Alcoholics Anonymous.*
10. Schaberg, William H *Writing the Big Book: The Creation of A.A..*
11. A.A. General Service Office. *Alcoholics Anonymous Comes of Age: A Brief History of A. A.,* 96.

Tradition 1 Sources

1. A.A. General Service Office.. 1952. *Twelve Steps and Twelve Traditions*. 1991. New York City: Alcoholics Anonymous World Services, Inc., 129.
2. Ibid, 189.
3. Ibid, 129 – 131.
4. McCarthy, Katherine. 1984. "Early Alcoholism Treatment: The Emmanuel Movement and Richard Peabody." *Journal of Studies on Alcohol* 45 (1): 59 – 74.
5. The A. A. Grapevine, Inc. 1988. *The Language of the Heart: Bill W.'s Grapevine Writings*. New York: The A. A. Grapevine, Inc., 116.
6. Ibid, 116.
7. Schaberg, William H. 2019. *Writing the Big Book: The Creation of A.A.* Las Vegas, NV: Central Recovery Press, 11.
8. A.A. General Service Office. 1984. *'Pass It On': The Story of Bill Wilson and How the A.A. Message Reached the World*. New York City: Alcoholics Anonymous World Services, Inc., 111 -131.
9. A.A. General Service Office. 1939. *Alcoholics Anonymous: The Story of How Many Thousands of Men and Women Have Recovered from Alcoholism*. Fourth Edition 2001. New York City: Alcoholics Anonymous World Services, Inc, 15.
10. A.A. General Service Office. 1980. *Dr. Bob and the Good Oldtimers: A Biography, with Recollections of Early A.A. in the Midwest*. New York: Alcoholics Anonymous World Services, Inc., 69.
11. Schaberg, William H. 2019. *Writing the Big Book: The Creation of A.A.* Las Vegas, NV: Central Recovery Press, 26. (Early Fellowship numbers vary, depending on who provided the estimate.)
12. Ibid, 27.
13. Ibid, 85 – 87.
14. Ibid, 103 – 104.
15. Ibid, 108.
16. Ibid, 187 – 190.
17. A.A. General Service Office. *Dr. Bob and the Good Oldtimers: A Biography, with Recollections of Early A.A. in the Midwest.*, 54.
18. A.A. General Service Office. 1957. *Alcoholics Anonymous Comes of Age: A*

Brief History of A. A. New York: Alcoholics Anonymous World Services, Inc., 160.
19 Schaberg, William H. *Writing the Big Book: The Creation of A.A.*, 167.
20 Ibid, 457.
21 Kurtz, Ernest. 1979. *Not-God: A History of Alcoholics Anonymous.* Expanded Edition 1991. Center City, MN: Hazelden., 69.
22 W., Bill. Talk on Writing the Big Book, Fort Worth, 1954.
23 Schaberg, William H. *Writing the Big Book: The Creation of A.A.*, 423 – 424.
24 Kurtz, Ernest. *Not-God: A History of Alcoholics Anonymous*, 69.
25 A.A. General Service Office. *Alcoholics Anonymous: The Story of How Many Thousands of Men and Women Have Recovered from Alcoholism*, 58 – 60.
26 Ibid, 58.
27 W., Bill. Talk on Writing the Big Book, Fort Worth, 1954.
28 Schaberg, William H. *Writing the Big Book: The Creation of A.A.*, 320 – 321.
29 A.A. General Service Office. *Alcoholics Anonymous: The Story of How Many Thousands of Men and Women Have Recovered from Alcoholism*, 17.
30 Schaberg, William H. *Writing the Big Book: The Creation of A.A.*, 578.
31 Ibid., 597 – 599.
32 A.A. General Service Office. *Alcoholics Anonymous Comes of Age: A Brief History of A. A.*, 177 – 179.
33 Schaberg, William H. *Writing the Big Book: The Creation of A.A.*, 601 – 602.
34 A.A. General Service Office. *Alcoholics Anonymous Comes of Age: A Brief History of A. A.*, 87.
35 Ibid, 94.
36 Ibid, 96.
37 Ibid, 192.
38 Ibid, 192 – 193.
39 Kurtz, Ernest. *Not-God: A History of Alcoholics Anonymous*, 238.
40 A.A. General Service Office. *Alcoholics Anonymous Comes of Age: A Brief History of A. A.*, 88.
41 Ibid, 88.

42 Ibid, 98.
43 Ibid, 98.
44 Ibid, 98.
45 A.A. General Service Office. *'Pass It On': The Story of Bill Wilson and How the A.A. Message Reached the World.*, 304.
46 A.A. General Service Office. *Alcoholics Anonymous Comes of Age: A Brief History of A. A.*, 203.
47 A.A. General Service Office. 1984. *'Pass It On': The Story of Bill Wilson and How the A.A. Message Reached the World*, 324.
48 A.A. General Service Office. *Twelve Steps and Twelve Traditions*, 130.
49 Alcoholics Anonymous World Service, Inc. 2021 – 2023. *The A.A. Service Manual combined with Twelve Concepts for World Service by Bill W.* New York, NY: Alcoholics Anonymous World Service, Inc.
50 A.A. General Service Office. *Alcoholics Anonymous: The Story of How Many Thousands of Men and Women Have Recovered from Alcoholism*, 18.
51 Ibid, 25.

Tradition 2 Sources

1 A.A. General Service Office. 1952. *Twelve Steps and Twelve Traditions.* 1991. New York City: Alcoholics Anonymous World Services, Inc, 132.
2 Ibid, 189.
3 Ibid, 132 – 138.
4 Schaberg, William H. 2019. *Writing the Big Book: The Creation of A.A.* Las Vegas, NV: Central Recovery Press.,563 -567.
5 Ibid, 563.
6 Ibid, 565 – 566.
7 A.A. General Service Office. 2018. "The "God" Word: Agnostic and Atheist Members in A.A." Pamphlet P-86." New York, NY: Alcoholics Anonymous World Services, Inc., 7.
8 Kurtz, Ernest. 1979. *Not-God: A History of Alcoholics Anonymous.* Expanded Edition 1991. Center City, MN: Hazelden, 185.
9 A.A. General Service Office. *Twelve Steps and Twelve Traditions*, 28.
10 Ibid, 109.
11 A.A. General Service Office. 1939. *Alcoholics Anonymous: The Story of*

How Many Thousands of Men and Women Have Recovered from Alcoholism. Fourth Edition 2001. New York City: Alcoholics Anonymous World Services, Inc., 219 – 231.
12 Kurtz, Ernest. *Not-God: A History of Alcoholics Anonymous,* 185.
13 Schaberg, William H. *Writing the Big Book: The Creation of A.A.,* 604.
14 Kurtz, Ernest. *Not-God: A History of Alcoholics Anonymous.,* 136.
15 Schaberg, William H. *Writing the Big Book: The Creation of A.A.,* 604.
16 Kurtz, Ernest. *Not-God: A History of Alcoholics Anonymous.,* 136.
17 A.A. General Service Office. "The "God" Word: Agnostic and Atheist Members in A.A.", Introduction.
18 A.A. General Service Office. "The "God" Word: Agnostic and Atheist Members in A.A.", Introduction.
19 A.A. General Service Office. *Alcoholics Anonymous: The Story of How Many Thousands of Men and Women Have Recovered from Alcoholism,* 47.
20 Ibid, 567 – 568.
21 A.A. General Service Office. 1984. *'Pass It On': The Story of Bill Wilson and How the A.A. Message Reached the World.* New York City: Alcoholics Anonymous World Services, Inc., 324.
22 A.A. General Service Office. *'Pass It On': The Story of Bill Wilson and How the A.A. Message Reached the World,* 306.
23 A.A. General Service Office. *Twelve Steps and Twelve Traditions,* 132.
24 Schaberg, William H. *Writing the Big Book: The Creation of A.A,* 70.
25 Ibid, 70.
26 Ibid, 70n.
27 Ibid, 127.
28 Ibid, 177, 424.
29 Ibid, 600.
30 Ibid, 600.
31 Ibid, 600.
32 Ibid, 70.
33 Ibid, 69.
34 Ibid, 1 – 3.
35 A.A. General Service Office. *'Pass It On': The Story of Bill Wilson and How the A.A. Message Reached the World,* 314.

36 Ibid, 314 – 315.
37 Ibid, 271.
38 Schaberg, William H. *Writing the Big Book: The Creation of A.A*, 100.
39 A.A. General Service Office. *'Pass It On': The Story of Bill Wilson and How the A.A. Message Reached the World*, 322.
40 Ibid, 322.
41 Ibid, 322.
42 Ibid, 324.
43 Ibid, 324.
44 A.A. General Service Office. 1957. *Alcoholics Anonymous Comes of Age: A Brief History of A. A.* New York: Alcoholics Anonymous World Services, Inc., 211.
45 Ibid, 211.
46 Ibid, 212.
47 A.A. General Service Office. *'Pass It On': The Story of Bill Wilson and How the A.A. Message Reached the World*, 349.
48 Ibid, 349.
49 Ibid, 349.
50 See the A.A. Literature Catalog **https://www.aa.org/assets/en_US/aa-catalog.pdf**
51 A.A. General Service Office. 2019. "The A.A. Group ... Where It All Begins: How a Group Functions. How to Get Started Pamphlet P-16." New York, NY: Alcoholics Anonymous World Services, Inc., 28 – 29.
52 A.A. General Service Office. *Alcoholics Anonymous: The Story of How Many Thousands of Men and Women Have Recovered from Alcoholism*, 17.
53 Ibid, 13.
54 Ibid, 84.
55 A.A. General Service Office. 2019. "The A.A. Group ... Where It All Begins: How a Group Functions. How to Get Started Pamphlet P-16.", 13.

Tradition 3 Sources

1 A.A. General Service Office. 1952. *Twelve Steps and Twelve Traditions*. 1991. New York City: Alcoholics Anonymous World Services, Inc., 139.

2 Ibid, 189.
3 Ibid, 139 – 145.
4 A.A. General Service Office. 1939. *Alcoholics Anonymous: The Story of How More than One Hundred Men Have Recovered from Alcoholism.* Reproduction published by The Anonymous Press. New York: Works Publishing Company., 25.
5 A.A. General Service Office. 1939. *Alcoholics Anonymous: The Story of How Many Thousands of Men and Women Have Recovered from Alcoholism.* Fourth Edition 2001. New York City: Alcoholics Anonymous World Services, Inc., 15 -16.
6 Ibid, 16.
7 A.A. General Service Office. 1980. *Dr. Bob and the Good Oldtimers: A Biography, with Recollections of Early A.A. in the Midwest.* New York: Alcoholics Anonymous World Services, Inc., 58.
8 Ibid, 60.
9 Ibid, 58.
10 Ibid, 218.
11 Ibid, 218.
12 P., Wally. 2001. *Back to Basics: The Alcoholics Anonymous Beginners' Meetings.* Second Edition. Tucson, AZ: Faith with Works Publishing Company., 7.
13 P., Wally. *Back to Basics: The Alcoholics Anonymous Beginners' Meetings*, 11 – 15.
14 Ibid, 11.
15 A.A. General Service Office. 1957. *Alcoholics Anonymous Comes of Age: A Brief History of A. A.* New York: Alcoholics Anonymous World Services, Inc., 102.
16 Ibid, 102.
17 Schaberg, William H. 2019. *Writing the Big Book: The Creation of A.A.* Las Vegas, NV: Central Recovery Press., 142.
18 Ibid, 142.
19 A.A. General Service Office. *Alcoholics Anonymous: The Story of How Many Thousands of Men and Women Have Recovered from Alcoholism.*, 229.
20 A.A. General Service Office. *Twelve Steps and Twelve Traditions*, 145.
21 A.A. General Service Office. *Alcoholics Anonymous: The Story of How Many Thousands of Men and Women Have Recovered from Alcoholism.*, 229.

22 Ibid, 230.
23 Ibid, 230.
24 Schaberg, William H. 2019. *Writing the Big Book: The Creation of A.A.* Las Vegas, NV: Central Recovery Press., 176f.
25 Ibid, 348.
26 A.A. General Service Office. *Dr. Bob and the Good Oldtimers: A Biography, with Recollections of Early A.A. in the Midwest.*, 98.
27 Schaberg, William H. 2019. *Writing the Big Book: The Creation of A.A.* Las Vegas, NV: Central Recovery Press., 348.
28 Ibid, 348.
29 Ibid, 349.
30 Ibid, 349f.
31 Ibid, 349.
32 A.A. General Service Office. *Dr. Bob and the Good Oldtimers: A Biography, with Recollections of Early A.A. in the Midwest.*, 242.
33 A.A. General Service Office. 2021. *A Visual History of Alcoholics Anonymous: An Archival Journey.* New York: Alcoholics Anonymous World Services, Inc., 60.
34 Ibid, 61.
35 Schaberg, William H. 2019. *Writing the Big Book: The Creation of A.A.* Las Vegas, NV: Central Recovery Press., 350.
36 A.A. General Service Office.. *Alcoholics Anonymous: The Story of How Many Thousands of Men and Women Have Recovered from Alcoholism,* 161.
37 A.A. General Service Office. 1984. *'Pass It On': The Story of Bill Wilson and How the A.A. Message Reached the World.* New York City: Alcoholics Anonymous World Services, Inc., 317.
38 Ibid, 317.
39 Ibid, 316.
40 Ibid, 316.
41 Ibid, 318.
42 Borden, Audrey. 2007. *The History of Gay People in Alcoholics Anonymous: From the Beginning.* Binghamton, New York: The Haworth Press, Inc., 15 – 16.
43 Ibid, 13.

44 Ibid, 13.
45 Ibid, 20.
46 Ibid, 20.
47 Ibid, 21.
48 Ibid, 22.
49 A.A. General Service Office. *Twelve Steps and Twelve Traditions*, 142.
50 Ibid, 141.
51 Ibid, 189.
52 A.A. General Service Office. 2019. "A.A. Tradition: How it Developed by Bill W. Pamphlet P-17." New York: Alcoholics Anonymous World Services, Inc., 11 – 14.
53 Ibid, 13.
54 Ibid, 13.
55 Ibid, 13 – 14.
56 Ibid, 14.
57 A.A. General Service Office. 2019. "The A.A. Group ... Where It All Begins: How a Group Functions. How to Get Started Pamphlet P-16." New York, NY: Alcoholics Anonymous World Services, Inc., 13.

Tradition 4 Sources

1 A.A. General Service Office. 1952. *Twelve Steps and Twelve Traditions*. 1991. New York City: Alcoholics Anonymous World Services, Inc., 146.
2 Ibid, 189.
3 Ibid, 146 – 149.
4 A.A. General Service Office. 2019. "The Twelve Traditions Illustrated P-43." New York, NY: Alcoholics Anonymous World Services, Inc., July., n.p., Fourth Tradition.
5 A.A. General Service Office. 1957. *Alcoholics Anonymous Comes of Age: A Brief History of A.A.* New York: Alcoholics Anonymous World Services, Inc., 87.
6 Ibid, 82.
7 Ibid, 82.
8 Ibid, 82.
9 A.A. General Service Office. *Twelve Steps and Twelve Traditions.*, 146.

10 Ibid, 103.
11 Ibid, 103.
12 Kurtz, Ernest. 1979. *Not-God: A History of Alcoholics Anonymous.* Expanded Edition 1991. enter City, MN: Hazelden., 113
13 A.A. General Service Office. 1984. *'Pass It On': The Story of Bill Wilson and How the A.A. Message Reached the World.* New York City: Alcoholics Anonymous World Services, Inc., 29 – 30.
14 Ibid, 219.
15 A.A. General Service Office. *Alcoholics Anonymous Comes of Age: A Brief History of A. A..*, 22.
16 Ibid, 88.
17 Ibid, 25.
18 Ibid, 25.
19 Ibid, 25.
20 Ibid, 105.
21 Ibid, 105.
22 Ibid, 105.
23 Ibid, 96.
24 Ibid, 96.
25 A.A. General Service Office. 1939. *Alcoholics Anonymous: The Story of How Many Thousands of Men and Women Have Recovered from Alcoholism.* Fourth Edition 2001. New York City: Alcoholics Anonymous World Services, Inc., 161.
26 A.A. General Service Office. *'Pass It On': The Story of Bill Wilson and How the A.A. Message Reached the World,* 316.
27 Borden, Audrey. 2007. *The History of Gay People in Alcoholics Anonymous: From the Beginning.* Binghamton, New York: The Haworth Press, Inc., 90.
28 Ibid, 90.
29 Ibid, 90 – 91.
30 Ibid, 22.
31 A.A. General Service Office. 2019. "The A.A. Group … Where It All Begins: How a Group Functions. How to Get Started Pamphlet P-16." New York, NY: Alcoholics Anonymous World Services, Inc., 12.

32 A.A. General Service Office. *Alcoholics Anonymous Comes of Age: A Brief History of A. A.*., 105.
33 Akron AA. n.d. *Akron AA Pamphlets/Meeting Aids.* Accessed 07 20, 2022. https://akronaa.org/product-category/pamphlets/.
34 Alcoholics Anonymous Cleveland. n.d. *Shop [Literature].* Accessed 07 20, 2022. https://www.aacle.org/shop/page/3/.
35 Kurtz, Ernest. *Not-God: A History of Alcoholics Anonymous.*, 51.
36 Akron Area AA Intergroup Council. n.d. "Second Reader for Alcoholics Anonymous." Akron, OH: Akron Area AA Intergroup Council., 11.
37 Akron Area AA Intergroup Council.. n.d. "Spiritual Milestones in Alcoholics Anonymous." Akron, OH: Akron Area AA Intergroup Council., 3.
38 A.A. General Service Office. *Twelve Steps and Twelve Traditions.*, 147.
39 A.A. General Service Office. *Alcoholics Anonymous Comes of Age: A Brief History of A. A.*., 203.
40 Ibid, 106.
41 Ibid, 1.
42 Kurtz, Ernest. *Not-God: A History of Alcoholics Anonymous.*, 126 – 127.
43 A.A. General Service Office. *Twelve Steps and Twelve Traditions*, 123.
44 Ibid, 189.
45 Ibid, 189.
46 Ibid, 189.
47 Ibid, 189.

Tradition 5 Sources
1 A.A. General Service Office. 1952. *Twelve Steps and Twelve Traditions.* 1991. New York City: Alcoholics Anonymous World Services, Inc., 150.
2 Ibid, 190.
3 Ibid, 150 – 154.
4 A.A.General Service Office. 1939. *Alcoholics Anonymous: The Story of How Many Thousands of Men and Women Have Recovered from Alcoholism.* Fourth Edition 2001. New York City: Alcoholics Anonymous World Services, Inc., 95.

5 Ibid, 60.
6 Schaberg, William H. 2019. *Writing the Big Book: The Creation of A.A.* Las Vegas, NV: Central Recovery Press., 26.
7 Ibid, 81.
8 Ibid, 81 – 82.
9 Ibid, 87.
10 Ibid, 250.
11 The A. A. Grapevine, Inc. 1988. *The Language of the Heart: Bill W.'s Grapevine Writings.* New York: The A. A. Grapevine, Inc., 83.
12 Ibid, 82 -83.
13 Ibid, 83.
14 A.A. General Service Office. 2019. "The A.A. Group ... Where It All Begins: How a Group Functions. How to Get Started Pamphlet P-16." New York, NY: Alcoholics Anonymous World Services, Inc., 7.
15 A.A. General Service Office. 1957. *Alcoholics Anonymous Comes of Age: A Brief History of A. A.* New York: Alcoholics Anonymous World Services, Inc., 106.
16 Ibid, 106.
17 Ibid, 106.
18 Ibid, 106.
19 Ibid, 107.
20 Kurtz, Ernest. 1979. *Not-God: A History of Alcoholics Anonymous.* Expanded Edition 1991. Center City, MN: Hazelden., 28 – 29.
21 Ibid, 28.
22 Ibid, 29.
23 Ibid, 29.
24 A.A. General Service Office. *Alcoholics Anonymous: The Story of How Many Thousands of Men and Women Have Recovered from Alcoholism.*, 18.
25 Ibid, 193 – 199.
26 Ibid, 246 – 257.
27 Ibid, 258 – 267.
28 Ibid, 94.
29 Ibid, 95.

30 A.A. General Service Office. "The A.A. Group ... Where It All Begins: How a Group Functions. How to Get Started Pamphlet P-16," 29.
31 Ibid, 8.
32 A.A. General Service Office. *Alcoholics Anonymous: The Story of How Many Thousands of Men and Women Have Recovered from Alcoholism.*, 89.
33 A.A. General Service Office. 1994. "What Does 'Crosstalk' Have to Do with Our Primary Purpose?" *Box 459: News and Notes From the General Service Office of A.A.*, Holiday Issue.
34 Ibid, 2.
35 Ibid, 2.
36 Ibid, 2.
37 Ibid, 2.
38 Ibid, 2.
39 Brown, Sally, and David R. Brown. 2001. *A Biography of Mrs. Marty Mann: The First Lady of Alcoholics Anonymous.* Center City, MN: Hazelden, 106 – 107.
40 A.A. General Service Office. *Alcoholics Anonymous: The Story of How Many Thousands of Men and Women Have Recovered from Alcoholism,* 200 – 207.
41 Ibid, 207.
42 Brown, Sally, and David R. Brown. *A Biography of Mrs. Marty Mann: The First Lady of Alcoholics Anonymous.* Center City, 263.
43 Ibid, 266.
44 Ibid, 266.
45 Ibid, 267.
46 A.A. General Service Office. *Twelve Steps and Twelve Traditions*, 151, 153.
47 Ibid, 190.
48 The A. A. Grapevine, Inc. *The Language of the Heart: Bill W.'s Grapevine Writings*, 116.
49 Ibid, 116.
50 Ibid, 116.
51 Ibid, 116.
52 Ibid, 116.
53 Ibid, 116.

Tradition 6 Sources

1. A.A. General Service Office. 1952. *Twelve Steps and Twelve Traditions*. 1991. New York City: Alcoholics Anonymous World Services, Inc., 155.
2. Ibid, 190.
3. Ibid, 155 – 159.
4. A.A. General Service Office."A.A. Tradition: How it Developed by Bill W. Pamphlet P-17.", 155.
5. A.A. General Service Office. 1939. *Alcoholics Anonymous: The Story of How Many Thousands of Men and Women Have Recovered from Alcoholism*. Fourth Edition 2001. New York City: Alcoholics Anonymous World Services, Inc., xiii – xiv.
6. A.A. General Service Office. 1980. *Dr. Bob and the Good Oldtimers: A Biography, with Recollections of Early A.A. in the Midwest*. New York: Alcoholics Anonymous World Services, Inc., 155.
7. Schaberg, William H. 2019. *Writing the Big Book: The Creation of A.A.* Las Vegas, NV: Central Recovery Press, 436.
8. Ibid, 436.
9. A.A. General Service Office. 1980. *Dr. Bob and the Good Oldtimers: A Biography, with Recollections of Early A.A. in the Midwest*. New York: Alcoholics Anonymous World Services, Inc., 154 – 155.
10. Ibid, 218.
11. A.A. General Service Office. *Alcoholics Anonymous: The Story of How Many Thousands of Men and Women Have Recovered from Alcoholism*, xv – xvi.
12. Ibid, xx.
13. Ibid, 572.
14. A.A. General Service Office. 1984. *'Pass It On': The Story of Bill Wilson and How the A.A. Message Reached the World*. New York City: Alcoholics Anonymous World Services, Inc., 320.
15. Ibid, 320.
16. Brown, Sally, and David R. Brown. 2001. *A Biography of Mrs. Marty Mann: The First Lady of Alcoholics Anonymous*. Center City, MN: Hazelden., 180.
17. A.A. General Service Office. *'Pass It On': The Story of Bill Wilson and How the A.A. Message Reached the World*, 320.
18. Ibid, 320.

19 A.A. General Service Office. 2019. "A.A. Tradition: How it Developed by Bill W. Pamphlet P-17." New York: Alcoholics Anonymous World Services, Inc., 24.
20 Ibid, 24 – 25.
21 Brown, Sally, and David R. Brown. *A Biography of Mrs. Marty Mann: The First Lady of Alcoholics Anonymous,* 212 – 213.
22 Schaberg, William H. *Writing the Big Book: The Creation of A.A.,* 98.
23 Ibid, 98 – 99.
24 Ibid, 295 – 296.
25 Ibid, 296.
26 Ibid, 296.
27 Ibid, 296.
28 A.A. General Service Office."A.A. Tradition: How it Developed by Bill W. Pamphlet P-17.", 25.
29 Ibid, 19.
30 Ibid, 19.
31 A.A. General Service Office. *Twelve Steps and Twelve Traditions,* 190.
32 A.A. General Service Office."A.A. Tradition: How it Developed by Bill W. Pamphlet P-17.", 21.
33 A.A. General Service Office. *Twelve Steps and Twelve Traditions.,* 190.
34 A.A. General Service Office."A.A. Tradition: How it Developed by Bill W. Pamphlet P-17.", 20.
35 A.A. General Service Office. *Twelve Steps and Twelve Traditions.,* 190.
36 A.A. General Service Office."A.A. Tradition: How it Developed by Bill W. Pamphlet P-17.", 20.
37 A.A. General Service Office. *Twelve Steps and Twelve Traditions.,* 190.
38 A.A. General Service Office."A.A. Tradition: How it Developed by Bill W. Pamphlet P-17.", 20.
39 A.A. General Service Office."A.A. Tradition: How it Developed by Bill W. Pamphlet P-17.", 21 – 22.
40 General Service Office, *Relationship between A.A. and Clubs.* 02/25/2022. Accessed 05/28/2022 https://www.aa.org/sites/default/files/literature/MG-3A_Relationship_AA_%26_Clubs%20EN.pdf.
41 A.A. General Service Office. 1957. *Alcoholics Anonymous Comes of Age: A*

Brief History of A. A. New York: Alcoholics Anonymous World Services, Inc., 109.

Tradition 7 Sources
1 A.A. General Service Office. 1952. *Twelve Steps and Twelve Traditions.* 1991. New York City: Alcoholics Anonymous World Services, Inc., 160.
2 Ibid, 190 – 191.
3 Ibid, 160 – 165.
4 Schaberg, William H. 2019. *Writing the Big Book: The Creation of A.A.* Las Vegas, NV: Central Recovery Press, 92.
5 Ibid, 92.
6 Ibid, 92 – 93.
7 A.A. General Service Office. 1939. *Alcoholics Anonymous: The Story of How Many Thousands of Men and Women Have Recovered from Alcoholism.* Fourth Edition 2001. New York City: Alcoholics Anonymous World Services, Inc., 136 – 150.
8 Finan, Christopher M. 2017. *Drunks: An American History.* Boston, MA: Beacon Press, 233 -234.
9 Schaberg, William H. *Writing the Big Book: The Creation of A.A.*, 93.
10 Ibid, 98.
11 Ibid, 109.
12 Ibid, 236.
13 Ibid, 238.
14 Ibid, 236 – 237.
15 A.A. General Service Office. *Twelve Steps and Twelve Traditions*, 147 – 149.
16 Schaberg, William H. *Writing the Big Book: The Creation of A.A.*, 237.
17 Ibid, 266.
18 Ibid, 266.
19 Ibid, 267.
20 Ibid, 109.
21 Ibid, 297 – 301.
22 Ibid, 298.
23 Ibid, 304.
24 Ibid, 308 – 314.

25 Ibid, 314.
26 A.A. General Service Office. 1984. *'Pass It On': The Story of Bill Wilson and How the A.A. Message Reached the World.* New York City: Alcoholics Anonymous World Services, Inc., 235.
27 Schaberg, William H. *Writing the Big Book: The Creation of A.A.*, 298f, 313.
28 A.A. General Service Office. *Twelve Steps and Twelve Traditions*, 166.
29 Schaberg, William H. *Writing the Big Book: The Creation of A.A.*, 551.
30 Ibid, 314.
31 Ibid, 302.
32 A.A. General Service Office. *'Pass It On': The Story of Bill Wilson and How the A.A. Message Reached the World*, 236.
33 Schaberg, William H. *Writing the Big Book: The Creation of A.A.*, 302.
34 Alcoholics Anonymous World Service, Inc. 2021 – 2023. *The A.A. Service Manual combined with Twelve Concepts for World Service by Bill W.* New York, NY: Alcoholics Anonymous World Service, Inc., 95.
35 A.A. General Service Office. 1980. *Dr. Bob and the Good Oldtimers: A Biography, with Recollections of Early A.A. in the Midwest.* New York: Alcoholics Anonymous World Services, Inc., 269.
36 A.A. General Service Office. *'Pass It On': The Story of Bill Wilson and How the A.A. Message Reached the World*, 236.
37 Schaberg, William H. *Writing the Big Book: The Creation of A.A.*, 92.
38 Ibid, 93.
39 A.A. General Service Office. *'Pass It On': The Story of Bill Wilson and How the A.A. Message Reached the World*, 255.
40 A.A. General Service Office. 1957. *Alcoholics Anonymous Comes of Age: A Brief History of A. A.* New York: Alcoholics Anonymous World Services, Inc., 193.
41 A.A. General Service Office. *Alcoholics Anonymous Comes of Age: A Brief History of A. A.*, 193.
42 Ibid, 194.
43 Ibid, 194.
44 A.A. General Service Office. *'Pass It On': The Story of Bill Wilson and How the A.A. Message Reached the World*, 255 -256.

45 Ibid, 257.
46 A.A. General Service Office. 2019. "A.A. Tradition: How it Developed by Bill W. Pamphlet P-17." New York: Alcoholics Anonymous World Services, Inc., 31.
47 A.A. General Service Office. *'Pass It On': The Story of Bill Wilson and How the A.A. Message Reached the World.* 257.
48 Borden, Audrey. 2007. *The History of Gay People in Alcoholics Anonymous: From the Beginning.* Binghamton, New York: The Haworth Press, Inc., 23.
49 The Washington Post. 2018. "Alcoholics Anonymous Original Manuscript Sells for $2.4 Million to NFL Team Owner." *The Washington Post*, May 6. Accessed February 17, 2022. https://www.washingtonpost.com/news/retropolis/wp/2018/03/09/lost-for-decades-the-alcoholics-anonymous-original-manuscript-will-be-auctioned-for-millions/.
50 A.A. General Service Office. 2019. "The A.A. Group ... Where It All Begins: How a Group Functions. How to Get Started Pamphlet P-16." New York, NY: Alcoholics Anonymous World Services, Inc., 21.
51 General Service Office Quarterly Report (accessed 01/21/2023): https://www.aa.org/quarterly-reports-from-gso.
52 A.A. General Service Office. *Alcoholics Anonymous Comes of Age: A Brief History of A. A.*, 111.
53 Ibid, 111 – 112.
54 The A. A. Grapevine, Inc. 1988. *The Language of the Heart: Bill W.'s Grapevine Writings.* New York: The A. A. Grapevine, Inc., 83.
55 Ibid, 84.

Tradition 8 Sources

1 A.A. General Service Office. 1952. *Twelve Steps and Twelve Traditions.* 1991. New York City: Alcoholics Anonymous World Services, Inc., 160.
2 Ibid, 191.
3 Ibid, 166 – 171.
4 A.A. General Service Office. 1939. *Alcoholics Anonymous: The Story of How Many Thousands of Men and Women Have Recovered from Alcoholism.* Fourth Edition 2001. New York City: Alcoholics Anonymous World Services, Inc., xxvii.

5   A.A. General Service Office. *Twelve Steps and Twelve Traditions*, 109.
6   Clancy, Tom, Carlton Cuse, and Graham Roland. 2019. *Tom Clancy's Jack Ryan*. Directed by Phil Abraham.
7   Schaberg, William H. 2019. *Writing the Big Book: The Creation of A.A.* Las Vegas, NV: Central Recovery Press., 97.
8   Ibid, 98
9   Ibid, 241.
10 Ibid, 550 – 551.
11 Ibid, 100.
12 See in this study, Tradition Seven.
13 A.A. General Service Office. 1984. *'Pass It On': The Story of Bill Wilson and How the A.A. Message Reached the World.* New York City: Alcoholics Anonymous World Services, Inc., 229.
14 Ibid, 230.
15 Ibid, 230.
16 Ibid, 230 – 231.
17 Ibid, 231.
18 Ibid, 231.
19 Ibid, 231.
20 Ibid, 222.
21 Ibid, 223.
22 A.A. General Service Office. 1980. *Dr. Bob and the Good Oldtimers: A Biography, with Recollections of Early A.A. in the Midwest.* New York: Alcoholics Anonymous World Services, Inc., 269.
23 A.A. General Service Office. 1984. *'Pass It On': The Story of Bill Wilson and How the A.A. Message Reached the World*, 322 – 323.
24 Ibid, 323.
25 A.A. General Service Office. 2019. "A.A. Tradition: How it Developed by Bill W. Pamphlet P-17." New York: Alcoholics Anonymous World Services, Inc., 32.
26 A.A. General Service Office. 1957. *Alcoholics Anonymous Comes of Age: A Brief History of A. A.* New York: Alcoholics Anonymous World Services, Inc., 115 – 116.
27 Ibid, 116.

28 Ibid, 116.
29 A.A. General Service Office. 2019. "The A.A. Group ... Where It All Begins: How a Group Functions. How to Get Started Pamphlet P-16." New York, NY: Alcoholics Anonymous World Services, Inc., 37 – 38.
30 Alcoholics Anonymous World Service, Inc. 2021 – 2023. *The A.A. Service Manual combined with Twelve Concepts for World Service by Bill W.* New York, NY: Alcoholics Anonymous World Service, Inc., 6.
31 Alcoholics Anonymous World Service, Inc. 2021 – 2023. *The A.A. Service Manual combined with Twelve Concepts for World Service by Bill W.*, 72.
32 A.A. General Service Office. 2022. "Estimates of A.A. Groups and Members as of December 31, 2021, SM F-53." Accessed January 22, 2023. https://www.aa.org/estimates-aa-groups-and-members. The figures cited in the text are approximated from this data.
33 Alcoholics Anonymous World Service, Inc. 2021 – 2023. *The A.A. Service Manual combined with Twelve Concepts for World Service by Bill W.*, 72 – 73.
34 Ibid, 72.
35 Ibid, 5.
36 Alcoholics Anonymous Conference-Approved Literature and Other A.A. Material 2020, https://www.aa.org/assets/en_US/aacatalog.pdf, 52 – 55.
37 Ibid, 72.
38 Alcoholics Anonymous World Service, Inc. 2021 – 2023. *The A.A. Service Manual combined with Twelve Concepts for World Service by Bill W.*, 74 – 75.
39 A.A. General Service Office. 2022. "Estimates of A.A. Groups and Members as of December 31, 2021, SM F-53.
40 A.A. General Service Office. 2022. "Estimates of A.A. Groups and Members as of December 31, 2021, SM F-53." Accessed January 22, 2023. https://www.aa.org/estimates-aa-groups-and-members. The figures cited in the text are approximated from this data.
41 A.A. General Service Office. 2019. "Your AA General Service Office, F-6." New York, NY: Alcoholics Anonymous World Services, Inc., 4.
42 2020 World Services Report. *The Purpose of our Service: Sobriety within Everyone's Reach.* The 26th World Service Meeting (A Virtual Event).

Accessed January 22, 2023. https://www.aa.org/sites/default/files/literature/f-150_26th_WSM_finalreport_2020.pdf (See page 53 for Turkey's report.).
43 A.A. General Service Office. "The A.A. Group … Where It All Begins: How a Group Functions. How to Get Started Pamphlet P-16," 34 – 35.
44 General Service Office, Archives, email dated 09/21/2021.
45 Alcoholics Anonymous World Service, Inc. *The A.A. Service Manual combined with Twelve Concepts for World Service by Bill W.*, 86.
46 Ibid, 63.

Tradition 9 Sources

1 A.A. General Service Office. 1952. *Twelve Steps and Twelve Traditions*. 1991. New York City: Alcoholics Anonymous World Services, Inc., 172.
2 Ibid, 191 – 192.
3 Ibid, 172 – 175.
4 A.A. General Service Office. 1957. *Alcoholics Anonymous Comes of Age: A Brief History of A. A.* New York: Alcoholics Anonymous World Services, Inc., 140.
5 Ibid, 140.
6 A.A. General Service Office. *Twelve Steps and Twelve Traditions*, 174 – 175.
7 A.A. General Service Office. *Twelve Steps and Twelve Traditions*, 174.
8 Ibid, 191.
9 A.A. General Service Office. 2019. "The A.A. Group … Where It All Begins: How a Group Functions. How to Get Started Pamphlet P-16." New York, NY: Alcoholics Anonymous World Services, Inc., 13 – 24.
10 Ibid, 12 – 13.
11 A.A. General Service Office. *Twelve Steps and Twelve Traditions*, 146 – 147.
12 A.A. General Service Office. "The A.A. Group … Where It All Begins: How a Group Functions. How to Get Started Pamphlet P-16," 13.
13 Ibid, 24.
14 Ibid, 23 – 24.
15 Ibid, 26.
16 Ibid, 25 – 26.
17 Ibid, 23.

18 Ibid, 26 – 27.
19 A.A. General Service Office. 2019. "A.A. Guidelines." Alcoholics Anonymous World Services, Inc., January. Accessed January 22, 2023. https://www.aa.org/aa-guidelines-conferences-conventions-and-roundups.
20 A.A. General Service Office. *Twelve Steps and Twelve Traditions,* 191.
21 Ibid, 22 -23, 37 – 38.
22 Ibid, 22.
23 A.A. General Service Office. *Twelve Steps and Twelve Traditions,* 172.
24 Alcoholics Anonymous World Service, Inc. 2021 – 2023. *The A.A. Service Manual combined with Twelve Concepts for World Service by Bill W.* New York, NY: Alcoholics Anonymous World Service, Inc., 4.
25 Ibid, 4.
26 Alcoholics Anonymous World Service, Inc. *The A.A. Service Manual combined with Twelve Concepts for World Service by Bill W.,* 3.
27 Alcoholics Anonymous World Service, Inc. *The A.A. Service Manual combined with Twelve Concepts for World Service by Bill W.,* 4 – 5.
28 Ibid, 34.
29 A.A. General Service Office. *Twelve Steps and Twelve Traditions,* 191.
30 Alcoholics Anonymous World Service, Inc. *The A.A. Service Manual combined with Twelve Concepts for World Service by Bill W.,* 40, 49, 63.
31 A.A. General Service Office. *Twelve Steps and Twelve Traditions,* 175.
32 A.A. General Service Office. *Alcoholics Anonymous Comes of Age: A Brief History of A. A.,* 210.
33 Ibid, 210.
34 Ibid, 210.
35 Ibid, 212.
36 Kurtz, Ernest. 1979. *Not-God: A History of Alcoholics Anonymous.* Expanded Edition 1991. Center City, MN: Hazelden, 130.
37 Ibid, 130.
38 Ibid, 130.
39 Ibid, 130.
40 Ibid, 130.
41 Ibid, 130 – 131.
42 Ibid, 131.

43 Ibid, 131.
44 Ibid, 131.
45 Ibid, 138 – 142.
46 Ibid, 138 – 140.
47 A.A. General Service Office. 1984. *'Pass It On': The Story of Bill Wilson and How the A.A. Message Reached the World*. New York City: Alcoholics Anonymous World Services, Inc., 395.
48 Kurtz, Ernest. *Not-God: A History of Alcoholics Anonymous*, 139 – 140.
49 Ibid, 140.
50 Ibid, 140.
51 Alcoholics Anonymous World Service, Inc. *The A.A. Service Manual combined with Twelve Concepts for World Service by Bill W.*, C2.
52 Kurtz, Ernest. *Not-God: A History of Alcoholics Anonymous*, 140.
53 A.A. General Service Office. 2005. *Alcoholics Anonymous 70 Years of Growth: 2005 A.A. International Convention, Toronto, Ontario, Canada, June 30-July 3, 2005*. New York: Alcoholics Anonymous World Services, Inc., 60.
54 A.A. General Service Office. 2019. *Our Great Responsibility: A Selection of Bill W.'s General Service Conference Talks, 1951 – 1970*. New York, NY: Alcoholics Anonymous World Services, Inc., 46.
55 A.A. General Service Office. *'Pass It On': The Story of Bill Wilson and How the A.A. Message Reached the World*, 396.
56 Alcoholics Anonymous World Service, Inc. *The A.A. Service Manual combined with Twelve Concepts for World Service by Bill W.*, 52.
57 A.A. General Service Office. *Twelve Steps and Twelve Traditions*, 191 – 192.
58 A.A. General Service Office. *Alcoholics Anonymous Comes of Age: A Brief History of A. A.*, 120.

Tradition 10 Sources

1 A.A. General Service Office. 1952. *Twelve Steps and Twelve Traditions*. 1991. New York City: Alcoholics Anonymous World Services, Inc., 176.
2 Ibid, 192.
3 Ibid, 176 – 179.
4 Ibid, 155.

5   Ibid, 176.
6   Ibid, 192.
7   A.A. General Service Office. 1957. *Alcoholics Anonymous Comes of Age: A Brief History of A. A.* New York: Alcoholics Anonymous World Services, Inc., 87.
8   Ibid, 87.
9   Kaufmann, Kevin. 2011. *Rigorous Honesty: A Cultural History of Alcoholics Anonymous 1935-1960.* Dissertations. 73. https://ecommons.luc.edu/luc_diss/73., 161 – 162.
10 Ibid, 159 – 160.
11 Ibid, 160.
12 Ibid, 164 – 165.
13 A.A. General Service Office. 1984. *'Pass It On': The Story of Bill Wilson and How the A.A. Message Reached the World.* New York City: Alcoholics Anonymous World Services, Inc., 274.
14 A.A. General Service Office. *Twelve Steps and Twelve Traditions*, 38 – 39.
15 A.A. General Service Office. 1939. *Alcoholics Anonymous: The Story of How Many Thousands of Men and Women Have Recovered from Alcoholism.* Fourth Edition 2001. New York City: Alcoholics Anonymous World Services, Inc., 17.
16 Ibid, 65 – 66.
17 A.A. General Service Office. *Twelve Steps and Twelve Traditions*, 129.
18 Ibid, 130.
19 Ibid, 130.
20 A.A. General Service Office. *Alcoholics Anonymous: The Story of How Many Thousands of Men and Women Have Recovered from Alcoholism*, 19.
21 McCarthy, Katherine. 1984. "Early Alcoholism Treatment: The Emmanuel Movement and Richard Peabody." *Journal of Studies on Alcohol* 45 (1): 59 – 68.
22 Schaberg, William H. 2019. *Writing the Big Book: The Creation of A.A.* Las Vegas, NV: Central Recovery Press., 436.
23 A.A. General Service Office. *Alcoholics Anonymous Comes of Age: A Brief History of A. A.*, 2 – 3.
24 Kurtz, Ernest. 1979. *Not-God: A History of Alcoholics Anonymous.* Expanded Edition 1991. Center City, MN: Hazelden., 117.

25 A.A. General Service Office. *Alcoholics Anonymous: The Story of How Many Thousands of Men and Women Have Recovered from Alcoholism*, 571.
26 Kurtz, Ernest. *Not-God: A History of Alcoholics Anonymous*, 34.
27 McCarthy, Katherine. "Early Alcoholism Treatment: The Emmanuel Movement and Richard Peabody." *Journal of Studies on Alcohol* 45 (1): 62.
28 Kurtz, Ernest. *Not-God: A History of Alcoholics Anonymous*, 34.
29 A.A. General Service Office. 2019. "The A.A. Group ... Where It All Begins: How a Group Functions. How to Get Started Pamphlet P-16." New York, NY: Alcoholics Anonymous World Services, Inc., 39.
30 A.A. General Service Office. 2018. "The A.A. Member – Medications & Other Drugs P-11." New York, New York: Alcoholics Anonymous World Services, Inc., 4.
31 A.A. General Service Office. 2018. "A.A. for Alcoholics with Mental Health Issues – and their sponsors P-87." New York, New York: Alcoholics Anonymous World Services, Inc., 41.
32 A.A. General Service Office. *Alcoholics Anonymous: The Story of How Many Thousands of Men and Women Have Recovered from Alcoholism*, 28.
33 Schaberg, William H. *Writing the Big Book: The Creation of A.A.*, 436.
34 A.A. General Service Office. *Alcoholics Anonymous Comes of Age: A Brief History of A. A.*, 309.
35 Conlon, Leon S. 1997. "Griffen v. Coughlin: Mandated AA Meetings and the Establishment Clause." *Journal of Church and State* 39 (3): 431.
36 Ibid, 447.
37 Barron, James. 1996. "Saying A.A. Is Religious, Court Lets Inmate Skip It." *New York Times*, June 12. Accessed January 22, 2023 https://www.nytimes.com/1996/06/12/nyregion/saying-aa-is-religious-court-lets-inmate-skip-it.html.
38 Ibid.
39 A.A. General Service Office. 2018. "The "God" Word: Agnostic and Atheist Members in A.A. Pamphlet P-86." New York, NY: Alcoholics Anonymous World Services, Inc., Introduction.
40 A.A. General Service Office. *Twelve Steps and Twelve Traditions*, 147.
41 Ibid, 147.
42 Kurtz, Ernest. *Not-God: A History of Alcoholics Anonymous*, 115 – 116.

43 Ibid, 116.
44 Ibid, 116.
45 Ibid, 116.
46 Ibid, 117.
47 Ibid, 117.
48 A.A. General Service Office. *Alcoholics Anonymous Comes of Age: A Brief History of A. A.*, 126.
49 *Something to Live For*, Film, 1952 Paramount Pictures. Accessed January 22, 2023. https://en.wikipedia.org/wiki/Something_to_Live_For_(film).
50 A.A. General Service Office. *Alcoholics Anonymous Comes of Age: A Brief History of A. A.*, 126.
51 Ibid, 126.
52 Ibid, 127.
53 Ibid, 126 – 127.
54 Kurtz, Ernest. *Not-God: A History of Alcoholics Anonymous*, 137.
55 Ibid, 136.
56 Ibid, 136.
57 A.A. General Service Office. *'Pass It On': The Story of Bill Wilson and How the A.A. Message Reached the World*, 368 – 375.
58 Ibid, 368 – 375.
59 Kurtz, Ernest. *Not-God: A History of Alcoholics Anonymous*, 137.
60 A.A. General Service Office. *'Pass It On': The Story of Bill Wilson and How the A.A. Message Reached the World*, 388 – 391.
61 Ibid, 390.
62 Ibid, 390 – 391.
63 United States Senate. July 23, 24, and 25, 1969. *The Impact of Alcoholism: Hearings before the Special Subcommittee on Alcoholism and Narcotics of the Committee on Oabor and Public Welfare*. U. S. Senate, 91st Congress, 1st Session, on Examination of the Impact of Alcoholism, Washington, D.C.: U. S. Government Printing Office.
64 United States Senate. September 27, 1988. "Causes and Consequences of Alcohol Abuse Senate Hearing 100-834 Pt. 2." Committee on Governmental Affairs, 100th Congress, Second Session, Part 2, Washington, D. C., 3.

65 Ibid, 115.
66 Ibid, 114.
67 Ibid, 113.
68 A.A. General Service Office. "The A.A. Group ... Where It All Begins: How a Group Functions. How to Get Started Pamphlet P-16.", 39.
69 A.A. General Service Office. *Twelve Steps and Twelve Traditions*, 176.
70 Ibid, 178.
71 Ibid, 178.

Tradition 11 Sources

1 A.A. General Service Office. 1952. *Twelve Steps and Twelve Traditions*. 1991. New York City: Alcoholics Anonymous World Services, Inc., 180.
2 Ibid, 192.
3 Ibid, 180 – 183.
4 A.A. General Service Office. 1939. *Alcoholics Anonymous: The Story of How Many Thousands of Men and Women Have Recovered from Alcoholism*. Fourth Edition 2001. New York City: Alcoholics Anonymous World Services, Inc., xiii.
5 Kurtz, Ernest. 1979. *Not-God: A History of Alcoholics Anonymous*. Expanded Edition 1991. Center City, MN: Hazelden., 104.
6 Ibid, 84.
7 Ibid, 85.
8 Ibid, 85 – 86.
9 Ibid, 86.
10 A.A. General Service Office. 1980. *Dr. Bob and the Good Oldtimers: A Biography, with Recollections of Early A.A. in the Midwest*. New York: Alcoholics Anonymous World Services, Inc., 252.
11 Kurtz, Ernest. *Not-God: A History of Alcoholics Anonymous*, 85.
12 Ibid, 86.
13 Ibid, 87.
14 Ibid, 87.
15 Brown, Sally, and David R. Brown. 2001. *A Biography of Mrs. Marty Mann: The First Lady of Alcoholics Anonymous*. Center City, MN: Hazelden., 180 – 181.

16 A.A. General Service Office. 1984. *'Pass It On': The Story of Bill Wilson and How the A.A. Message Reached the World.* New York City: Alcoholics Anonymous World Services, Inc., 310.
17 Ibid, 310.
18 Ibid, 310.
19 Ibid, 310 – 311.
20 The A. A. Grapevine, Inc. 1988. *The Language of the Heart: Bill W.'s Grapevine Writings.* New York: The A. A. Grapevine, Inc., 215.
21 A.A. General Service Office. 1957. *Alcoholics Anonymous Comes of Age: A Brief History of A. A.* New York: Alcoholics Anonymous World Services, Inc., 130.
22 Ibid, 130.
23 Ibid, 131.
24 The A. A. Grapevine, Inc. *The Language of the Heart: Bill W.'s Grapevine Writings*, 94.
25 A.A. General Service Office. *'Pass It On': The Story of Bill Wilson and How the A.A. Message Reached the World*, 308 – 309.
26 Ibid, 309.
27 Ibid, 309.
28 Ibid, 309.
29 Ibid, 309.
30 Ibid, 314.
31 Ibid, 314.
32 A.A. General Service Office. *Twelve Steps and Twelve Traditions*, 192.
33 Ibid, 192.
34 Ibid, 192.
35 A.A. General Service Office. 2018. "Understanding Anonymity Pamphlet P-47." New York, NY: Alcoholics Anonymous World Services, Inc., 12.
36 Ibid, 5.
37 A.A. General Service Office. 2019. "Anonymity Online and Digital Media SM F-197." February. https://www.aa.org/sites/default/files/literature/assets/smf-197_en.pdf.
38 Continental European Region of Alcoholics Anonymous. *Anonymity is so*

fragile, you can break it with one finger. Accessed January 22, 2023. https://alcoholics-anonymous.eu/anonymity-online-2019/.
39 Continental European Region of Alcoholics Anonymous. *Online Anonymity and Meeting Safety.* Accessed January 22, 2023. https://alcoholics-anonymous.eu/online-meeting-safety-and-anonymity/. See also, Online Zoom Meeting Hosting Guidelines and Good practice for listing online meetings.
40 A.A. General Service Office. 2019. "A.A. Tradition: How it Developed by Bill W. Pamphlet P-17." New York: Alcoholics Anonymous World Services, Inc., 47.

Tradition 12 Sources

1 A.A. General Service Office. 1952. *Twelve Steps and Twelve Traditions.* 1991. New York City: Alcoholics Anonymous World Services, Inc., 184.
2 Ibid, 192.
3 Ibid, 184 – 187.
4 Ibid, 192.
5 Ibid, 192.
6 A.A. General Service Office. 2019. "The A.A. Group … Where It All Begins: How a Group Functions. How to Get Started Pamphlet P-16." New York, NY: Alcoholics Anonymous World Services, Inc., 9.
7 Kurtz, Ernest. 1979. *Not-God: A History of Alcoholics Anonymous.* Expanded Edition 1991. Center City, MN: Hazelden., 51.
8 Schaberg, William H. 2019. *Writing the Big Book: The Creation of A.A.* Las Vegas, NV: Central Recovery Press., 172.
9 Ibid, 172.
10 Ibid, 531 – 532.
11 A.A. General Service Office. 1984. *'Pass It On': The Story of Bill Wilson and How the A.A. Message Reached the World.* New York City: Alcoholics Anonymous World Services, Inc., 307.
12 Kurtz, Ernest. *Not-God: A History of Alcoholics Anonymous,* 100 – 101.
13 Ibid, 101.
14 Ibid, 101.

15 A.A. General Service Office. 1957. *Alcoholics Anonymous Comes of Age: A Brief History of A. A.* New York: Alcoholics Anonymous World Services, Inc., 135.
16 Ibid, 135.
17 Ibid, 135.
18 Ibid, 135.
19 The A. A. Grapevine, Inc. 1988. *The Language of the Heart: Bill W.'s Grapevine Writings.* New York: The A. A. Grapevine, Inc., 111.
20 A.A. General Service Office. *Alcoholics Anonymous Comes of Age: A Brief History of A. A.*, 136.
21 A.A. General Service Office. *Twelve Steps and Twelve Traditions*, 41.
22 Ibid, 125.
23 The A. A. Grapevine, Inc. *The Language of the Heart: Bill W.'s Grapevine Writings*, 14.
24 Ibid, 15.
25 A.A. General Service Office. *Twelve Steps and Twelve Traditions*, 130.
26 A.A. General Service Office. *Alcoholics Anonymous Comes of Age: A Brief History of A. A.*, 132.
27 Ibid, 136.
28 A.A. General Service Office. *'Pass It On': The Story of Bill Wilson and How the A.A. Message Reached the World*, 237.
29 Ibid, 238.
30 Ibid, 307.
31 The A. A. Grapevine, Inc. *The Language of the Heart: Bill W.'s Grapevine Writings*, 13.
32 A.A. General Service Office. *'Pass It On': The Story of Bill Wilson and How the A.A. Message Reached the World*, 311.
33 Ibid, 312 – 313.
34 Ibid, 313 -314.
35 Ibid, 313.
36 A.A. General Service Office. 2019. "A.A. Tradition: How it Developed by Bill W. Pamphlet P-17." New York: Alcoholics Anonymous World Services, Inc., 45.
37 Ibid, 45.

38 Ibid, 45.
39 Ibid, 45.
40 A.A. General Service Office. *Alcoholics Anonymous Comes of Age: A Brief History of A. A.*, 43.
41 Ibid, 43.
42 Ibid, 43.
43 A.A. General Service Office. *Twelve Steps and Twelve Traditions*, 132.
44 A.A. General Service Office."The A.A. Group … Where It All Begins: How a Group Functions. How to Get Started Pamphlet P-16.", 8.
45 A.A. General Service Office. 2018. "Understanding Anonymity Pamphlet P-47." New York, NY: Alcoholics Anonymous World Services, Inc., 6.
46 The A. A. Grapevine, Inc. *The Language of the Heart: Bill W.'s Grapevine Writings*, 216.
47 Kurtz, Ernest. *Not-God: A History of Alcoholics Anonymous*, 197.
48 Ibid, 197 – 198.
49 Ibid, 197 – 198.
50 Ibid, 198.
51 Alcoholics Anonymous World Service, Inc. 2021 – 2023. *The A.A. Service Manual combined with Twelve Concepts for World Service by Bill W.* New York, NY: Alcoholics Anonymous World Service, Inc., II.
52 Ibid, 40.

Epilogue Sources

1 A.A. General Service Office. 2019. "The A.A. Group … Where It All Begins: How a Group Functions. How to Get Started Pamphlet P-16." New York, NY: Alcoholics Anonymous World Services, Inc., 31.
2 Ibid, 31.

CPSIA information can be obtained
at www.ICGtesting.com
Printed in the USA
BVHW041654030723
666727BV00004B/252